STUDIES IN WAR, SOCIETY,
AND THE MILITARY

You Can't Fight Tanks
with Bayonets

Psychological Warfare
against the Japanese Army
in the Southwest Pacific

Allison B. Gilmore

University
of Nebraska Press

Lincoln & London

∞

First Bison Books printing: 2000
Most recent printing indicated by the last digit below:
10   9   8   7   6   5   4   3   2   1

Library of Congress Cataloging-in-Publication Data
Gilmore, Allison B., 1959–
You can't fight tanks with bayonets: psychological warfare against the Japanese army in the
Southwest Pacific / Allison B. Gilmore.
p.   cm.—(Studies in war, society, and the military)
Includes bibliographical references and index.
ISBN 0-8032-2167-3 (cloth: alk. paper)
ISBN 0-8032-7089-5 (pa.: alk. paper)
1. World War, 1939–1945—Propaganda. 2. World War, 1939–1945—Psychological aspects.
3. Propaganda, American—History—20th century. 4. World War, 1939–1945—Oceania.
5. National characteristics, Japanese. I. Title. II. Series.
D810.P7U5 1998   97-29975
940.54'8673—dc21   CIP

To Roger, Ronni, and Emma

Contents

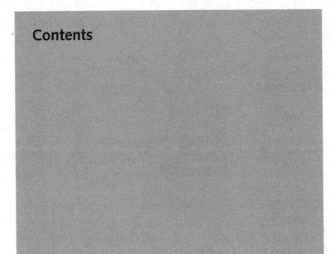

Illustrations

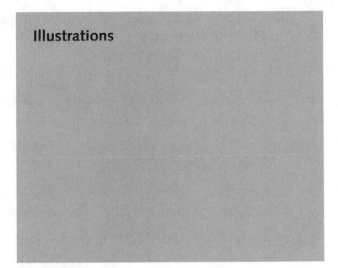

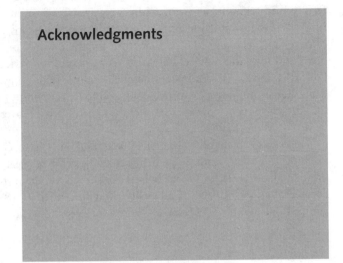

Acknowledgments

I wish to begin by thanking Bob Sandberg and Frank Hallgren, who served with the Psychological Warfare Branch in the Southwest Pacific and had the rare foresight and generosity of spirit to accumulate and donate a spectacular collection of Allied propaganda materials to the University of Nebraska's Special Collections. Without their vision this book would never have been written. I am especially indebted to Peter Maslowski for introducing me to the joys of military history and for his moral support and professional advice over many years. Thanks also to Allan R. Millett for the rigor of the academic program he oversees at Ohio State University and the superb example of scholarly excellence he sets for everyone around him.

I owe a great debt of gratitude to two archivists at the National Archives—Will Mahoney, who managed to locate the official records of PWB after three other staff members had assured me they did not exist; and Timothy K. Nenninger, who maneuvered several of the illustrations for this book through the tangled bureaucracy of the archives in record time. I also wish to thank the entire staff of the MacArthur Memorial Archives, who made working there both pleasurable and exceedingly productive, especially Edward J. Boone (now retired), James Zobel, Jeffrey Acosta, and Col. Lyman H. Hammond. Thanks also to the U.S. Army Center of Military History for the Dissertation Year Fellowship, which enabled me to conduct much of the research for this book; to the faculty and administration of Ohio State University–Lima, who have supported the completion of this project in every way possible; and to Michael J. Hogan and Mansel Blackford for their words of encouragement and insightful advice. I am also very grateful to Mark Parillo and Edward J. Drea, who read portions of the manuscript and offered valuable suggestions for its improvement, and to Roger Nimps for his skillful editing, patient confidence, and thoughtful advice over what has been a very long haul.

I also wish to thank my parents, Max and Eula Mae Gilmore, for teaching me that nothing worth achieving comes easily, and my brothers, Guy, Scott, and Mark, who have shown me the importance of perseverance in the face of adversity. And finally, to my very special family, Roger, Ronni, and Emma—thanks for everything, you're the best.

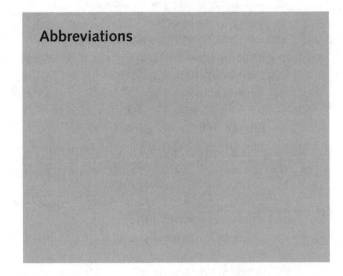

Abbreviations

ADVATIS Advanced Allied Translator and Interpreter Section
AFHQ Allied Forces Headquarters
AGS Allied Geographical Section
AIB Allied Intelligence Bureau
AMF Australian Military Forces
APWC Allied Political Warfare Committee
ATIS Allied Translator and Interpreter Section
CB Central Bureau
CBI China-Burma-India
CCS Combined Chiefs of Staff
CIAA Office of the Coordinator of Inter-American Affairs
CINCPAC Commander-in-Chief, Pacific
CINCPOA Commander-in-Chief, Pacific Ocean Areas
COI Office of the Coordinator of Information
ETO European Theater of Operations
FEAF Far East Air Forces

FEC	Far East Command
FELO	Far Eastern Liaison Office (Australian)
FMAD	Foreign Morale Analysis Division
G-2	U.S. Army Military Intelligence
GHQ	General Headquarters
I&E	Information and Education Section
IJA	Imperial Japanese Army
JCS	Joint Chiefs of Staff
JICPOA	Joint Intelligence Center, Pacific Ocean Areas
JPWC	Joint Psychological Warfare Committee
MIS	Military Intelligence Service
MMBA	MacArthur Memorial Bureau of Archives
MOI	Ministry of Information (British)
MRBC	Mobile Radio Broadcasting Company
NARA	U.S. National Archives and Records Administration
NCO	Noncommissioned officer
ONI	Office of Naval Intelligence
OSS	Office of Strategic Services
OWI	Office of War Information
PID	Political Intelligence Department (British)
POW	Prisoner of war
psywar	Psychological warfare
PWB	Psychological Warfare Branch
PWBLO	Psychological Warfare Branch liaison officer
PWD	Psychological Warfare Division
R&A	Research and Analysis Branch
SACO	Sino-American Cooperative Organization
SACSEA	Supreme Allied Command, Southeast Asia
SCAP	Supreme Commander Allied Powers
SEATIC	Southeast Asia Translation and Interrogation Center
SHAEF	Supreme Headquarters Allied Expeditionary Force
SWPA	Southwest Pacific Area
USAAF	United States Army Air Forces
USAFFE	United States Army Forces in the Far East

You Can't Fight Tanks
with Bayonets

Introduction

In November 1944, during a lull in the intense fighting so characteristic of the Pacific War, a Japanese soldier made the following entry in his diary: "I won't go so far as to say it is absolutely impossible but I don't think we can win the war with Japanese spirit alone."[1] Although the average GI would have found these words of little interest or importance, they were immensely heartening to Allied propagandists charged with the task of inducing demoralization among enemy combatants. For this seemingly insignificant diary entry and many others akin to it provided evidence that soldiers of the Imperial Japanese Army (IJA) were losing confidence in their ability to win the "Greater East Asia War" and recognizing the vital importance played by material factors in wartime. Similar statements proffered by Japanese prisoners of war (POWs) and found in documents retrieved from battlefields throughout the Pacific were important sources of intelligence for psychological warfare personnel, whose job it was to hasten Japan's defeat by waging a propaganda campaign to diminish Japanese confidence in their ability to achieve victory.

Historians have written hundreds of volumes about World War II. Many of them analyze various aspects of the Pacific War, and some examine the subject of psychological warfare (psywar), but rarely do these two lines of scholarly inquiry intersect. The bulk of the studies of psychological operations in World War II pertain to the European Theater of Operations (ETO). John W. Dower's *War without Mercy: Race and Power in the Pacific War* assesses the impact of racial hatred, cultural stereotypes, and psychological factors on the conduct of the Pacific War. Yet his treatment of wartime atrocities, Japanese adherence to "death before dishonor," and Americans "obsessed with the task of slaughter" reveals only part of the story.[2] Although he refers to the surrender of demoralized Japanese soldiers, the subject is peripheral to his work. This is understandable given his focus, yet one is left with a very clear impression that such occurrences were extraordinarily rare and insignificant events. More problematic is Dower's assertion that Americans in decision-making positions were so singularly unimpressed with the idea of waging a serious propaganda campaign against the Japanese that "such ideas had little impact."[3] In fact, this is not the case. Psywar was not an afterthought on the part of Allied military commanders, nor was it always perceived as some "impractical plaything of effete civilians."[4] In their attempts to demoralize Japanese troops Allied propagandists in the Southwest Pacific alone disseminated nearly 400 million propaganda leaflets and witnessed the capture of approximately 19,500 Japanese prisoners.

The dearth of historical inquiry into the conduct of psywar against the Japanese likely results from assumptions that deserve closer scrutiny. One such assumption seems to be that psywar could not have been effective against an enemy so thoroughly indoctrinated in a tradition that emphasized "death before dishonor" and the supreme virtues of loyalty to the emperor, unquestioning obedience to one's superiors, and self-sacrifice in the service of the nation. To be sure, soldiers in the IJA were thoroughly imbued with these values. But just as it did not prevent them from experiencing defeat on the battlefield, military indoctrination did not safeguard the emperor's soldiers from the ill effects of demoralization. The evidence shows that as the war progressed and Allied military successes mounted, morale among Japanese combatants markedly declined and Japanese soldiers became increasingly susceptible to the Allied war of words.

Pacific War narratives provide graphic images of the brutal fighting in the Pacific, the atrocities committed by combatants, and the fight-to-the-death mentality that dominated among all fighting men in what has been characterized as a savage race war. Taken as a whole, this literature attributes to the war in the Pacific inherently different qualities from those that prevailed in other theaters during World War II, with the possible exception of the fighting on the eastern front. Integral to this way of thinking is the idea that despite the horror that inevitably accompanies warfare, combatants elsewhere somehow managed to retain a sense that the enemy was human, to remember that the ultimate goal was victory over the enemy rather than its extermination, and to adhere to ethical standards deemed essential among civilized people even in wartime. Not so in the Pacific, where American propagandists dehumanized the enemy and thus encouraged his extermination, where GIs' bigotry led them to callously and regularly mutilate the corpses of enemy dead, and where Japanese soldiers became human grenades and charged willingly, even gratefully, to their death in the service of their emperor. One is led to believe that the Pacific War was peculiarly repugnant as it pitted the IJA, with its fanatical obsession with the principle of "death before dishonor," against an American army "obsessed with the task of slaughter" and "notoriously reluctant to take prisoners."[5] The resultant kill-or-be-killed psychology gave rise to egregious behavior on the part of both armies and a level of inhumanity that far exceeded the norm even in an era when total war was accepted as both legitimate and necessary.

Admittedly, there is much evidence that most Japanese fought to the death rather than surrender and that Allied troops were reluctant to take Japanese prisoners. It is also clear that issues of race influenced the nature of the fighting in the Pacific. Nor should one discount the atrocities committed by combatants of every nationality during the Pacific War. The purpose of this study is not necessarily to shatter that image of the Pacific War, though it behooves us all to recognize that brutality, atrocities, and hatred of the other, however reprehensible, are integral to warfare. My purpose is to further our understanding of that war by revealing the existence of another, very different facet of the fighting in the Pacific—the propaganda war. This is not another story of how racial hatred produced implacable enemies. It is the story of Allied propagandists who strove to go beyond the prevailing racial stereotypes and arrive at a more sophisticated understanding of the enemy as individual human beings with discernible strengths and weaknesses. It is the story of Allied efforts to discover the factors that contributed to high morale among Japanese soldiers in order to devise means of eroding that morale and thus bring the war to an end short of exterminating the enemy to a man. In some ways it is the story of how psywar personnel attempted to convince Japanese and Americans alike that their assumptions about the other were misleading and counterproductive. In short, it is the story of a war of words that required propagandists to know the enemy in ways fundamentally different from the way infantrymen, who fought the Japanese with conventional weapons, knew them.

Ironically, perhaps, while propagandists on the American home front were creating an image of the Japanese fighting man as either subhuman or superhuman, propagandists in operational theaters were employing a fundamentally different approach. Allied personnel involved in psywar sought to understand and communicate with Japanese soldiers on a human and personal level rather than view them as an aggregate of identically fanatical automatons irrevocably committed to a lost cause. They recognized that soldiers everywhere are most concerned with the practical necessities of survival in combat, such as food, water, ammunition, weapons, air and naval support, and capable leadership. As the war progressed these necessities were in short supply throughout the IJA, and propagandists had abundant opportunities to exploit such deficiencies.

The present work examines one aspect of the extensive and varied propaganda efforts of the United States and its allies in the Pacific War, namely, psychological warfare as it was waged against the IJA in the Southwest Pacific Area (SWPA). It focuses on combat propaganda, that is, informational activities conducted in support of military operations and intended to demoralize Japanese combatants. It examines Allied efforts to manipulate the thoughts of the enemy and describes the "mind war" as the men who conducted it perceived their work, namely, as one aspect of the multifaceted war against Japan. It delineates the objectives of the psywar campaign, outlines the process by which propaganda was devised, evaluates the policies that guided its creation, and offers a number of criteria for judging its success. It also sheds light on the nature of the IJA's spiritual training and indoctrination by assessing both the strengths and the vulnerabilities of Japanese morale and shows how Allied propagandists exploited enemy weaknesses and devised ways to manipulate the core truths of Japanese military indoctrination.

The relative successes of the propaganda war against Japan must be attributed to the principles that guided and molded it. In this regard it is imperative to understand the philosophy that prevailed among SWPA propagandists: the raison d'être of the psywar apparatus was to contribute to Allied victory by exacerbating the demoralization that inevitably accompanies battlefield losses. Propagandists played a supporting role in the Pacific War. "Psychological warfare," said Brig. Gen. Bonner F. Fellers, head of the Psychological Warfare Branch (PWB), SWPA, "can proceed no faster than winning armies."[6] The work of propagandists was to build on the foundations laid by armed forces, to add salt to the wounds already inflicted by combat troops. In order to succeed, therefore, propagandists had to work closely with friendly forces in the field. The greater the cooperation between the forces wielding armaments and those wielding words, the greater the likelihood of success. A high level of cooperation also results, however, in making it more difficult to assess the impact of psychological operations, which cannot be judged apart from the conventional forces they augment. Nonetheless, the task is not impossible, for intelligence agencies accumulated much information pertinent to an assessment of Japanese morale and how it was affected by propaganda.

Two policies were central to Allied psywar operations: to tell the truth and to refrain from criticizing the Japanese emperor. The strategy of truth was designed primarily to establish and maintain the credibility of information disseminated by the Allies. It enabled propagandists to establish trust between themselves and the Japanese troops they hoped to influence. It dictated that psywarriors induce despair within the enemy's ranks by distributing accurate information. It prohibited the use of the "big lie," which was so typical of the informational programs of both Nazi Germany and imperial Japan. In a number of instances the strategy of truth significantly limited what propagandists could say. It was very difficult, for example, for propagandists to adhere to the strategy of truth and at the same time design propaganda that would mitigate the Allied policy of unconditional surrender. In the final analysis, however, it was an effective cornerstone of the campaign. Allied propaganda remained credible because it conformed to the real-life experiences of Japanese soldiers.

The decision not to criticize the Japanese emperor was also astute. Rather than blaming the emperor for the devastating results of the war, which would have alienated the target audience, Allied propaganda portrayed the emperor as an unwitting victim of the militarists who controlled Japan, whose policies were leading Japan down the path to destruction. Like the strategy of truth, portraying the emperor as a victim made Allied propaganda more credible to Japanese soldiers, who revered the emperor to such an extent that they could not bring themselves to hold him responsible for the debacle that was the Pacific War.

The primary objective of the psywar campaign against the IJA in the Southwest Pacific was to induce demoralization among Japanese combatants and thus hasten Japan's defeat. Because the leading cause of demoralization was military defeat, Allied propagandists devised a plan of attack to capitalize on the combat successes of Allied armed forces. By distributing a propaganda barrage that continually focused the attention of enemy troops on the deteriorating military situation, Allied propagandists sought to convince Japanese forces in the field that Japan's defeat was inevitable. The Allied propaganda war also aimed at convincing Japanese soldiers that the longer they continued to fight the greater the destruction of their beloved homeland would be.

Although SWPA propagandists communicated with enemy troops in a variety of ways, leaflets were their primary weapon. A textual analysis of these leaflets reveals that Allied propaganda fell into four general categories. Divisive propaganda aimed at exacerbating preexisting tensions between various constituencies of Japan's armed forces. In particular, it exploited interservice rivalries and the strained relations between officers and enlisted men within the IJA. Subversive propaganda sought to undermine the confidence of the enemy by questioning the core truths of Japanese military indoctrination. For example, it challenged enemy soldiers' belief that they were fighting for a righteous cause, that "Japanese spirit" was sufficient to ensure Japan's victory, that Japan's military leaders were acting in accordance with the will of the emperor, and that death on the battlefield was infinitely superior to life as a POW. Enlightenment propaganda was designed to give Japanese troops a more accurate picture of the enemy they were fighting as well as the objectives of the war from an Allied perspective. Finally, Allied propagandists sought to foment despair among Japanese troops by providing them with indisputable evidence that Japan was losing the war. Propaganda of despair relied in large part on the dissemination of war news that illustrated Japan's declining military fortunes and emphasized the Allies' superior material, industrial, and human resources. The most prevalent theme of

Allied propaganda was the material superiority of the Allied powers. In every facet of their propaganda campaign propagandists assaulted the Japanese maxim that the power of the Japanese spirit was sufficient to overcome Allied material superiority. For this reason, the Japanese diarist who began to doubt that Japanese spirit alone could secure victory was particularly reassuring to propagandists.

The Allied propaganda war achieved varying degrees of success. Enlightenment propaganda, for example, was never particularly persuasive. Mere words failed to convince Japanese troops that GIs were really compassionate human beings who would never shoot a surrendering soldier or torture a POW or that Allied war aims were legitimate. Likewise, subversive propaganda generally failed to convince Japanese soldiers that the concept of "death before dishonor" was irrational and outmoded. On the other hand, there is evidence that as the war progressed Japanese soldiers did begin to question the notion that the unique spirit of Japanese soldiers was sufficient to overcome all odds, that Japan's military leaders were faithfully and capably implementing the will of the emperor, and that the goals of the "Greater East Asia War" were pure. The results of divisive propaganda were quite promising: tensions between enlisted men and their officers became a significant problem, and army personnel became increasingly critical of the Imperial Navy.

In the end, the propaganda of despair was the key to achieving the stated objectives of the Allied psywar campaign, for an army pervaded by a sense of despair loses its cohesion and fighting effectiveness, is more subject to defeatism, and succumbs more easily to the debilitating effects of enemy propaganda. An examination of Japanese documents recovered during the Pacific War and its aftermath, the testimony of Japanese POWs, and the wartime analysis of Allied intelligence agencies provides evidence of declining Japanese morale, discipline, and combat effectiveness in addition to an increasing incidence of surrender and desertion. Research also indicates that Japanese combatants found Allied propaganda more convincing as the war continued and that Japan's high command expressed concern over the perfidious influence of enemy propaganda, which was said to be infecting the minds of the emperor's soldiers with "dangerous ideas."

Demoralization among Japanese combatants was directly related to their experiences on the battlefield. Successive military defeats combined with the debilitating effects of supply shortages eroded the confidence and stamina of Japanese troops. That combat troops become demoralized as battlefield conditions deteriorate is a truism. My purpose here is not so much to argue that Japanese morale declined as the war progressed, although that is most certainly the case and much of the evidence presented in this volume supports that conclusion. I am more directly concerned with examining how Allied propagandists uncovered the sources of Japanese morale and devised appropriate methods for undermining it, as well as providing some tentative conclusions about the extent to which the loss of morale among Japanese combatants in the Southwest Pacific can be attributed to Allied psychological warfare operations.

1 Tracing the Historical Roots of Propaganda in Wartime

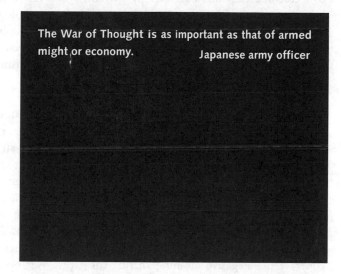

> The War of Thought is as important as that of armed might or economy.   Japanese army officer

        Two thousand years ago the Chinese philosopher Sun Tzu, in his classic treatise *The Art of War*, recognized the impact of psychological factors on the conduct of military operations. Sun Tzu argued that it was a superior general who could "render others' armies helpless without fighting" and "overcome opponents by dispiriting them rather than by battling with them." Some nineteen centuries later, Carl von Clausewitz analyzed the internal dynamics of warfare in his *On War*, which placed the "analysis of psychological forces at the very center of the study of war." Clausewitz emphasized the critical wartime role of "immaterial forces" such as morale, spirit, genius, and enthusiasm for the cause. He said that while these moral elements of war "can be neither counted nor classified," they "constitute the spirit which permeates the whole being of war."[1]

        Indeed, the nature and outcome of warfare, as of any human endeavor, are largely dependent on the individual talents and cumulative experiences of the people who engage in it. To study the material and technological aspects of modern warfare to the exclusion of its emotional, spiritual, and intellectual elements is foolish. The very existence of war requires that one possess not only the physical means to sustain an armed struggle but a mentality that predisposes one to initiate it or persevere in it. It follows, then, that hostilities cease when one of these two essential elements has been destroyed—when one combatant no longer possesses either the physical means or the psychological will to carry on the fight. The purpose of combat operations is to physically destroy the enemy's physical and material ability to make war. The objective of psychological operations is to erode his will to continue the fight.

■   ■   ■

Despite a centuries-long awareness of the vital role psychological factors play in wartime, the term *psychological warfare* is a product of the twentieth century. J. F. C. Fuller, a British officer and military strategist, was the first to use the term, in his *Tanks in the Great War, 1914–1918*, published in 1920, in which he assessed the impact of armor on warfare.

In World War I efforts to manipulate the mind of the enemy were commonly referred to as *propaganda*, a word that originated during the Counter Reformation in reference to the propagation of the Catholic faith. In its original context *propaganda* was essentially a neutral term. It contracted a negative meaning during the Great War because of the popular outrage over the belligerents' systematic efforts to manipulate the attitudes and ideas of friends, foes, and neutrals. By the 1930s the word conjured up notions of evil forces intent on brainwashing the unsuspecting.

And yet, perceptions of the "good" or "evil" content of a particular message have nothing to do with whether it is propaganda. Propaganda is merely a form of persuasive communication. It is designed to persuade the target audience to respond to a particular issue or idea either favorably or unfavorably. By contrast, *information* denotes a balanced representation of available facts and opinion (the two must be identified as such) presented so as to encourage the audience to reach its own conclusions rather than to persuade it to adopt a prescribed point of view. What distinguishes propaganda from information is the intent of the communicator, not the content of the message. Just as propaganda is not categorically evil, neither is it synonymous with the dissemination of lies. Again, the key is the intent of the communicator, not the content of the message. Propagandists may make use of falsehoods if they increase the persuasiveness of the argument. As a general rule, however, truth (or at least half-truth) is crucial to propaganda's success, for falsehoods, if discovered, destroy the credibility of the communicator as well as the message and thus subvert the propagandist's purpose.

In wartime, propaganda serves one of three purposes: it increases support for the war effort among friendly peoples, encourages neutrals either to remain unaligned or to become allies, or diminishes an enemy's will to remain in the war. The predispositions of the target population thus establish the parameters of wartime propaganda. Within those parameters the precise aim of the message determines its content. Propaganda may encourage the audience to take immediate action or simply provide the enemy with discouraging news. In any case, wartime propaganda plays a supporting role, for its primary purpose is to facilitate a nation's efforts to achieve military victory.

Psychological warfare, or psywar, has as many definitions as there are psywar specialists. Simply stated, psywar, when it is directed against an enemy population, is merely a label for nonviolent activities aimed at destroying the enemy's will to continue the fight. It is an aspect of war that attacks the enemy psychologically rather than physically. It must be pursued in combination with the political, economic, and military dimensions of a total war effort. Psywar operations are intended to achieve military advantages without the direct application of violence. Propaganda (i.e., persuasive communication) is simply the instrument most frequently used to gain such advantages.

Propaganda in warfare, like the military operations it augments, is often divided into two broad categories, strategic and tactical. *Strategic propaganda* focuses on long-range goals at the highest psychological level, such as the gradual but continuous demoralization of the enemy or the mobilization of support for one's own war effort. It is most commonly directed at audiences outside the immediate combat area. *Tactical propaganda* comprises informational activities that accompany combat operations. It is most often aimed at enemy combatants and may be designed to elicit immediate results of tactical advantage on the battlefield. Nonetheless, "tactical" propaganda operations ("tactical" in that they are conducted against enemy troops in combat areas) are very often designed to achieve long-range, that is "strategic," objectives, such as the gradual demoralization of enemy combatants. For this reason, it is more accurate to use the term *combat propaganda* for informational activities conducted against enemy forces in the field.

.   .   .

During World War I state-organized propaganda campaigns became an integral part of national war efforts. Of course "the war to end all wars," to use the rhetoric of the day, did not achieve that lofty objective. It did, however, produce a blueprint for much of the wartime propaganda disseminated during World War II, by which time propaganda in support of a nation's military effort was referred to as psychological warfare.

Propaganda in World War I served three purposes. It mobilized hatred of the enemy, sought the support of neutral nations (in this contest the British won the grand prize—American participation in the war as an Associated Power to the Entente), and attacked the morale of enemy military forces and civilian populations. American propaganda efforts during World War I focused on mobilizing support on the home front, embracing an idealistic rhetoric that complimented Wilsonian diplomacy. The heightened expectations elicited by "the war to end all wars" plummeted with the subsequent peace, creating a postwar disillusionment that, among other things, engendered a widespread aversion to propaganda. American propaganda organizations, and their British counterparts for that matter, were immediately disbanded at the end of World War I. Nonetheless, some scholars writing during the interwar period concluded that propaganda had become an integral part of twentieth-century warfare and thus demanded greater attention, not less.[2] Largely as a result of American antipathy to the use of propaganda, the knowledge and experience gained during the war in the area of informational activities was quickly diverted into such newly developing fields as public relations and advertising. For the United States, the postwar foreign policy of noninterventionism paralleled a similar inward-looking trend in the sphere of persuasive communication.

The outbreak of World War II found the United States unprepared to mobilize its communications resources, whereas the Nazis and the Soviets had fully developed and formidable propaganda capabilities. Yet rapid mobilization in times of crisis, the dominant feature of U.S. military planning throughout its history, was once again called upon to correct the deficiencies resulting from peacetime neglect. Overlooked in peacetime, psywar planning and operations commenced after the outbreak of war on an ad hoc basis.

. . .

To understand the structure of the propaganda war in the Southwest Pacific requires some knowledge of the complex bureaucratic apparatus created by the United States to wage psywar on a global scale. The organizational structure first created in 1942 produced a confusing array of jurisdictional divisions, bureaucratic squabbles, and ultimately an exceedingly confusing network of interrelated agencies charged with performing information activities both at home and abroad. In the beginning, President Franklin D. Roosevelt authorized the creation of two civilian agencies, the Office of War Information (owi) and the Office of Strategic Services (oss), to conduct information programs and other strategic services (in other words, propaganda and psywar operations). owi emerged from a 13 June 1942 executive order, which called on it to "formulate and carry out, through the use of the press, radio, motion picture and other facilities, information programs designed to facilitate the development of an informed and intelligent understanding, at home and abroad, of the status and progress of the war effort and of the war policies, activities and aims of the government."[3] owi consisted of a Domestic Branch to disseminate information internally and an Overseas Operations Branch responsible for informational activities in all foreign nations except those in Latin America, which was the province of the Office of the Coordinator of Inter-American Affairs (ciaa).

Theoretically, the functions of oss, formerly known as the Office of the Coordinator of Information (coi), did not conflict with those of owi. oss was to collect "secret and strategic information in foreign countries" and to perform "general miscellaneous strategic services abroad, other than the dissemination of information by radio, leaflets, etc."; the latter activities were part of owi's domain.[4] Nevertheless, interagency disputes soon developed over the dissemination of information abroad. Much of the controversy resulted from conflicting interpretations of what constituted propaganda as opposed to psychological warfare. oss Director William Donovan perceived intelligence gathering, propaganda, and psywar operations as three sequential steps leading up to the application of military force. Conventional attack, according to Donovan, first required intelligence penetration of enemy nations. The analysis and processing of this intelligence provided the background for the second step, which he defined as propaganda designed to weaken the enemy's will to resist. Finally, psywar entailed special operations such as sabotage and subversion, followed by commando raids and guerrilla uprisings to thoroughly soften up the enemy's territory in preparation for conventional military attack.[5] Donovan argued that OWI should be in charge of propaganda, which he defined as open, general informational activities, while OSS should have responsibility for psywar, which he regarded as activities tied more closely to combat operations.

In March 1943 the rivalry between OWI and OSS over which agency had control of overseas propaganda culminated in another executive order that confirmed OWI's control of overseas information and propaganda programs. A 13 March executive order instructed OWI to "plan, develop, execute . . . foreign propaganda activities involving dissemination of information."[6] In other words, OWI was to conduct "white" propaganda operations, while OSS continued its activities in covert ("black") propaganda and other "special services," such as unconventional warfare, guerrilla activities behind enemy lines, interaction with resistance groups, sabotage, and subversion. More importantly for this study, however, Roosevelt's executive order confirmed what theater commanders had established in practice, namely, that all propaganda activities executed in a theater of military operations were subject to the theater commander's control.

Military control of psywar operations was seen as essential for two reasons. First, combat propaganda had to be closely linked with military operations since it existed to serve specific strategic or tactical purposes. Second, effective psywar required access to military plans and intelligence, and theater commanders deemed the presence of independent psywar units a security risk. For pragmatic reasons, then, they demanded operational control over all activities and personnel within their respective theaters in order to better coordinate psywar activities, however defined, with military operations and to clarify civilian propagandists' subordinate relationship to military personnel.

While theater commanders exercised operational control over psywar, the War Department's Military Intelligence Division (G-2) directed and coordinated the army's informational activities to ensure conformance with Joint Chiefs of Staff (JCS) and State Department policies. Within the War Department, psywar activities were handled successively by several different agencies. From June 1941 to January 1942, PWB of G-2 supervised psywar operations. The Special Study Group inherited this function in January 1942. Three months later, in March 1942, the Military Intelligence Division once again shifted authority over the army's psywar activities to a newly created agency, the Psychological Branch. The Military Intelligence Division itself experienced a change in March

1942, when the War Department divided it into two parts: an operational unit and a policy-making unit. The operational unit, known as the Military Intelligence Service (MIS), assumed authority over the Psychological Branch at this time.

The Psychological Branch published daily summaries and special studies of foreign propaganda and helped plan leaflet-dropping campaigns conducted by overseas commands. It also prepared plans and an instruction manual for combat propaganda teams and supervised the activation of such teams. In December 1942 the Psychological Branch was replaced by the Foreign Press Section, which persisted for nearly a year.

The War Department created the Propaganda Branch in November 1943, when it assumed the functions of the Foreign Press Section. The Propaganda Branch, which lasted until the end of the war, had the longest administrative life of all of the War Department's psywar-related agencies. Its principal mission was to coordinate the War Department's diverse propaganda activities and ensure that both OWI and OSS activities conformed to JCS and State Department policies. The chief of the Propaganda Branch represented the U.S. Army on the JCS Joint Psychological Warfare Committee (JPWC). In short, the Propaganda Branch was the controlling federal agency for government information and propaganda activities abroad. It had access to all policy directives and information about future operations and thus fulfilled the need for coordination between OWI, OSS, and the War Department's propaganda agencies in the field.[7]

Inevitably, these complex bureaucratic entanglements did not produce uniform psywar structures at the various theater headquarters. Rather, a variety of organizational relationships emerged between OWI's Overseas Branch, OSS, and theater psywar units.[8] In the ETO, for example, Gen. Dwight D. Eisenhower created the Psychological Warfare Branch, Allied Forces Headquarters (PWB, AFHQ) in December 1942 to participate in the North African campaign. In this instance, PWB, AFHQ incorporated OWI, OSS, the Political Intelligence Department (British) (PID), and the Ministry of Information (British) (MOI). Eisenhower's integration of the British and American forces in psywar paralleled the interallied cooperation achieved in military operations. In February 1944 General Eisenhower enlarged PWB, AFHQ and gave it a new title— Psychological Warfare Division, Supreme Headquarters Allied Expeditionary Forces (PWD, SHAEF). Like its forerunner, PWD, SHAEF comprised both American and British military and civilian personnel. In the ETO, then, OWI and OSS functioned as service agencies for operations in the combat zone.

The head of PWD, Brig. Gen. Robert McClure, maintained close ties to SHAEF headquarters to ensure Eisenhower's control over psywar operations. The War Department's Propaganda Branch functioned as the liaison agency between the War Department and PWD. McClure also had four deputies, each representing one of the civilian agencies that contributed personnel to PWD (OWI, OSS, and the two British organizations).[9]

SHAEF's overall objective was to destroy Germany's armed forces. To assist SHAEF, PWD was "to destroy the fighting morale of our enemy, both at home and on the front." The Mobile Radio Broadcasting Company (MRBC) served as the basic army field operating unit for psywar in the ETO. MRBCS were normally broken up into smaller teams that worked in direct support of front-line combat units. MRBCS also employed staff from both British and American military and civilian organizations concerned with psywar. PWD operated under a chain of command that began with the respective heads of the Allied nations as represented by the Combined Chiefs of Staff (CCS) and descended through the commander of the joint headquarters at SHAEF to PWD. This command structure ensured that both British and American policies shaped propaganda operations in the ETO.[10]

In the war against Japan the theater commanders again defined the form psywar operations would take and determined what agencies would be involved in its conduct. In the China theater, for example, Gen. Joseph Stilwell directed that the Sino-American Cooperative Organization (SACO), which operated as an intelligence and guerrilla-warfare unit, coordinate OSS activities. Beginning in April 1944 OSS served as a tactical intelligence-gathering agency for Maj. Gen. Claire L. Chennault's Fourteenth Air Force. Not until February 1945, after Stilwell was replaced by Lt. Gen. Albert C. Wedemeyer, did OSS begin to operate directly under the commanding general as an independent agency in charge of clandestine operations. OWI's operations in China emanated from its headquarters in Chungking, under the direction of F. MacCracken Fisher, and focused on leaflet operations aimed at Japanese troops as well as Chinese, French, Annamese, Manchurian, Korean, and Taiwanese civilians.[11]

Adm. Chester Nimitz employed the services of OWI in the North and Central Pacific Areas but did not allow OSS to operate there. He left the decision whether these organizations would be permitted to function in the South Pacific to Adm. William Halsey. In March 1943 Nimitz, his operations staff, and an OWI representative attended a series of meetings to discuss the creation of an OWI Pacific command team. The OWI representative later wrote, "There was evidenced a general lack of belief in the worthwhileness of OWI efforts along propaganda lines and covert doubt as to its general usefulness." Yet, he stressed, Nimitz himself was "not unsympathetic to propaganda warfare . . . and is willing to give us a fair shake in his theater." Halsey, on the other hand, was described as interested only in "fighting, fighting, fighting, and regards psychological warfare as some impractical plaything of effete civilians."[12] That impression was apparently correct, for in the end Halsey refused both OWI and OSS clearance to operate under his command.

OWI did not establish a presence in Nimitz's command until March 1944, when it opened an overseas branch in Honolulu and began full-scale propaganda activities. From Hawaii OWI worked under the jurisdiction of the Joint Intelligence Center, Pacific Ocean Areas (JICPOA), operating jointly with Nimitz's Psychological Warfare Section, created in June 1944. OWI, however, maintained an independent identity from the Psychological Warfare Section, unlike in SWPA.[13]

■ ■ ■

On 18 April 1942 the War Department established General Headquarters, Southwest Pacific Area (GHQ, SWPA) in Melbourne, Australia, and appointed Gen. Douglas MacArthur supreme commander. The area encompassed Australia, the Bismarck Archipelago, New Guinea, the Solomons, the Netherlands East Indies (exclusive of Sumatra), and the Philippine Islands. SWPA was an "integrated, combined headquarters," wielding operational control over all Allied ground, sea, and air forces and employing staff officers from air, ground, and naval forces of the United States, Great Britain, Australia, and the Netherlands. The subordinate tactical headquarters were also interallied in nature and consisted of the Allied Land Forces, under an Australian commander (Gen. Thomas Blamey), and the Allied Air Forces and Allied Naval Forces, both under American commanders (Maj. Gen. George Kenney after August 1942 and Vice Adm. Herbert F. Leary).

Many authors have criticized MacArthur for mistrusting OWI and rejecting OSS. Their criticisms are misguided, however, since informational and intelligence activities were ongoing when MacArthur arrived in

Australia. Independent guerrilla resistance movements spontaneously arose in the Philippine Islands, and the Royal Australian Navy had formed a network of coastwatchers to monitor and report on Japanese movements in the Pacific even before the outbreak of war in Europe. Although some attribute MacArthur's disaffection for OWI to his belief that it was part of an "administrative conspiracy" working against him and argue that he absolutely refused to permit OSS to operate in the Southwest Pacific, Maj. Gen. Charles A. Willoughby, MacArthur's chief intelligence officer, maintained that MacArthur did not so much refuse its services as decide that he simply did not have time to wait for its help. OSS did not operate in SWPA for good reason. Since the Allied Intelligence Bureau (AIB), its Australian counterpart, was already well established in the area, MacArthur simply integrated it into a new theater organization under his command, allowing a successful unit to continue without disruption. As MacArthur's chief of staff put it, the combination of AIB, the Allied Translator and Interpreter Section (ATIS), the Allied Geographical Section (AGS), and the Central Bureau (CB) provided SWPA with its own office of strategic services.[14]

In July 1942 MacArthur's headquarters directed AIB to "obtain and report information of the enemy in the SWPA, and in addition, where practical . . . weaken the enemy by sabotage and destruction of morale, and . . . render aid and assistance to local efforts in the same end in enemy-occupied territories." Also in July, GHQ created the Far Eastern Liaison Office (FELO) as Section D of AIB. FELO's mission was to plan and direct propaganda operations against the Japanese and to the inhabitants of enemy-occupied territories in SWPA. An Australian "comptroller" (Col. C. G. Roberts) who was also the Australian Army's military intelligence director controlled AIB's activities and was responsible to G-2, GHQ, SWPA. Thus, Australia combined the functions of OSS and OWI into one military intelligence agency.[15]

FELO operated almost exclusively in British and Dutch territories, unilaterally until June 1944. It was only after the Allied victory at Hollandia (New Guinea), and in preparation for the invasion of the Philippine Islands, that MacArthur established an American psywar unit, the Psychological Warfare Branch, Southwest Pacific Area (PWB, SWPA). At that time PWB incorporated several FELO personnel as well as approximately twenty-four OWI staff members into its organizational structure. The chief of OWI in SWPA, Frederic S. Marquardt, supervised OWI's limited activities from Brisbane, Australia. Marquardt had been born in the Philippine Islands of American parents (his father had been director of education in the Philippines) and had been a newsman in Manila for many years. Not only was he intimately acquainted with Filipino culture and language but he had many friends on MacArthur's staff, who proved to be valuable links between owi and GHQ.[16]

MacArthur also created the office of military secretary to take charge of the new pwb and report to him personally on developments in the propaganda field, then appointed Brig. Gen. Bonner F. Fellers to fill the position. Fellers wrote in his official report on psywar in swpa that MacArthur established pwb when he did for two specific reasons. First, prior to the Allied victory at Hollandia, Japanese military successes precluded an effective psywar campaign. The function of psychological operations "is to exploit military victories," said Fellers. "Psychological warfare can proceed no faster than winning armies." His second reason was also a consequence of the military situation. The Allied occupation of Hollandia secured a harbor from which to launch the long-awaited Philippine campaign, and psywar was deemed "an essential adjunct to the sweep into the Philippines." pwb thus originated out of military necessity and throughout its existence functioned to exploit military victories.[17]

. . .

The propaganda devised by pwb in the Southwest Pacific did not differ markedly from what was employed in other theaters of the war. And taken as a whole the substance of World War II propaganda was not radically different from that of World War I (with one exception: the atrocity propaganda so prevalent during World War I was noticeably absent from World War II). In both wars belligerents disseminated combat propaganda designed to spread discouragement, incite defeatism, and encourage disintegration. In both wars combat propaganda generally focused on advertising one's own military victories and publicizing the enemy's losses and relied primarily on divisive propaganda themes designed to disrupt the unity of the enemy coalition and exploit schisms within the enemy's ranks. Perhaps the most significant difference between World War I and World War II propaganda operations was the method of distribution, for the advent of air power enabled nations at war to deliver news, information, and propaganda in mass quantities to even the most remote areas of the globe. It is also worth remembering that for the United States, which entered World War I only in 1917 and then directed the bulk of its propaganda at the home front, the conduct of psywar against enemy populations was a new undertaking.

During World War II the Allies engaged in psywar operations against the Axis in every operational theater of the war. The strategic objectives of the propaganda war against enemy combatants were the same throughout: to diminish their fighting spirit and thus hasten Allied victory. Despite the similar goals, the organizational structures created to conduct psywar in operational theaters were complex and varied. Moreover, the Allied propaganda war was of necessity a multidimensional undertaking since it attempted to influence a wide variety of people. Because propagandists appealed to numerous civilian populations in addition to enemy troops, Allied psywar operations were multinational, multilingual, and multidimensional. The Allies waged a series of distinct propaganda wars conditioned by theater command structures, by the pace of Allied military progress, and, above all else, by the Allied understanding of the enemy culture.

2 Building a Psychological Warfare Capability on Australian Foundations

> From the outset, it was insisted on in FELO that every leaflet and other propaganda weapon should give only those aspects which could be proved. Exaggeration, even in its mildest forms, was not approved, the attitude being that, if we were once caught out in a lie, we should find it very difficult to live down that lie and our value would at once diminish.
>
> FELO officer

Psychological warfare operations in the Southwest Pacific can be divided roughly into two time periods. Prior to June 1944 the Australian agency known as the Far Eastern Liaison Office, or FELO, was the Allied organization responsible for disseminating information to both enemy troops and civilian populations in the theater. Although OSS did not function in SWPA, OWI representatives became involved in psywar operations at an early date through their association with FELO. Until mid-1944 General MacArthur allowed the Australian agency to dominate information activities, even to the point of rejecting an OWI request to send a representative directly to GHQ for fear of incurring the hostility of the Australians. The second phase of the propaganda war began in June 1944 when MacArthur authorized the creation of a new psywar agency. Thereafter, American military personnel became responsible for coordinating the theater's propaganda operations.

MacArthur established PWB in June 1944 in anticipation of the long-awaited Allied invasion of the Philippine Islands. To MacArthur's way of thinking, the fighting of the previous two and a half years had been directed toward this objective, and his near obsession with returning to the

Philippines as a mighty conqueror influenced his attitude toward propaganda operations as well. As the invasion of the Philippines became imminent MacArthur determined that the time was right for his headquarters to take a more active role in psywar operations. Yet it was the Australians that established the foundations for PWB's subsequent successes, for FELO personnel trained the novice American propagandists in the theory and methods of psywar as they had waged it prior to the summer of 1944.

.   .   .

FELO was originally part of AIB, though it was soon separated from that agency and became a "semi-independent" organization under the command of the Australian Chiefs of Staff and led by Comdr. J. C. R. Proud, of the Royal Australian Naval Reserve. Under that arrangement FELO came under the authority of the commander, Allied Land Forces, Gen. Thomas Blamey, while the Australian minister for external affairs provided political direction for propaganda matters in accordance with the advice of the Australian Political Warfare Committee. Nonetheless, FELO retained a close association with AIB and frequently detached field operatives to AIB units.[1]

FELO's objectives were to lower the morale of enemy forces, mislead the enemy about Allied military intentions, and persuade civilians in enemy-occupied territories to assist the Allies. To achieve these goals FELO created mobile propaganda units, disseminated leaflets, and engaged in some radio broadcasting. It also sent agents into enemy-occupied areas to enlist native support and collect field intelligence. Most FELO personnel were drawn from the Australian Military Forces (AMF), though the other Australian services and the Netherlands also contributed manpower. From an original strength of only 5 men FELO expanded to more than 470 people by the end of the war. Although a small number of civilians were employed to perform technical and professional roles, FELO was by design a military organization. It was believed that an organization dominated by civilians would be "incapable of appreciating the difficulties of operations conducted in the field, or the state of mind of the troops against whom they were operating."[2] Given the relative success with which PWB subsequently combined the skills of OWI civilians and military personnel, this concern was perhaps ill-founded. Nevertheless, FELO drew its human resources from the various military services operating in the theater, believing that this would result in better propaganda and closer ties between propagandists and the combat forces they augmented.

FELO's first leaflet drop occurred in August 1942, when the United States Army Air Forces (USAAF) distributed Japanese-language news bulletins announcing the Allied victory in the Battle of Coral Sea. FELO was subsequently involved in more intensive leaflet campaigns in Buna and Sanananda (New Guinea), and thereafter the majority of combat missions flown in the theater included the scattering of propaganda materials on enemy troops. During the war FELO operated primarily in areas under the jurisdiction of the Australian, British, and Dutch governments, disseminating more than 58 million leaflets in six different languages and several native dialects.

OWI became involved in propaganda operations in August 1942, when its representatives were instructed to cooperate with the Australian Political Warfare Committee and work under the control of the American minister to Australia. OWI's Overseas Branch established its Australian outpost in Sydney at this time.[3] OWI policymakers wanted one of their representatives assigned to MacArthur's headquarters to "work directly with, and under the direction of, the American theater commander," as was being done in Eisenhower's command. But MacArthur rejected OWI's request, preferring OWI to continue to act under the direction of the American minister to Australia and in cooperation with FELO. MacArthur contended that the Australians were very "sensitive" about their prerogatives with regard to propaganda activities in SWPA and might become "resentful and suspicious" if OWI were permitted a more independent role. He did, however, "anticipate the possibility" that an OWI representative might be attached to GHQ when it came time to initiate the Philippines campaign.[4]

By mid-1943 all OWI propaganda was being created in collaboration with a branch of the armed services and required the approval of GHQ, SWPA before distribution. Prior to the creation of PWB in mid-1944, OWI focused "almost entirely" on raising the morale of Australians, keeping them informed of the American war effort, and supplying FELO with leaflets as requested by various military commands. OWI's informational activities consisted of radio broadcasts on Australian networks, the creation of U.S. information libraries in Australia and New Zealand, and the distribution of news publications, posters, exhibits, filmstrips, and documentary films.[5]

When MacArthur approved the creation of PWB in June 1944, it began to oversee all psywar operations in the theater. Yet it was FELO that laid the foundations for the propaganda war against Japan. What Australian propagandists had learned through trial and error became PWB's guiding principles. Indeed, FELO provided a number of its own personnel to serve as the nucleus of what became PWB and trained the first contingent of American operatives in the theater. FELO training, coordinated by its director, Proud, stressed both psywar methods and the need to understand the target audience. It began by teaching American psywar personnel about Japan. The course included assessments of the "racial sources" and cultural characteristics of the Japanese people and lectures on Japanese history. Because FELO also propagandized indigenous populations in the Netherlands East Indies, New Guinea, and elsewhere in SWPA, Comdr. Proud lectured on the history and culture of these peoples as well.

Effective psywar operations required proper timing, said the head of FELO. "The right leaflet at the right place at the right moment is the crux of the whole program." The second requirement was intimately related to timing: psywar must be perceived as "one of the fighting forces," a weapon to be used operationally in light of local situations. Proud drilled into his students that successful psywar began with the collection of intelligence relevant to a particular operational area. It then proceeded through a planning stage six to eight weeks prior to the start of a military campaign, which focused on determining the enemy's weaknesses based on current intelligence. Once the enemy's weaknesses were pinpointed, propaganda was devised to exploit specific vulnerabilities. According to Proud, propaganda initially should be very subtle in nature. With the passage of time and the further weakening of the enemy, propaganda should become more blatant, "until the propaganda at the final stage becomes bold and outright." Proud insisted that proper timing was essential throughout the process, for if the propaganda became too bold before the enemy was sufficiently weakened by the application of military force, it would fail to achieve its objective.[6]

FELO instructors delineated ten basic rules for propaganda directed at Japanese combatants. Japanese language leaflets must be written in a style that was "paternal but not cold," avoided any semblance of condescension, and appealed to Japanese emotions in a gently persuasive manner. Propaganda should not offend or humiliate the reader, should not be boastful, should never place blame on the target audience, and should leave the impression that the Allies appreciated the good in the

Japanese people, who had been forced into war by the militaristic aggression of their leaders. Leaflet writers were told never to force the enemy into a corner without providing a way out and to convince the Japanese that death in battle was not man's "proper destiny." Finally, they should make sure that every word and phrase was sincere, suggest the possibility of a bright future when the war ended, and produce materials that encouraged Japanese to draw their own conclusions rather than subjecting them to the answers that seemed clear to Allied propagandists.

FELO's training regimen outlined three stages in the development of an effective psywar campaign. The first stage began with the opening air offensive, at which time propaganda leaflets should seek to create doubts and suspicions in the enemy's mind regarding the war situation. FELO suggested that propagandists achieve this objective by disseminating news bulletins summarizing Allied victories in local areas. War news should include maps and photographs to illustrate in the starkest manner possible the adverse military situation facing the Japanese army. Operatives should also create doubt by pointing out the failures of Japan's military leaders that had led to the army's current difficulties and the isolation of Japanese forces in the South Pacific. In a similar vein, propagandists should highlight Japan's isolation by discussing the lack of support provided by its European allies in an effort to raise questions about the wisdom and foresight of Japan's leaders. FELO instructors also encouraged leaflets demonstrating the superiority of Allied production as well as the moral qualities and spiritual determination of Allied troops. Finally, Phase 1 operations included leaflets describing developments in the Japanese home islands to produce nostalgia among troops.

Phase 2 commenced, according to FELO, "when the aerial activity over the area has reached a pitch of intensity" such that it was clear that the "Allied attack is imminent." During this phase leaflet drops should occur after the Allies had landed in the vicinity of the target audience, but in areas not yet under attack. The objective of this phase of the campaign was the same as that of the first phase: to diminish enemy morale and erode fighting efficiency. Leaflets were to emphasize Allied air and sea superiority and deficiencies in Japan's lines of communication and supply. Attacks on Japan's military leaders continued, but the focal point was the failure of local commanders to repulse Allied landings. Phase 2 leaflets should also criticize Japanese naval and air forces for failing to protect ground troops, thus creating dissension and distrust among the Japanese armed services. War news outlining Allied successes in other areas of the Pacific should continue thereby disabusing the enemy of the notion that although they were losing ground, Japanese forces elsewhere were succeeding. Phase 2 operations also included leaflets designed to break down Japanese aversion to surrender by emphasizing Allied adherence to the Geneva Convention's regulations for the treatment of prisoners and supplying pictures and stories illustrating the humane treatment of Japanese already in captivity.

Phase 3 operations occurred in areas where Allied troops had landed and made contact with the enemy. Propaganda in this stage sought to make surrender a credible option to Japanese troops. FELO instructors advised concentrating on the immediate circumstances facing enemy soldiers, in particular the prevalence of disease, food and supply shortages, officer desertion, and other vulnerabilities known through intelligence channels to encumber the enemy's efficiency. "Spot news" replaced more general war news in this phase of the campaign. Spot news drew attention to Allied military successes in the region and the immediate consequences for Japanese troops. Leaflets containing spot news often acknowledged the relentless nature and devastating impact of Allied bombing and strafing in the area. Phase 3 operations also included surrender appeals; leaflets encouraged Japanese troops to cease resistance and explained how to surrender safely. By way of conclusion, FELO representatives declared that the "intelligent selection of leaflets and their effective distribution" was the most vital aspect of propaganda operations. As a consequence, they stressed the key role played by aircrews, who distributed the bulk of Allied propaganda, and the importance of maintaining friendly relations with them.

■   ■   ■

When MacArthur approved the creation of PWB in June 1944 its mission was to facilitate the retaking of the Philippines, and its objectives were identical to FELO's: to weaken the enemy's will to resist, influence oppressed peoples to cooperate with the Allies, and mislead the enemy in an effort to further military operations. PWB used the same media as FELO: news publications, leaflets, radio, and public-address systems. However, PWB personnel did not engage in field intelligence work, though they made excellent use of intelligence gathered by a multitude of other agencies. The essential difference between PWB and FELO was that PWB was an American operation targeting the Philippines and FELO was an Australian agency operating in areas under British, Australian, and Dutch jurisdiction.

In July 1944 PWB selected seventeen U.S. Army officers and twenty enlisted men to undergo basic training with FELO. These thirty-seven men became the nucleus of PWB, along with nine members of FELO who were brought into the organization at MacArthur's headquarters in Brisbane. Also at this time OWI personnel (previously in Sydney) were brought to GHQ, where they assisted PWB with psywar operations. Thereafter the practical relationship between FELO and PWB was one of "technical supervision and coordination of the dissemination of information to the enemy." FELO continued to conduct propaganda operations outside the Philippines throughout the war and remained under the control of the commander of the Allied Land Forces (Blamey). It never became an integral part of PWB, GHQ, though FELO personnel sometimes joined PWB units in the field. GHQ's decision to have American propagandists trained by experienced Australians demonstrates its confidence in FELO's expertise. That PWB planners consulted both FELO and OWI, as well as ATIS (whose vital role in the propaganda war will be discussed in later chapters), when shaping theater policies and objectives also illustrates GHQ's dependence upon Australian psywar and intelligence agencies.[7]

MacArthur's military secretary, Brig. Gen. Bonner F. Fellers, functioned as the theater's chief psywar officer. A 1918 graduate of West Point, Fellers apparently developed an interest and some expertise in Japanese military affairs during his program of study at the Command and General Staff School, where he produced a study entitled "The Psychology of the Japanese Soldier" in 1935. This study outlined his thinking about the IJA in the 1930s and contained ideas that continued to hold sway throughout his tenure as head of PWB. Fellers joined MacArthur's staff during the latter's tenure as military adviser to the Philippine government prior to the outbreak of the Pacific War. During this time Fellers established a personal relationship with MacArthur and undoubtedly solidified his interest in Asian affairs as well. Between 1940 and October 1943, when he joined MacArthur's staff in Australia, Fellers served as U.S. military attaché to Egypt, as an army instructor on desert warfare, and as a War Department representative to OSS's Planning Group. As early as August 1941, however, Fellers wrote to MacArthur of his desire to serve with him, referring to the "Orient" as his "first love." Not until September 1943, after Gen. George C. Marshall had alerted

MacArthur to Fellers's continued interest in serving at GHQ, SWPA, was Fellers reassigned with MacArthur's approval.[8]

As military secretary and head of PWB, Fellers planned and directed the U.S. propaganda war, monitored FELO activities, and coordinated the relationship between propagandists and Allied combat forces. He also functioned as a liaison with psywar personnel working elsewhere in the Pacific and Asia. On 2 August 1944 Fellers completed the "Basic Military Plan for Psychological Warfare in the Southwest Pacific Area," which became the guiding force behind PWB operations. It established the organization's goals, methods, and procedures and defined psychological warfare as "all activity directed against the enemy except guerrilla and orthodox warfare, and physical sabotage." The purpose of psywar, according to Fellers, was to further the military effort by weakening the fighting spirit of the enemy and thus hasten Japan's decision to surrender. To this end, Fellers stated, combat propagandists should strive to do three things: inspire despair among Japanese troops, discredit Japan's militaristic leaders, and make the enemy "surrender conscious."[9]

From the beginning Fellers insisted that taking Japanese prisoners was a secondary goal. In September 1944, for example, an OSS memo sent to Fellers concerning his "Basic Military Plan" declared that "the major object of psychological warfare against the Japanese soldier is to induce surrender." Fellers's marginal notations on the memo made it absolutely clear that he rejected that interpretation of his military plan. He wrote that such an emphasis was "WRONG!" In Fellers's opinion, the major object with regard to the Japanese soldier was "to weaken resistance and undermine morale."[10] In his scheme of things, surrender was a secondary consideration. Nonetheless, Fellers's "Basic Military Plan" stated that combat propagandists should not only make Japanese "surrender conscious" but also encourage them to "seek self-preservation." Perhaps Fellers doubted whether Japanese soldiers could be induced to surrender and therefore minimized the importance of taking prisoners in order not to set himself up for failure. Regardless, the notion that one can determine the relative success of a psywar campaign simply by counting the number of prisoners taken fails to take into account a variety of other evidence, most of which is more subtle and infinitely less quantifiable though nonetheless significant. Certainly, POW statistics are one criterion worth examining, but given that PWB's stated goal was to induce demoralization, the degree to which PWB propaganda induced surrender should not be overemphasized.

Fellers's "Basic Military Plan" established three functional divisions within PWB: the Collation Section, the Planning Department, and the Production Section. Situated between these three sections and the Office of the Military Secretary in the chain of command was the executive officer, Col. J. Woodall Greene. As executive officer, Greene implemented Fellers's plans and policies, supervised administration, and coordinated the work of the three section chiefs and the field units. He also composed the "Weekly Military Plan for Psychological Warfare," designed to achieve the organization's objectives in light of the changing military situation. Each week's plan was submitted to Fellers for his approval, then distributed to the Collation, Planning, and Production divisions to ensure a coordinated effort. The Collation Section compiled pertinent information from intelligence agencies operating throughout the Pacific and Asia and used it to ascertain Japanese psychological vulnerabilities. It then presented to the Planning Department clearcut objectives to guide PWB in exploiting those vulnerabilities.[11]

The Planning Department was responsible for shaping and timing psywar operations. It relied on the Collation Section's intelligence and the weekly military plans to develop weekly schedules for English- and Japanese-language radio broadcasts and the distribution of leaflets and newspapers. Planning Department schedules were designed so that propaganda activities coalesced into a unified program. The Planning Department also censored PWB output to safeguard military information and ensure conformity with GHQ policies. After receiving the executive officer's approval, the planners issued instructions to the Production Section in the form of weekly directives. The Production Section then produced newscasts, leaflets, news sheets, and magazines accordingly.[12]

Colonel Greene's weekly military plans also provided guidance on future propaganda operations related to anticipated developments. For example, leaflet texts and radio broadcasts announcing the surrender of Germany and the consequent isolation of Japan were in readiness at forward areas throughout the theater as early as March 1945 to allow for immediate distribution to Japan's armed forces. Other anticipatory planning, such as the preparation of leaflets in April 1945 announcing Soviet Russia's declaration of war on Japan, enabled PWB to respond to important developments as they occurred.[13]

The whole process was designed to ensure that the propaganda war was as thoroughly planned as conventional military operations. Fellers outlined four essential steps in psywar planning. First, propagandists must have a "detailed knowledge of enemy psychology." Understanding the enemy would lead naturally to the second step, which was a "recognition of enemy psychological vulnerabilities." Third, planners must select "decisive psychological objectives," and finally, they must present the "facts clearly, logically and properly timed."[14]

The executive officer and the Collation, Planning, and Production divisions were located at GHQ. They focused on long-range planning, coordination of theaterwide programs, and the production of leaflets that were sufficiently general to allow for widespread distribution. The exploitation of rapidly changing local situations was the purview of PWB field units assigned to lower echelons. If local conditions called for the creation of new propaganda material, PWB's field units were equipped to produce it, though detached units were instructed to use material already on hand (at PWB, GHQ or army headquarters) whenever possible.

PWB units attached to the Sixth and Eighth Armies produced leaflets for general distribution in their respective areas of operation and also responded to special requests from the corps and division level for leaflets applicable to more limited situations. Keeping in mind the weekly military plans developed by PWB, GHQ, Sixth and Eighth Army planners created their own schedules for producing and distributing propaganda in light of the opportunities created by tactical military successes.

On the basis of Fellers's "Basic Military Plan," PWB, GHQ assigned tactical missions to the Sixth and Eighth Armies and the Far East Air Forces (FEAF), then detached PWB field units to combat units throughout SWPA, where they became responsible for the conduct of psywar in their respective sectors. Once a field unit was detached from PWB, GHQ it became responsible to that unit rather than to PWB. At the army level, for example, the ranking intelligence officer (G-2) was responsible for PWB personnel and programs in his sector. All PWB detached personnel were "directed and guided by the desires of the particular unit to which they are assigned, the desires of the particular G-2 of the unit." Intelligence officers at the army level then dispatched smaller units to the various corps, and so on. In short, each army had a PWB field unit. Each corps had its own, smaller psywar unit, which was responsible for doing work at the corps level and reporting results up the chain of command to GHQ. FEAF headquarters also had a PWB unit, as did each bomb wing. Although precise numbers are elusive, it appears that PWB consisted of no more than two hundred persons at any one time during the war.[15]

The army G-2 not only carried out GHQ's plans for that area but initiated psywar activities it thought necessary or desirable within its jurisdiction. The army-level G-2, in turn, delegated his responsibility down to corps. When army G-2 relegated its authority, however, it did not free itself of responsibility for that sector. Since a corps had limited means of transmitting and distributing propaganda, it always had recourse to army headquarters, which conducted operations beyond the corps' scope. Any unit could initiate psywar operations in its own sector and call on the next higher echelon for assistance if it lacked the means to carry them out unilaterally. As a result, divisions often initiated psywar, but if they were incapable of accomplishing a particular mission they called on the corps, which generally relied on cub planes for propaganda dissemination. If a cub plane was insufficient, the corps would call on army headquarters for assistance. An army sometimes requested that special leaflets intended for widespread distribution be printed at GHQ. In such instances GHQ had no input regarding the leaflet's content unless it violated a principle of the military secretary's "Basic Military Plan."[16]

PWB field units specialized in conducting propaganda operations of a tactical nature since they were more familiar with the circumstances confronted by the Japanese troops in their area than was PWB, GHQ. While the field units could produce their own material, they also had access to the leaflets created by all other PWB units. Field units were informed of the leaflets produced elsewhere in SWPA and kept a ready supply of these leaflets for rapid dissemination when appropriate situations arose. PWB officers attached to each army headquarters also responded to requests from other detachments for leaflets originating in their units. Thus, the executive officer (Greene) distributed leaflets produced by PWB, GHQ to all field units. Sixth and Eighth Armies' PWB officers, Captains Paul T. Anderson and Alfred G. Hall, provided the same service for detachments throughout the theater.

The ranking intelligence officer of each unit controlled psywar operations and could refuse to distribute materials he deemed inappropriate. In order to ensure compliance with the G-2's wishes, PWB field officers kept PWB, GHQ informed of material that failed to gain the approval of the G-2 and, if possible, explained why specific leaflets were rejected.[17] In this way PWB ensured that the G-2 retained ultimate authority over psywar operations and learned of problems inherent to particular leaflets, thus enabling propagandists to correct deficiencies in their output. In a similar manner, PWB, GHQ and its field units exchanged valuable information regarding fluctuations in enemy morale and the impact of morale operations. In other words, while field units made use of the Collation and Planning divisions' weekly directives and pronouncements concerning trends and patterns in the enemy's morale, they also forwarded to PWB, GHQ their own observations on the status and results of psywar operations at the front lines and their perceptions of trends in enemy morale.[18]

Sixth Army PWB was established in September 1944 at Hollandia, where it immediately began producing leaflets for the Philippine invasion. PWB field units arrived at subordinate task forces (Fourteenth Corps, Tenth Corps, and First Cavalry Division) by 1 October 1944. Each of these units came equipped with an "advance kit of leaflets" designed for distribution during landing operations and sufficient to carry on propaganda work while Sixth Army PWB reestablished production facilities following the invasion. In the Sixth Army, PWB's field unit was directed by Col. H. V. White, the unit's G-2. It functioned as a reproduction unit to produce and disseminate leaflets, pamphlets, and news bulletins and included specialists in typesetting, printing, and layout as well as artists and cartoonists. The field unit provided the intelligence branch with psywar data as well as the capability to create printed material and make front-line broadcasts.

The "Basic Sixth Army Plan for Psychological Warfare" was approved by the Sixth Army's chief of staff in September 1944. It described the Sixth Army's PWB operations as "comparable to air support." It called for strategic "softening up" of Japanese troops for a considerable period of time preceding landing operations, to be followed by tactical propaganda accompanying combat forces and serving as a parallel to "close air support." The objective of "strategic" propaganda, according to the Sixth Army plan, was to demoralize troops by fostering doubt about Japan's ability to win battles and thus win the war. Then "tactical" propaganda would erode morale further by emphasizing Japan's battlefield losses pursuant to the Allied invasion of the Philippines. Sixth Army headquarters (HQ) was responsible for the "softening up" phase, while tactical propaganda was conducted in one of three ways. First, leaflets designed to exploit predictable situations were produced in advance at Sixth Army headquarters. Second, PWB liaison officers assigned to advancing units asked headquarters to produce specific leaflets to take advantage of military situations as they arose in the field. Sixth Army HQ then produced and distributed such leaflets to the bomber groups that provided air support to the requesting unit. Finally, field units produced and distributed their own leaflets via cub planes, naval support aircraft, or leaflet shells. Sixth Army HQ encouraged propagandists in the field to assume the initiative for tactical leafleting to alleviate the burden carried by those at HQ. The Sixth Army plan for psywar also envisioned the creation of a Japanese-language newspaper as a regular, biweekly publication for general distribution to the IJA. The first issue of the *Rakkasan News* (Air Drop, or Parachute, News), as it was called, was disseminated in March 1945.[19]

The 308th Bomb Wing's psywar team, for example, consisted of four PWB personnel detached from the Sixth Army. Their activities fell into three broad categories. First, the ongoing long-term propaganda campaign against enemy troops behind the front lines. The 308th field unit conducted these operations in accordance with the Sixth Army's policies but chose its own targets and leaflets.[20] Second, the bomb wing's field unit used ground-support aircraft to make leaflet drops on front-line troops. On average the 308th's flight crews flew five missions per week, each averaging 225,000 leaflets. Ground-support aircraft dropped propaganda leaflets (a maximum of 8,000 per sortie) on smaller targets in the front lines. Finally, propagandists with the 308th fulfilled requests for local leaflet drops made by combat units in the area. Liaison planes or artillery shells were used to reach targets less than one mile in length.[21]

Although other theaters had Monroe leaflet bombs (specially designed leaflet-dropping devices used for air drops), PWB, SWPA packaged most of its leaflets in one-foot-square parcels wrapped with twine. This type of packaging significantly reduced the amount of control an individual had over the time of dispersal. It also made the aircrew's job more difficult since they had to cut the twine and loosen the leaflets manually before release. Nonetheless, PWB disseminated millions of leaflets in this manner, and they apparently landed on the intended target much of the time.[22]

To assist with leaflet distribution PWB appointed air liaison officers to serve with air force units. Liaison officers were crucial since PWB, GHQ was initially located in Australia, where it produced millions of leaflets for general distribution over the vast expanse of the Southwest Pacific. The logistical problems associated with the movement of these leaflets from MacArthur's headquarters to forward bases were immense. Thus, PWB personnel were assigned to forward areas to oversee not only the acquisition of leaflet supplies but also the coordination of leafleting operations with the intelligence and operations officers commanding each air unit.[23] PWB teams came equipped with a small Davidson press or mimeograph machine to produce leaflets applicable to local situations, as well as a public-address system for front-line broadcasting.[24]

The function of air liaison officers was to ensure that propaganda leaflets were dropped on the designated targets. This task required, above all else, amicable relations between the liaison officer and the air-crews. It was frequently the case that PWB field units first had to convince the army air forces of the value of psywar before active cooperation was forthcoming. Liaison officers also monitored the available intelligence on the status of enemy morale and troop dispositions in order to ensure that leaflets were directed at appropriate targets. Frequent contact with the operations officer enabled liaison officers to keep abreast of current and future air assaults and plan leaflet drops accordingly. Field experience proved that propagandists should maintain a variety of leaflets in close proximity to airplanes in order to respond quickly to changing situations as flight paths were often altered shortly before takeoff. Since air liaison officers instructed aircrews where to drop leaflets, they had to familiarize themselves with scheduled flight paths. The quantity of leaflets disseminated during each sortie was carefully determined to ensure that the extra weight of the leaflet bundles did not interfere with the plane's takeoff and the physical act of leaflet dispersal did not consume more than approximately five minutes of the crew members' time in the air. Air liaison personnel also questioned the crew upon its return concerning precisely where the leaflets had been dropped and whether there had been any observable results.

It was not unusual for PWB officers to accompany aircrews on leaflet-dropping missions so that the crew members' attention would not be diverted from their primary bombing mission. In so doing, PWB officers acquired firsthand knowledge of dropping techniques, a precise measure of where the leaflets went, a feel for the geographic area over which they had flown for future reference, and a larger "payload" since they could disseminate nearly twice as many leaflets as they could ask crew members to drop. Active participation in dropping missions also earned PWB a greater respect from aircrews by demonstrating PWB officers' willingness to risk their own lives in fulfilling the mission. In addition, air liaison officers could assist crew members with their conventional duties on board the plane as a way of furthering good relations.[25]

Because the attitudes of intelligence officers were vital to the success of psywar, it was imperative that propagandists keep them informed of their activities. Propagandists therefore created up-to-date displays of their work, including translations of leaflet texts, maps showing the extent of leaflet drops, and summaries of the results of their efforts. Telling air and ground forces about psywar's contributions to the war against Japan thus became an integral part of PWB operations.

Convincing the army that psychological warfare was valuable, however, required proof that it had beneficial results. And beneficial results could only be attained if the propaganda was indeed persuasive to Japanese troops. As a consequence, Allied propagandists struggled with two rather daunting tasks during much of the war: educating friendly forces about the value of psywar operations and getting to "know the enemy" in ways that would enable them to influence his thoughts and actions. Allied propagandists' pursuit of these objectives is the subject of the following chapter.

3 Getting to Know the Enemy

The Soldier and the Sailor should consider loyalty their essential duty . . . and bear in mind that duty is weightier than a mountain, while death is lighter than a feather.

Imperial Rescript
to Soldiers and Sailors

The importance of "knowing one's enemy" is a well-established principle of war, but a realistic appraisal of the psychological strengths and vulnerabilities of an enemy nation requires trained experts, effective intelligence networks, skilled linguists, and experienced propagandists. Yet early in the war Allied experts on Japan were scarce, intelligence estimates rarely focused on assessing enemy morale, and few propagandists knew Japanese. In short, Allied propagandists came to "know the enemy" gradually and learned the art of propaganda by trial and error.

Early in the war propagandists were constrained both by Japan's overwhelming military successes and by Allied indifference to morale operations. Psychological warfare is effective only when it is coupled with successful combat forces. As General Fellers said, psychological warfare "can proceed no faster than winning armies." Propagandists knew that the abysmal military defeats suffered by the Allies during the first six months of the war had created an enemy that was anything but receptive to propaganda devices.

The propaganda war also suffered from skepticism within the Allied ranks. Once the Allies stopped the Japanese advance in the summer of 1942 and moved to the offensive, combat propagandists began their own campaign, but their work lacked credibility in the eyes of many of their compatriots, who viewed the war of words as a waste of time. In part this view stemmed from an obsession with Japanese "treachery" and the assumed adherence to the ideal of "death before dishonor." The all too pervasive conclusion within the Allied camp was that Japanese soldiers did not surrender and were impervious to psychological manipulation. As a result, combat forces sometimes tolerated rather than encouraged psywar operations. Through much of the war, then, propagandists not only prosecuted a war of words against Japan but also directed an information campaign to prove the value of combat propaganda to their own forces.

It is also clear that propagandists in swpa suffered from their own ineptitude during the preliminary stages of their work. Early propaganda texts were simplistic and provoked laughter among Japanese readers but not much else. Moreover, leaflet writers often failed to use the Japanese language properly, and this too limited their effectiveness. Allied propagandists never fully solved the problems created by the language barrier, though, as we shall see, it was eventually ameliorated by the use of Japanese linguists and pows. But in the early years propagandists too often alienated Japanese soldiers instead of attracting a faithful audience of readers.

Allied propagandists quickly became aware of the deficiencies in their output and struggled to upgrade the thematic content of propaganda as well as the linguistic and artistic components of leaflet texts. They also began gradually to earn some respect within their own military services. The most significant reason for the increasing influence of Allied propaganda, however, was that Allied battlefield successes gradually transformed an overconfident Japanese military machine into an army of physically weakened men who were vulnerable to psychological attack. The interplay of these three factors made a successful Allied propaganda campaign possible. As the war progressed, Japanese troops became demoralized, less disciplined, and more surrender-conscious. Propagandists amassed such evidence to support their claims that psywar had something to contribute to the war against Japan, and as the evidence mounted, more and more people within the Allied camp began to see psywar as a credible weapon. With increased credibility came greater institutional support. As their operations expanded and elicited more favorable results, psywar operatives sought to dispel once and for all the notion among Allied combatants that all Japanese were invulnerable to propaganda appeals and determined to die on the battlefield. PWB, for example, launched an extensive program to educate Allied troops about the objectives and results of the propaganda war and to convince fighting forces of the value of Japanese prisoners, who were immensely helpful to the Allies.

Such internal dynamics aside, propagandists struggled throughout the war to develop methods and messages that would reach the intended audience both physically and intellectually. They soon realized that getting the written word to enemy troops was considerably easier than writing words that insinuated themselves into the enemy's mind. The tough-mindedness of the target population was the single biggest obstacle to successful psywar in SWPA, for the IJA possessed fundamental and formidable psychological strengths that sustained soldiers in the field.

The remarkable determination of Japanese combatants to fulfill their duty was nearly matched by a similar level of devotion among civilians. The apparent unity of Japan during the war led outsiders to conclude that there was something inherent in the Japanese race that produced an all-consuming nationalism. Yet the notion that it is possible to define something as elusive as a national character is controversial. In the 1940s social scientists produced a profusion of national-character studies in an effort to understand better the characteristic attitudes and predilections not only of Japanese but of diverse peoples around the world.[1] Underlying these studies was the assumption that the people of a particular nation held in common certain values and behaviors that, taken together, served to define their national character. Many social scientists ran amok in what critics have since described as "whole-culture" analyses. That is, many analysts succumbed to the fallacy that the entire population of a nation has identical viewpoints, predictable behavior patterns, and equivalent value systems as a result of a common national experience.

Although it is possible to identify certain predispositions based on a nation's history and culture, the consequent tendency of whole-culture analyses was to think in terms of "the Japanese," for example, rather than in terms of human beings with personalities uniquely their own who just happened to be Japanese in nationality. Certainly the Japanese themselves engaged in their own brand of whole-culture analysis during the war. The examples of Japanese claiming for themselves certain inbred qualities that made the Japanese nation superior to all others and enabled its citizens to "endure adverse circumstances grimly and with resolution" are profuse. Japanese writers discussed "our virile national mentality," "our intrinsic national virtue," and Japan's "national spirit of self-denial." Japanese leaders often asserted that the nation functioned as "one hundred million hearts beating as one," and by 1945 these same leaders predicted that the Japanese en masse would willingly perform the ultimate act of loyalty as "one hundred million [died] together." Japanese rhetoric thus seemed to validate the Western tendency to see the Japanese as a million imprints from the same woodcut rather than as individuals.[2]

The notion of a Japanese national character influenced propagandists, who needed to develop an awareness of "things Japanese" but at the same time recognize that the enemy consisted of millions of individuals. On the one hand, they had to understand Japan and its people if they hoped to influence Japanese troops; on the other hand, they had to bear in mind that the goal of their work was to demoralize the enemy. This required propagandists to elicit the desired response—loss of morale—from individuals, which they hoped would then spread to larger groups. SWPA propagandists had to use their understanding of "the Japanese" to appeal separately, for example, to Japanese enlisted men, who did not generally think and behave in the same ways as officers. Similarly, the attitudes of the rank and file varied according to their age, personality, level of education, whether their upbringing had been rural or urban, and their wartime experiences. At the risk of falling prey to the problems inherent to a "whole-culture" analysis, what follows is a synopsis of the conclusions of a few prominent postwar scholars on the sources of Japanese unity and devotion to the war effort.

■ ■ ■

In the fifty-odd years since the outbreak of the "China Incident" in 1937 and the Pacific War that followed, historians have attempted to show not only why Japan's leaders embarked on a course of action that led to the most devastating of defeats but why Japanese fought so tenaciously and for so long. For while it is not unusual for military and political leaders to encourage their armed forces to fight to the death, few nations in history have come as close to fulfilling that ideal as Japan did during the Pacific War. All soldiers must learn to accept the possibility of their own death in battle. In most armies this fact is muted for morale's sake, but in the Japanese army death on the battlefield was touted as tantamount to deification. Therein lies a remarkable point of contrast, for in this respect, as in many others, the IJA managed to turn what was for other combatants a grim reality into an idealized virtue.

Postwar scholars have debated the extent to which the Showa emperor (Hirohito) was responsible for the war in Asia and the Pacific and the extent to which the Japanese people should be held accountable for its disastrous results, as well as whether justice was served at the International Military Tribunal for the Far East. There is little question, however, that during the war the emperor was not only an emotionally powerful symbol of imperial Japan but a unifying force in the empire's drive to establish its dominance over Asia. Likewise, most scholars agree that the imperial institution was thoroughly manipulated by Japan's military leaders, who sought to ensure popular support for an aggressive foreign policy in the early 1930s and selfless devotion to an extended war effort after 1937. And whether or not one accepts the idea of collective responsibility, there is no question that the dogged determination of the Japanese people to fulfill their duty as they saw it enabled Japan to persist in the war far longer than logic would dictate. These three forces—the central role of the imperial institution, the prestige and power of Japan's armed forces, and the duty-bound nature of the citizenry—are central to an assessment of why the Japanese people, soldiers and civilians alike, were able and willing to withstand the onslaught of the Allied powers for nearly four long years.

Japan's success in creating a sense of nation and sustaining a unified war effort was largely the result of the success with which Japanese elites revived ancient myths, manipulated traditional values, and inculcated the population with a virulent nationalist ideology. In the decades following the Meiji Restoration of 1868, which ostensibly restored the Japanese emperor to his rightful exalted position in society, Japanese leaders set out to create a national identity in place of the regional affiliations and loyalties that prevailed under the feudal structure of the shogunate. The Japanese emperor became the fundamental symbol of modern Japan and the focus of what was characterized during the war as an "emperor cult" and in postwar scholarship as the "emperor system."

Japan's modern ideology portrayed the emperor not only as the symbol of national unity and national progress—the very "embodiment of

Japanese modernity"—but also as the "repository of Japanese traditions" and the symbolic head of the Japanese national family.[3] During
the 1930s, Japanese ultranationalists molded the existing ideological
constructs in ways that enabled them to harness the energy of the nation
and direct it toward achieving what they saw as the great mission of the
Japanese race: dominance of the Far East. The ultranationalists and the
militarists who led the nation into war in China and the Pacific did so in
part by manipulating the symbolism and the person of the emperor and
portraying their aggressive foreign policy and schemes of Pacific con-
quest as the imperial will.

In postwar Japan, as well as in the West, the "ideology of the emperor
system" emerged as a prominent subject of study as scholars attempted
to provide reasoned explanations for Japan's wartime actions. The explanations that have emerged generally define Japanese "mythohistory,"
which was inseparably linked to the emperor system, as a prime culprit
in Japan's descent from the "liberal 1920s" into the abyss of ultranation-
alism and militarism of the thirties and forties. The constituent elements
of this mythohistory were a belief in the divine origins of the emperor,
an unbroken line of imperial succession, racial superiority and spiritual
indomitability, and the concept of nation as family. *In toto*, these attributes were said to make Japan unique among the nations of the world
and its people unparalleled in strength of character and purity of spirit.
These racial and spiritual factors, together with a historic mission to
create a new order that would enable all Asian peoples to occupy their
proper place, free from the brutality and moral corruption of the Western colonial powers, were the driving forces behind Japanese ultrana-
tionalist ideology, forces John Dower captures in the phrase "myth, morality, and mission."[4]

The imperial institution was the central feature of this mythohistory,
for the emperor was the foundation of a national cultural identity. The
mythohistory began with what the West viewed as the exceedingly peculiar Japanese version of the creation story, which portrayed the emperor as the divine, direct descendent of the Sun Goddess and the Japanese people, by virtue of their relationship to the emperor, as members
of a superior race. And because the line of imperial succession, which
according to this mythology began in 660 B.C., remained unbroken, the
emperor was a "deity incarnate." Moreover, Japanese adherence to a code
of civil and military morality that stressed duty, loyalty, and patriotism
ensured a national citizenry that no foreign country could match. Wide-

spread acceptance of this brand of morality produced an incomparable strength of will. No other people could claim such a unique heritage or equal the racial purity and moral righteousness of the Japanese.

The Japanese nation-family and "proper place" were other prominent features of the Japanese cultural landscape. Organized hierarchically, the Japanese family became a metaphor for the nation, the empire, and, ultimately, the new order that would emerge in Asia as Japan, the leading race, enlarged its empire to encompass Greater East Asia. Hierarchy was the basis for an orderly and harmonious society and began with the family unit. The emperor thus served as the head of the entire Japanese nation-family, a father figure to whom all loyalty and devotion was owed and whose superior position was unquestioned. Proper-place theories required the creation of a hierarchy of nations in which the Japanese, as the leading race under the authority of a semidivine emperor, would lead the Asian "family of peoples."[5]

Ultranationalists portrayed the creation of this family, otherwise known as the Greater East Asia Co-Prosperity Sphere as a righteous mission, ostensibly one that had historical roots reaching back through the centuries to the time of the first emperor, Jimmu Tenno, who purportedly ascended the throne in 660 B.C. The emperor Jimmu is credited with enunciating the principle of *hakko ichiu* (literally, the eight corners of the world under one roof), the notion that Japan possessed a divine mission to "bring all races and nations of the world under 'one roof'" and "lead the whole world along the path of virtue." The Japanese worldview thus assumed the existence of inequalities that dictated a proper place in both interpersonal and international relations.[6]

In 1882 and 1890 the proper place of Japanese soldiers, sailors, and civilians was decreed in two imperial rescripts. Together, the Imperial Rescript to Soldiers and Sailors (1882) and the Imperial Rescript on Education (1890) were designed to inculcate among the masses a sense of nation, something lacking in feudal Japan but essential in modern times. They were a clear expostulation of Japanese civil and military morality as envisioned by its leaders. According to both, the virtues of loyalty and patriotism were the structural mainstays of the edifice erected around Japan's imperial institution.

The ideal conduct of Japanese subjects was defined by the central government and bequeathed to the people as imperial pronouncements. Implementation, however, was accomplished at the local level, where family and community pressure to uphold traditional Japanese values, school curriculums as advanced by the Ministry of Education, and the imperial armed forces served as mechanisms for inculcating national-ism, spreading civil morality, and promoting the interests of the nation's military establishment. Given that universal education and national conscription became part of the fabric of Japanese life in 1872 and 1873, respectively, primary schools and the army touched the lives of nearly all Japanese by the twentieth century.

Education was a key element in the creation of a loyal, patriotic, even subservient Japanese citizenry. Civil morality as defined in 1890 was propagated among the masses via universal education, which was de-creed in 1872 as an essential characteristic of modern nations. Saburo Ie-naga, a prominent scholar and historian of the Pacific War, was himself a product of the Japanese education system, although he completed his education in the period of "Taisho democracy" and thus escaped the most blatant period of indoctrination. He argues that the education re-script "was issued in a bid to inculcate total submissiveness to the politi-cal authority presided over by the emperor" and that the resultant cur-riculum was "slanted toward unconditional obedience" to the state. Schools were consciously designed to achieve national conformity—to inculcate "Confucian feudal virtues"—by dictating not only the curricu-lum employed but the very textbooks studied by Japanese children (90 percent of elementary-age schoolchildren were enrolled by 1900). Thus, he says, the "standardized educational content stamped a uniform out-look on most Japanese minds."[7]

A key contributor to this uniformity of thought was the emphasis placed on veneration of the emperor. Already in the 1890s opening-day rituals in Japanese schools revolved around the reading of the Rescript on Education and veneration of the imperial photograph. Toshio Iritani, author of a recent book on Japanese group psychology during the war, asserts that by the 1930s and throughout World War II the primary ob-jective of education was to "indoctrinate children in Japanese national thought, and to unify the nation under the authority of the Emperor." Schools, writes Iritani, were the chief means by which "ideology infil-trated the daily lives of the people," and that ideology was directed to-ward the goal of heightening the "people's sense of pride in belonging to the national polity." He likewise cites the ever-present rituals centered around the person and office of the emperor. Typical morning cere-monies, for example, required that students bow toward the imperial palace, recite the imperial rescript, and then offer a pledge of allegiance to the emperor. Even the national anthem was entitled "The Emperor's Reign."

Postwar scholarship also reveals that from the time of the Sino-Japanese War in 1894–95 the state-controlled education system became increasingly militaristic in content. The "khaki-colored curriculum," as Ienaga calls it, stressed "submissiveness to authority and glorification of war." It imbued students with a sense of loyalty and devotion to the emperor and a desire to perform one's duties to the emperor and nation. Japanese students learned to take great pride in the military successes of Japan's armed forces. Students were regularly subjected to lessons about dying a glorious hero's death in battle, charging the enemy's positions with bravery, having no fear of death, or bringing honor to one's family by performing heroic deeds on the battlefield. And always, "a willingness to die in time of war was stressed as 'loyalty to the emperor and love of country.'" The militaristic and fascistic bent of Japanese education grew stronger in the decades after the Russo-Japanese War (1904–5), until by the fifth grade 50 percent of the curriculum was militaristic in nature, according to one recent analysis.[8]

Compulsory education did much to create a patriotic citizenry and foster a civil morality based on loyalty and filial piety. And just as the Rescript on Education laid the foundation for a national program of education, the Rescript to Soldiers and Sailors provided a detailed outline of what the emperor demanded of the armed forces. The emperor expected soldiers and sailors to display a great deal more of the same kind of virtues expected of civilians—more discipline, more obedience, more loyalty, a greater sense of duty, and a greater willingness to make the supreme sacrifice (one's life) in fulfilling one's obligations to the emperor and the nation. A uniform curriculum propagated via compulsory education ensured that young men recruited into the army already had a strong dose of "loyalty to the emperor and love of country." Military training and indoctrination merely reinforced those values.[9]

The IJA also adhered to a longstanding no-surrender policy. In 1908 the Japanese army's penal code dictated that for a commander to "allow his unit to surrender to the enemy without fighting to the last man" was an offense "punishable by death." The army's revised military law of 1942 specified a less harsh but still severe penalty: "a commanding officer who surrenders his troops to the enemy in combat, even though he has done his utmost, will be sentenced to a minimum of six months imprisonment." Japanese officers and enlisted men alike internalized the no-surrender policy, believing that "it was absolutely forbidden in the Japanese army to withdraw, surrender, or become a prisoner of war." As a consequence, the Japanese army has been "stigmatized as an army of fanatics run amok," though Japan's fighting forces merely consisted of men thoroughly trained to exhibit the qualities deemed necessary for success on the battlefield.[10]

"These five articles are the soul of Our soldiers and sailors," said the Meiji emperor in his Rescript to Soldiers and Sailors: loyalty, propriety, valor, faithfulness and righteousness, and simplicity. First, Japanese military morality demanded loyalty and devotion to duty above all else. "The soldier and sailor should consider loyalty their essential duty," said the rescript, "and bear in mind that duty is weightier than a mountain, while death is lighter than a feather." Second, soldiers and sailors must observe propriety by knowing their proper place in the hierarchy and fulfilling the obligations inherent to that position. For the rank and file, propriety meant obedience to one's superiors. Inferiors must obey their officers, said the rescript, and officers must treat subordinates with consideration. Third, Imperial soldiers must demonstrate true valor—personal bravery. Fourth, the armed services must be faithful and righteous. "Faithfulness implies the keeping of one's word, and righteousness the fulfillment of one's duty." And finally, soldiers and sailors should "make simplicity their aim" since "a fondness for luxurious and extravagant ways" is destructive of loyalty, bravery, martial spirit, and morale. Those who obeyed these instructions, concluded the rescript, would "fulfill your duty of grateful service to the country."

The introduction of conscription in 1873 made such "grateful service to the country" a universal obligation. Along with universal education, Japan's conscript army served as another powerful means of inculcating a code of morality among the people and inspiring a greater sense of nation. With the Meiji Restoration the feudal structure of society was abolished, including the regional military forces, members of the privileged samurai class who owed their loyalty to feudal lords. The introduction of national conscription was seen as a prerequisite for the creation of a modern mass army. Conscription also amounted to a social revolution, for it extended what had traditionally been the military morality of a privileged class to the entire nation. Even the lowliest of peasants was now called upon to exhibit courage, loyalty, bravery, obedience, frugality, and self-sacrifice in service to the emperor and trained to believe that to fail in his duties as a soldier was to bring dishonor not only upon himself but on his family, his community, and the nation.

Japan replaced a feudal military structure with a modern military organization when it implemented a system of national conscription, but conscripts were trained to become a cohesive fighting force not by imposing modern standards of conduct on them but rather by emphasizing traditional ones. Edward J. Drea argues that conscripts were imbued with "the rock-bottom values of a people conditioned over the centuries to accept a hierarchical social structure, clearly defined ranks and status, informal sanctions to avoid public embarrassment and humiliation, and, above all, identification of allegiance to the unit as allegiance to the emperor, thereby giving official approval to the concept of the unique and superior Japanese race."[11]

The Imperial Rescript to Soldiers and Sailors cemented the relationship between the emperor and the nation's armed forces, declaring the emperor to be Japan's supreme military commander and avowing that the two institutions were integral components of one living organism. "The supreme command of Our forces is in Our hands, and although We may entrust subordinate commands to Our subjects, yet the ultimate authority We Ourself shall hold and never delegate to any subject. . . . Soldiers and Sailors, We are your supreme Commander-in-Chief. . . . We rely upon you as Our limbs and you look up to Us as your head."[12] The glory of the empire thus depended on how well soldiers and sailors fulfilled their duties to their supreme commander, who was simultaneously the father of the Japanese family-nation and a living god to boot.

In innumerable ways military training and indoctrination sought to solidify the hold the emperor had on the army as an institution and soldiers as individuals. On a personal level, individual soldiers developed strong psychological attachments to the emperor, largely due to rigid indoctrination that emphasized loyalty and devotion to the emperor as a soldier's primary duty. Just as young schoolchildren learned through a variety of ritual behaviors to revere the emperor, soldiers and sailors were subjected to a regimen that constantly invoked displays of personal devotion to the emperor. Soldiers, for example, were daily required to study and recite the Rescript to Soldiers and Sailors and to bow toward the imperial palace. They had to memorize an abbreviated version of the rescript known as the "Five Principles of the Soldier." They were told that each unit's colors had been "royally bestowed" and that army equipment was a gift from the emperor himself. Through the overwhelming sense of personal responsibility to the emperor that was instilled in them, soldiers were induced to obey without question the orders of superiors, who were said to be carrying out imperial commands.[13]

The imperial army as an institution was also linked to the person of the emperor in a number of significant ways. And in the end, these links reinforced the perception that the IJA was indeed the "private army of the monarchy." According to the Constitution of 1889, the emperor was the supreme commander of the army and navy. He possessed the power to declare war and to make peace as well as the power to determine the size and mission of the nation's military establishment. In a constitutional sense, then, it was truly the "Emperor's Army," and orders issued by the Japanese high command "represented absolute orders issued by the monarch in his capacity as Commander in Chief."[14]

The Japanese cabinet was powerless to interfere in military decision making. For example, the army and navy chiefs of staff, who controlled military operations, reported directly to the emperor. This institutional arrangement maintained the appearance that all military matters were the purview of the emperor as supreme commander and that all operational orders were issued by the emperor through his subordinates. And since the chiefs of staff were independent of the war minister, the Japanese cabinet was unable to enforce its decisions concerning the nation's armed forces. The military members of the cabinet, the war and navy ministers, "wielded a life-or-death control over the fate of Cabinets."[15] If either minister became dissatisfied with cabinet policy making, he could terminate the existing government simply by resigning and forcing the creation of a new government. Thus, the IJA as an institution possessed unlimited power over its own internal affairs but also wielded great influence over the Japanese cabinet as well, and all by reason of its very special relationship to the emperor.

The army also maintained a significant power base within Japanese society. National organizations such as the Imperial Military Reserve Association, the Greater Japan Youth Association, and the Greater Japan National Defense Women's Association sought to imbue the population with soldierly values and patriotic sentiments. They were particularly effective at amalgamating traditional rural ideology with nationalistic and martial ideals. The army thus built up a social basis of support for militarism and an expansionist ideology. Local chapters of these national associations laid the foundation for the belief that "when one served his hamlet, he served his Emperor, army and nation; when one served the Emperor, army, and nation, he served the hamlet."[16]

The Japanese army also increased its prestige and influence by maintaining intimate ties to the local communities from which recruits were drawn and by representing itself as an extension of each soldier's family. The army thus was able to exploit the traditional Japanese virtues of filial piety and group loyalty and at the same time to provide soldiers with a sense of belonging. In theory, a soldier's military unit became the source of his well-being and the object of his devotion. Drea notes, for example, army rhetoric that portrayed military service as "the natural extension of the prewar Japanese family writ large, with all the trappings of respect for hierarchy and group versus individual identification implied in that institution." Even army regulations employed the ideal of the barracks as family: "The barracks is the soldiers' family where together soldiers share hardships and joys, life and death. . . . A family means that the company is one household in the one village that is the regiment. The heads of the household are the father and the mother. The company commander is a strict father, and the NCO a loving mother."[17]

District-based recruitment ensured that an individual remained closely linked to his community. Again, Drea emphasizes that a soldier could "not escape his peers and village by joining the army; they came along, and the consequent motivation not to disgrace one's family or village by delinquent military service was a powerful one." The army thus attempted to recreate a traditional family setting in institutionalized form among new recruits. The result, writes Drea, was that "all of these little loyalties to higher authority in this surrogate or substitute family, cultivated originally in one's own family, added up to the one great loyalty due to His Imperial Majesty, the emperor of Japan. For most conscripts it was a logical progression from the school curricula, which stressed the uniqueness of Japan because of the unbroken Imperial line."[18]

▪ ▪ ▪

Postwar scholarship reveals that the imperial institution, the education system, and the national conscript army were powerful forces for forming and directing the actions of the people in support of national objectives, including fighting and dying in the Greater East Asia War. But how much did wartime propagandists know about Japanese history and culture and its impact on the motivations and aspirations of its people? A great deal, at least by 1944. Propagandists' conclusions regarding Japanese wartime culture have proven to be amazingly cogent. John Dower asserts, for example, that the wartime studies prepared by social and behavioral scientists, many of which were examined by psychological warfare personnel, provided highly accurate assessments of the Japanese. Academics, says Dower, offered a "more balanced and empirical analysis of the Japanese national character" because they recognized that culture, not race, was the chief determinant of a people's conduct.[19]

The ways in which wartime propagandists accumulated knowledge of the Japanese enemy, appraised his strengths and weaknesses, and devised a plan of attack are the subject of the rest of this book, but it is worth noting at this juncture that long before the Japanese attack on Pearl Harbor the future head of PWB, SWPA produced an exceedingly interesting and insightful study of Japanese military psychology. Then Capt. Bonner F. Fellers wrote "The Psychology of the Japanese Soldier" in 1935 while completing his coursework at the Command and General Staff School at Fort Leavenworth, Kansas. Much of this study was later incorporated into his *Answer to Japan,* an orientation manual distributed to propagandists after he became head of PWB nearly a decade later.[20] Fellers's 1935 study argued that the Japanese people were becoming imbued with a "fanatical religious patriotism" as a result of manipulation of the imperial institution, control over the dissemination of information, and inculcation of militaristic values through schools and military indoctrination. He pointed out the pervasive influence of military men and martial values, frequently quoting Gen. Araki Sadao, an ardent nationalist who served as war minister, army minister, and education minister during the 1930s and who had written in 1934 of the need to propagate the "Soldier Spirit among the whole nation" and portrayed the army as a sacred instrument of the emperor and nation.

Fellers also concluded, much as postwar scholars would, that Japanese soldiers were not substantially different from the rest of the population. "The psychology of the Japanese soldier is the psychology of his people," he wrote. Japanese soldiers and civilians alike internalized a set of values based on loyalty to the emperor and devotion to nation, argued Fellers; they differed from Americans in that the Japanese army placed much greater emphasis on strength of will, offensive spirit, unquestioning obedience, and a psychology of sacrifice.

The IJA's psychology of sacrifice was predicated on a medieval samurai code that demanded "loyalty to death," wrote Fellers, who also described the practice of seppuku rather simply as a samurai custom designed to demonstrate absolute devotion. Modern-day soldiers, like the samurai before them, performed ritual suicide as a "means of preserving honor, or of expressing supreme and final moral protest against events over which they had no control." And since the Japanese army refused to acknowledge the legitimacy of POW status, seppuku became a respectable way of preserving one's honor when one was faced with impossible odds. Yet, the practice of seppuku was significant not so much in itself, argued Fellers, but because Japanese society revered those who performed the act as martyrs and immortalized them at the Yasukuni Shrine. For Fellers in 1935, as for many Americans during the Pacific War, the notion of "death before dishonor" became symbolic of the unity of the Japanese people in support of traditional practices that, at least from the conventional Western perspective, were antiquated, irrational, and suicidal.

Despite his conclusions that Japanese military training produced soldiers "with religious fanaticism burning in their souls" and "supreme confidence that with divine sanction they cannot lose," Fellers believed that the Japanese had deficiencies that might provide an enemy with opportunities for exploitation. The spirit of sacrifice so thoroughly ingrained in soldiers might be a source of weakness rather than strength, he said. Soldiers might become "crazed" when faced with great adversity and prove too willing to die for the emperor. Too much offensive spirit, suggested Fellers, might result in suicidal tactics and battlefields "strewn with entrails-Nipponese." When Japanese offensive spirit was combined with a determination to die an honorable death, one might even expect to witness suicidal air assaults on enemy "airplane carrier[s]." Thus, in a rather amazing demonstration of prescience, Fellers predicted the advent of what became known a decade later as the kamikaze attack.

Fellers also concluded that an overemphasis on strength of will or Japanese spirit was detrimental in that it had apparently convinced the Japanese that the power of one's will, rather than the power of military machines, was the key to success. "Japanese soldier psychology inspires confidence, but it is based on supremacy of man power over man power. Japan has never faced a determined army equipped to slaughter in the modern manner. Confronted by a thoroughly modern army, Japan's man army will be found to be as ineffective as were her Samurai warriors against Perry's black ships." The IJA had neglected to avail itself completely of modern technology and would soon discover, predicted Fellers, that "Shinto Spirit cannot stop machine-gun bullets." It is no coincidence that this became one of the dominant propaganda themes of Fellers's PWB in 1944–45. In an interesting cross-cultural comparison Fellers juxtaposed Japanese military indoctrination in the 1930s with French military philosophy prior to World War I. He foresaw similar results: "In 1914 the French, ignoring the effectiveness of automatic fire adopted the insane cry of 'Toujours l'attaque!' It was a thrilling appeal, like the beating of drums, but in the first forty-five days of the World War they lost 329,000 men. French fury did not defeat the enemy nor will Japanese fanaticism."

Fellers also maintained that the primary difference between American and Japanese soldiers was psychological: "In methods of thought," wrote Fellers, "the Japanese and the Americans are today as different as if each had always lived on different worlds." Americans depended on the power of machines, on "mechanical superiority," whereas the Japanese relied on spiritual superiority. "Infantry troops only can hold ground gained, but *economy of life* teaches that machines can best prepare the way for the infantry," argued Fellers (emphasis added). He insisted that the key to defeating Japan in war was to rely on machines to bear the brunt of the fighting in powerful counterattacks once Japan had expended its strength in aggressive offensives.

Fellers concluded that Japan had risen to power as a result of "intense national ambition to attain her destiny" and that the military establishment was prestigious and powerful because it was military prowess that had earned Japan status as a great power. Patriotism meant more to the Japanese than to any other people, he said, because patriotism combined religion with love of county, thus creating a united front of soldiers and civilians. Already by 1935 Fellers had concluded that the "Japanese soldier is better disciplined than a West Point cadet. He has the indifference toward death of the Mohammedan. He has an offensive spirit which makes the Furia Franchese of 1914 appear pale."

In the 1944 revision of the study *(Answer to Japan)* Fellers provided an extended review of enemy mythology (what postwar scholars refer to as "mythohistory"), highlighting the Japanese belief in their "divine origin, racial superiority, and Imperial Destiny" and explaining how each was connected to the imperial institution. These myths, said Fellers, were taught in schools as a "comprehensive system of moral training." As a result, "samurai teachings become the vehicle for the national faith" and the emperor has gained a "mystic hold" on his people. Fellers also blamed the Greater East Asia War on "gangster militarists" who used religion and the emperor as tools to achieve their expansionist ambitions. The gangster militarists had "duped their people," "betrayed their sacred Emperor," and created a "cauldron of religious patriotism." He also noted that during the Pacific War the traditional Japanese aversion to surrender as a violation of the soldier's code of honor had been heightened by the gangster militarists' claims that Japanese prisoners were not only disgraced in the eyes of their own people but tortured as a matter of course by their enemies. According to Fellers, death, rather than surrender, had become the "ultimate step in the spirit of aggressiveness" in wartime. Even so, the apparent fanaticism of the enemy did not necessarily translate into the need to exterminate all Japanese. Fellers argued that the emperor could be turned into an instrument to achieve peace, but first he had to be released from the hold of the militarists, whom Fellers incessantly portrayed as the real aggressors in this war. It is remarkable that in 1935 Fellers was already arguing that the imperial institution and the person of the emperor should not be belittled or attacked by foreigners in time of war. In this respect, as in a number of others, Fellers's report foreshadowed the heated debates of the 1940s over how to deal with the emperor during and after the war.

Fellers's writings shed light on some fundamental differences between Japanese and American society and reveal his understanding that these differences were the product of cultural, not racial, factors. American society inculcated a belief in the sanctity of human life, and thus its code of military honor did not include the same kind of emphasis on self-sacrifice that prevailed among Japanese soldiers. Americans learned to treasure their individual liberty and made heroes of inventors who devised ingenious mechanical solutions to everyday problems; Japanese learned to put the welfare of the group above their personal needs and to live life in such a way that they would be ever prepared for an honorable death. Americans demanded that the nation's armed forces rely on material superiority on the battlefield as a means to preserve human life, whereas Japanese emphasized the power of superior spirit to overcome all odds. Such contrasting perspectives reflect a basic difference in the two societies' underlying philosophies regarding the function of nation-states. For Americans, the state existed to protect the lives and liberties of the people; for Japanese in the 1930s and 1940s, the emperor's subjects existed to increase the power and prestige of the state.

. . .

The outbreak of war in Asia and then the Pacific turned the attention of academics, journalists, and scholars of various disciplines toward Japan. As the conflict in the Pacific raged, the propaganda war against Japan was molded by a multitude of studies produced by scholars working for organizations such as the OWI, OSS, FELO, and ATIS. In addition to General Fellers's own research on Japanese military psychology, wartime analyses provided propagandists in SWPA, as well as elsewhere in Asia and the Pacific, with greater insight into what motivated Japan's fighting forces the longer the war continued.

Wartime studies indicated that Japanese morale was sustained by several specific factors, namely, devotion to the emperor, racial pride, the samurai tradition, belief in Japan's divine mission and national destiny, and faith in the nation's military leaders. Like postwar scholars and Bonner Fellers in 1935, wartime propagandists concluded that these features of Japanese motivation were the result of cultural training and military indoctrination that taught young men to believe in the glory of martial spirit, the importance of patriotism, the necessity of unquestioning obedience to authority figures, and the virtue of loyalty.[21]

Allied propagandists learned of Japanese myths that glorified the emperor's divine origins and taught Japanese to see themselves as racially, spiritually, and militarily invincible from documents such as *Nippon Shindo Ron* ("The Way of the Subjects"). Issued in August 1941 by the Ministry of Education as a "handbook for young persons," *Nippon Shindo Ron,* like the Imperial Rescript to Soldiers and Sailors and the Imperial Rescript on Education, demanded that Japanese subjects adhere to the traditional virtues that made them a superior people: loyalty, patriotism, obedience to authority, and martial spirit.[22]

Studies produced during the war familiarized propagandists with Japanese confidence in *Yamato damashii,* a unique "Japanese spirit" that gave imperial subjects supreme determination and the ability to overcome all obstacles. The following speech, for example, taken from a captured Japanese army training manual, told Allied propagandists much about Japanese indoctrination:

> The Imperial Family is the light, the life, the pride of Japan. In truth, Japan is Japan and the Japanese are Japanese because of the Imperial Family. From this consciousness the Japanese spirit is born. A loyalty which utterly disregards the safety of the home and family, even one's own life, for the welfare of the country is born. This special Japanese spirit is something peculiarly

Japanese . . . we who possess this special Japanese spirit can accomplish our duty; but those who do not have it, perform only a superficial duty. Thus, in the arena of decisive battles, the issue between the enemy and ourselves is already decided.[23]

Thus, the emperor's divinity and Japanese racial and spiritual excellence simultaneously fostered a belief in military invincibility. Propagandists saw evidence of this sense of superiority in the statements of ultranationalists, who pointed out that Japan had never had a change in dynasty, had never been defeated in war, and had never been invaded successfully. These superlative accomplishments were attributed to the nation's adherence to an established and orderly social hierarchy. Propagandists thus learned that inequality was the rule of organized life in Japan and acknowledged the Japanese saying that in their nation rulers were always rulers and subjects were always subjects: "No subject has ever aspired to be ruler."[24]

Wartime propagandists saw Japanese military indoctrination for what it was—an extension of civil morality. Japanese cultural values emphasized unity, loyalty, and patriotism. Army training merely carried the process one step further to create soldiers determined to sacrifice their lives to fulfill the will of the emperor. The studies produced in the early 1940s emphasized the prominent role played by military men throughout Japanese history, underlined the position of prestige and power occupied by the IJA since the 1930s, and referred to the "mystic coalition" formed by the army and the emperor. They told of Japanese military leaders who had justified their control over the political life of the nation by portraying themselves as the guardians of ancient traditions, the instrument of the imperial will, and adherents to bushido, the moral code of conduct purportedly instituted by feudal samurai and carried on by the imperial armed forces.[25]

The IJA's efforts to gain popular support for its foreign aggrandizement by portraying itself as an army of the people were certainly familiar to Japan's enemies.[26] In 1932, for instance, the Japanese minister of war declared the army to be "matchless in the world. It is at once an Imperial and a national army. Once warriors were a privileged class; conscription was the greatest reform in a thousand years; it abolished the samurai caste, and all became equal in rights. . . . Our army is organized by the nation under the command of the Emperor and it is unique in the world."[27]

Researchers showed how the Japanese belief in *Yamato damashii* was incorporated into army training and instruction. *Seishin kyoiku,* or "spiritual training," instilled in soldiers self-denial and an ardent loyalty that glorified death for the emperor as life's greatest reward. To offer one's life to the emperor in order to ensure an enemy's defeat was the "highest privilege" of Japanese soldiers. Wartime sources likewise highlighted the Japanese focus on the overwhelming power of spiritual force, which encouraged soldiers to view death as a victory of the spirit. "The spirit is indestructible, and death is eternal life. Never must death be feared." After all, death in battle meant deification and immortality in the eyes of the Japanese nation.[28]

The IJA's battlefield conduct seemed to provide evidence of Japanese confidence that the spirit would be victorious over matter. "To match our training against their numbers and our flesh against their steel" was the slogan frequently used in indoctrination courses to instill in troops the proper attitude toward combat.[29] The following lyrics from a Japanese war song perhaps epitomize Japanese spirit:

Across the sea,
Corpses in the water;
Across the mountain,
Corpses heaped upon the field;
I shall die only for the Emperor,
I shall never look back.

Allied propagandists were certainly familiar with the imperial rescript's injunction that soldiers view death as "lighter than a feather." They saw evidence of the widespread belief in Japan's destiny as a great power in Asia, the Pacific, and beyond. They discovered very early in the war that most Japanese soldiers had an abiding faith in the righteousness of the cause for which they fought, having been convinced that it was the nation's destiny to unite East Asia under Japan's leadership. Propagandists were aware of Japanese rhetoric regarding the *hakko ichiu* principle and knew that it was used to portray the Greater East Asia Co-Prosperity Sphere as the nation's divine mission.[30]

"To bring together all the races of the world into one happy accord has been the ideal and the national aspiration of Japanese since the very foundation of their Empire," said an official Japanese spokesman in the early 1940s. "We deem this the great mission of the Japanese race to the world."[31] The creation of the Greater East Asia Co-Prosperity Sphere was the first step toward achieving Japan's national destiny, that is, to unite the universe under imperial Japanese rule. "The Way of the Subjects" testifies to Japan's uniqueness in this regard: "There is virtually no country in the world other than Japan having such a superb and lofty mission bearing world significance."

As one of the most influential of the Japanese ancients' historical exhortations, the principle of *hakko ichiu* thus gave a religious flavor to an expansionist foreign policy. It also made the army Japan's primary instrument for "propelling the development of her national destiny."[32] As a result, the IJA maintained a heightened state of morale because of its responsibilities not only as protector of the empire but as the emperor's instrument for the accomplishment of Japan's divine mission in the world.

As the confident representatives of an indestructible empire and as members of an army that received orders from a semidivine supreme commander, Japanese soldiers entered the Pacific War sure of the righteousness of their cause. Spiritual training produced highly motivated troops who were determined to fulfill their duty and certain of achieving the status of a deity if death on the battlefield should result. Wartime propagandists recognized these factors as giving enemy soldiers high morale, great confidence, and a sense of psychological well-being. It was this sense of well-being and these sources of high morale that they set out to destroy.

■   ■   ■

Allied psychological operations surfaced relatively late in the Pacific War, since the first prerequisite to effective psywar is the creation of a susceptible target audience, which can only be achieved by successful military operations. Any attempt to demoralize enemy troops that have experienced only success on the battlefield is useless, as victory inevitably results in high morale and greater optimism. To capture the target's attention, propaganda must focus on circumstances of personal interest and concern to the soldiers and operate on the level of his everyday thoughts. A soldier's primary concerns are the current military situation, the availability of food, water, and ammunition, and the caliber of his officers. Consequently, when troops are well supplied and victorious, there is very little enemy propagandists can do to undermine morale. The Foreign Morale Analysis Division (FMAD), a division of OWI created to study Japanese morale, consistently reported that "only military ac-

tion creates a situation where Japanese soldiers and sailors are influenced by Allied propaganda in the direction of weakened morale" and
compared military action to a "strong right fist" and propaganda to a
"much weaker left arm."[33]

FMAD studied the demoralizing effect of battlefield reverses on combat troops in several campaigns in SWPA. One such study of prisoners
taken during the fighting on New Guinea, Guadalcanal, New Britain,
and New Ireland focused on their faith in victory, their belief in the purpose of the war, and how they felt about Japan's mission in Asia, conditions on the home front, and the adequacy of food and supplies. The
results dramatically demonstrated that the prisoners who experienced
the severe battlefield conditions of New Guinea and Guadalcanal were
considerably less optimistic about the war situation as a whole than
those taken on New Britain or New Ireland, where the privations were
neither as severe nor as prolonged. FMAD concluded from their analyses
that Japanese troops forced to endure long, hard defensive campaigns
were significantly more pessimistic than fresh troops and that the "wors-
ening of their morale is produced primarily by military action." As one
prisoner put it, at the time of his capture the morale of his men had "just
about cracked. There is a world of difference between attacking and being attacked." The fighting in New Guinea produced one of FMAD's principal findings regarding the morale of Japanese forces. "In New Guinea,
where the campaign started out as a successful push against the unprepared Allies and gradually changed to defeat and rout for the Japanese
forces, there was a progressive shift from excellent morale on the part of
earlier captives to a state of hopelessness and despair in those taken during the last days."[34]

Clearly, propaganda would not have been particularly useful in the
first several months of the war, and in fact it was not attempted until August 1942. From that date until the end of 1943 Japanese-language propaganda consisted almost exclusively of news leaflets. Even after that date
psywar's usefulness depended upon the local successes of Allied combat
forces to increase the likelihood that propaganda would not fall upon
the deaf ears of confident and enthusiastic enemy soldiers. During the
Papuan phase of the New Guinea campaign, for instance, a study of Japanese morale showed an obvious downward trend in the fighting effectiveness and morale of enemy troops as the combat intensified and battlefield reverses mounted. No Japanese prisoners were taken in Papua
until September 1942, when the Australians launched their first counter-

attack, thus forcing the Japanese to retreat. Thereafter, surrenders increased until January 1943, when just prior to the collapse of Japanese resistance thirty-six POWs were taken, more than half the total number of prisoners taken during the entire campaign. The number of Japanese troops taken prisoner is not the only indicator of the collapse of Japanese morale, but it illustrates the correlation between the battlefield situation and military morale. Until Allied combat forces began to win convincing victories and inflict crushing blows upon enemy troops, propagandists had little opportunity to demoralize the Japanese. They did, however, distribute news leaflets early on in order to demonstrate the reliability of Allied information. By keeping enemy troops informed of the course of the war psywarriors hoped to convince the Japanese that the Allies spoke the truth, thus building a framework for future propaganda operations.[35]

Propagandists also had to deal with the fact that their work was not held in high esteem by the very military establishment whose combat successes they labored to exploit. They were forced to establish credibility not only with the enemy but with their own forces as well. The problems emanating from within the Allied military organization were twofold. First, a substantial portion of the officer corps saw little reason to expend time and effort on a war of words when success on the battlefield was obviously the decisive factor. Psywarriors strove to convince military commanders that although conventional operations were paramount, propaganda was a useful weapon that increased the impact of military victories on defeated enemy troops. Second, the majority of Allied military personnel believed propaganda was an exercise in futility as the Japanese were psychologically impervious to such ploys. Allied soldiers assumed that enemy troops were so thoroughly indoctrinated that they would be invulnerable to psychological manipulation and that they were imbued with a fanatical desire to die honorably on the battlefield. Many concluded from these suppositions that efforts to get the enemy to surrender were futile and that Japanese who attempted to surrender were in fact treacherous zealots intent upon inflicting damage upon the men to whom they feigned surrender. As a result, Allied troops frequently refused to accept as legitimate either combat propaganda or Japanese surrenders.

Allied officers' general attitude toward combat propaganda can best be described as indifferent rather than hostile. Their attention was properly focused on the conduct of military operations against the Japanese. They had little time and even less inclination to delve into the area of psywar, which was at best unfamiliar to them and at worst seen as unproductive. These attitudes were typified by General MacArthur's response to a telegram from the JCS in June 1943 regarding the nature of propaganda activities the general anticipated in his theater. "This headquarters has been completely engrossed in the planning and conduct of operations against the enemy in our immediate front," wrote MacArthur, "and has not, repeat not, made any study of possible propaganda programs."[36] MacArthur later created the PWB to facilitate the invasion of the Philippine Islands, but prior to that time he was satisfied to allow the Australians (FELO) almost free reign in this sphere of activity. And so it was with most commanding officers. The concern was primarily with combat operations and only secondarily, if at all, with propaganda work.

The situation confronted by combat propagandists naturally varied depending upon the unit to which they were detached. The key to successful relations lay with the intelligence officer, and in most cases intelligence personnel were quite amenable to psywar operations. PWB's executive officer, J. Woodall Greene, wrote to Fellers in September 1944 that PWB's field units had been well received and noted that "In each instance, the G-2 has been voluminous in his remarks about the necessity of Psychological Warfare in the field, and seems to be well pleased that GHQ has recognized this necessity and is providing a crew of experts and facilities to handle the program." Nonetheless, PWB personnel were sometimes treated with derision in the field. Capt. William R. Beard, head of the Tenth Corps PWB team, remarked in December 1944 that PWB had a "helluva big selling job to do yet, and we definitely need the cooperation of higher-ups. People just seem to laugh when you mention Psychological Warfare, but I suppose that is something we will just have to put up with."[37]

By way of contrast to the "disinterest, bordering upon antagonism" afforded Captain Beard at Tenth Corps, Capt. Alfred G. Hall (PWB officer for the Eighth Army) stated in early 1945 that the PWB representative detached to the First Cavalry Division had received the "best cooperation . . . and is presently preparing an orientation program for the troops of his division." Similarly, liaison officers assigned to the Fifth Air Force unanimously reported that aircrews were exceedingly cooperative when it came to propaganda operations. One report indicated that good relations were "secured in part by an informal orientation program, including the distribution of souvenir leaflets with translations and the posting on bulletin boards of official reports of the results of propaganda drops." Capt. James A. Matthews, Fifth Air Force Psychological Warfare Branch liaison officer (PWBLO), reported that PWB's efforts were wholeheartedly supported by the senior intelligence officer, that he had access to everything he needed, and that "units of the Fifth Air Force have cooperated to the limit of their tactical ability in carrying out Psychological Warfare leaflet missions."[38]

The Thirteenth Army Air Force and its subordinate bomb groups also demonstrated a strong willingness to work with PWB in conducting leaflet drops. Aircrews from the Thirty-eighth Bomb Group were described as regarding leaflet missions as a "worthy obligation rather than a concession." The Thirty-eighth PWBLO also noted that air personnel deemed propaganda leaflets valuable souvenirs and requested that psywarriors take care to keep "individual collectors' sets of leaflets and translations up-to-date."[39] In this and in many other ways Allied propagandists established good working relations with the combat personnel who were critical players in the propaganda war.

.   .   .

In October 1942 the AMF's Weekly Intelligence Review reported that only a few prisoners were taken in the fighting around Milne Bay but noted that "a few prisoners can save the lives of hundreds of our men." Not until 1944, however, did the Allies make a concerted effort to convince Allied troops that Japanese prisoners were a valuable commodity. As the propaganda war intensified to include a greater emphasis on provoking Japanese surrenders, propagandists initiated an information campaign to convince Allied combatants to take Japanese prisoners. The immediate impetus for the education program came from numerous reports of incidents in which Japanese soldiers advancing toward Allied lines and waving surrender passes were shot down by American or Australian troops. On 14 May 1944 General MacArthur sent a telegram to the commanding general of Alamo Force stating that an "investigation should be made of numerous reports reaching this headquarters that Japanese carrying surrender passes and attempting to surrender in Hollandia area have been killed by our troops." MacArthur concluded that "this situation must be corrected if propaganda for surrender is to be successful."[40]

Certainly MacArthur's interest in the problem inspired action, but psywar personnel had long been aware of such incidents. PWB's representative at Tenth Corps, Capt. William R. Beard, wrote Fellers that the success of propaganda campaigns aimed at eliciting Japanese surrenders was being "ruined by the front-line troops shooting (Japanese) when they made an attempt to surrender." He advised General Fellers to increase PWB's education program in an attempt to alleviate these problems. Beard bemoaned the fact that "our troops are still not familiar with the work we do" and seemed to be unaware of the value of prisoners. "Most people," Beard wrote, "think the Japanese is not psychologically vulnerable, but we know that he is. Part of our job is to make this known in the Army and Navy." He emphasized the need to establish contact with combat troops before they arrived at the front lines, for once they became involved in combat operations "it is almost impossible to reach them." Beard suggested that a portion of troop training be devoted to instruction on psychological warfare and the value of prisoners and that PWB furnish teams to provide such instruction.[41]

Allied troops clearly were indifferent or even hostile to the idea of taking Japanese prisoners. They believed that the enemy would never surrender willingly and that they deliberately feigned surrender only to deceive their enemies. Allied reluctance to take surrendering Japanese seriously is not surprising. Intelligence publications frequently referred to Japanese "cunning, treachery, fanaticism, and brutality" and warned American troops to "take nothing for granted in dealing with the Japanese."[42] The *Intelligence Bulletin* provided firsthand accounts of Japanese surrender ruses, such as the following:

A trick I saw the Japanese employ in Kwajalein was to send a lone soldier out of a pillbox, with hands raised as if in surrender. As five of our men went after him, the Japs in the pillbox shot about three of them. I saw them use this same ruse on several other occasions also.

The Japanese soldiers in the Admiralties were cagey and treacherous. Occasionally a Jap would come in with his hands up, offering to surrender; but when he was close enough, he would hit his helmet with a grenade he had tied to his wrist and had kept concealed in his hand. His object, of course, was to injure as many of us as possible while he was killing himself.

After the fighting had settled down, we began to run into Japs who used every type of deception. On one occasion a Jap on the crest of a hill started waving a white flag. When our troops ceased firing, he motioned to our men to come to him. As some of our men stood up, more Japs hidden around the base of the hill opened fire.[43]

Captain Beard, of Tenth Corps, asserted in January 1945 that the Allied press was "largely responsible for the detrimental attitude" of Allied troops toward taking prisoners. He maintained that the press, by emphasizing the idea that a Japanese soldier "fights until he can fight no longer, then commits Hara-Kiri," not only made heroes of the Japanese but confirmed the conception that surrender was simply unfathomable to the enemy. In so doing, the press, as well as some elements within the military establishment, reinforced a stereotype that was counterproductive to the objectives of psywar.[44]

The written word, however, was only part of the problem. The nature of the war between the Japanese and the Allies also contributed to the atmosphere of brutality that has been ascribed to the Pacific War. For example, Lt. Col. Arthur Murphy, an intelligence officer in the Australian army, wrote to the Sixth Army's PWB officer that

> the enemy and our forces have been fighting it out on a "no holds barred" basis for 3 years now. The enemy has shown no mercy (quite the reverse) to our soldiers when they are captured. As a result, our forces have and are still replying in kind. The enemy is fully aware of this and knows fully well that he has not the right to expect any mercy even though he should voluntarily surrender to our forces. Even if we could convince the enemy to surrender to our forces, it would be almost impossible to get our troops to accept this surrender.[45]

For these reasons Murphy concluded that his command had little use for the propaganda war.

PWB's Captain Beard expressed his dismay over the behavior of Allied troops as follows: "As for atrocities—we can't say with a straight face that the Japs are any worse than we are"; he went on to cite unofficial accounts of Japanese being killed while attempting to surrender or while in Allied hands. He concluded that the main obstacles to PWB's work were erected by "our own men" due to their "foolish hatred" and "lack of understanding" of the Japanese as well as their ignorance of psywar operations.[46]

Allied troops' reluctance to take prisoners played directly into the hands of Japanese propagandists, who maintained that Allied troops were brutal and had a policy of torturing Japanese prisoners. The take-no-prisoners mentality confirmed the Japanese belief that the Allies treated POWs no differently than they did and seriously impaired the credibility of Allied propaganda. Surrender appeals promised good treatment and adherence to the Geneva Convention's rules regarding POWs. When Allied troops violated those rules, they undermined the validity of all Allied statements and made a mockery of the strategy of truth. According to Beard, the policy of truth had to be implemented in action as well as on paper: "If something isn't done about the attitude of our men and officers toward taking prisoners and giving them a chance to be taken, we may as well pack up and quit trying because I feel that it is worse to tell the Jap that he will be given fair treatment in our leaflets and then have him shot as he attempts to surrender or as he lies wounded in a defenseless condition. We represent command and we can't afford to tell them that and have our men make liars out of our command."[47]

As early as May 1944 the Information and Education Section (I&E) of the United States Army Forces in the Far East (USAFFE) offered its services. Ken R. Dyke, chief I&E officer, declared in a letter to General Fellers that "a well planned and paralleling information campaign directed at our troops" was as important to the success of psywar as was the campaign directed at enemy troops. He concisely summed up the dilemma facing psywarriors as follows: "It's no use telling people what Americans are like, what they think, what they'll do if victorious—if when the first detachments of U.S. troops appear, they violate and contradict all the glowing virtues and sentiments given out by the propaganda machine. Let's make the troops part of the scheme—not through propagandizing them—but by telling the facts—and making them part of the *entire* military operation—psychological as well as tactical." Dyke requested permission from GHQ to reprint and distribute to all commanders in SWPA Fellers's *Answer to Japan,* the 1944 version of his earlier research on Japanese military psychology. Dyke believed it would serve as a useful foundation for a program designed to enlighten Allied combatants on the Japanese and the propaganda war directed against them. I&E then created a lecture series delineating precisely how psywar contributed to the war effort in SWPA, and by November 1944 it had furnished more than three hundred instructional kits containing leaflet texts and an accompanying outline for discussion to I&E officers throughout the theater.[48]

In this, as in all areas of psychological warfare, the attitude of the military leadership, especially intelligence officers, was crucial. Brig. Gen. Charles A. Willoughby, MacArthur's assistant chief of staff, G-2, recognized early on that the dissemination of surrender passes required "proper coordination with the troops in the area." In a letter to Col. H.

V. White, Sixth Army, G-2, Willoughby stated that the "first prerequisite" to the use of such leaflets was to inform Allied troops that surrender passes were being distributed in their sectors and emphasize the value of taking prisoners. He supported a "vigorous surrender program" but cautioned that "if a number of Japanese attempting to surrender are killed the whole effort will of course collapse."[49]

Colonel White demonstrated not only an understanding of the problem but a willingness to provide solutions. He informed Willoughby that the Sixth Army's intelligence personnel had "taken pains to inculcate in all personnel the necessity of taking prisoners because of the wealth of tactical information that can be gathered from them." He stated further that he did not believe there had been any "intentional killing of Japs who desired to surrender" to the Sixth Army, though the earliest surrender pass (created by FELO) was very small and "difficult to discern from any distance." White had discussed his concerns with the commander of FELO and suggested that a larger, more easily recognized leaflet be developed.[50]

In all likelihood White's statement concerning the absence of intentional killing of surrendering Japanese was based as much on wishful thinking as on fact. Nonetheless, his efforts to limit the number of such deplorable incidents through both heightened troop awareness and improved leaflet construction indicate that strides were being made to eliminate the perception that Japanese did not surrender and that psywar was a fruitless endeavor.

In September 1944 Colonel White told PWB that their efforts to demonstrate the worth of propaganda to Sixth Army personnel should be given "immediate priority." Similarly, Lt. Gen. Walter Krueger, commanding general of the Sixth Army, ordered that all American troops be "reminded repeatedly of the intelligence value of prisoners and the psychological factors involved in honoring surrender leaflets." Krueger acknowledged the increasing effectiveness of PWB's surrender propaganda and maintained that the killing of Japanese soldiers attempting to surrender not only negated PWB's efforts but encouraged the enemy to "fight to the bitter end," which was precisely what everyone wished to avoid.[51]

The campaign to make Allied troops aware of the objectives and successes of psywar and more "surrender conscious" took a variety of forms and was aimed at both ground and air forces.[52] Articles to familiarize Allied fighting forces with psywar were printed in a variety of publications, including *Yank, Newsmap, Maptalk,* and OWI's *Leaflet Newsletter.* These publications received wide distribution and contained articles such as "The Duties and Responsibilities of an Air Liaison Representative," "Orienting the Airman in Psychological Warfare," "A Short-Cut to Victory," and "The Value of Taking Prisoners." Summaries of psywar activities were regularly featured in the Allied Air Forces Intelligence Summary and other intelligence publications as well.

The information program discussed the role of propaganda in the war against Japan and the extent of its successes and made clear that it depended on the cooperation of Allied combatants. "A Short-Cut to Victory" outlined the benefits that accrued to GIS for every enemy that ceased resistance: every prisoner taken meant one less Japanese shooting at Allied troops and one less enemy to pursue. Since prisoners also divulged important tactical information, the article noted that the GI's favorite line, "The only good Jap is a dead one," should be accompanied by the thought that "a dead Japanese can do them no good," for the information provided by Japanese POWs might save the lives of many GIS and shorten the war. "We haven't the troops, the resources, or the time to kill them all," concluded the report. "Our short-cut to victory is through Japanese surrender."[53]

In addition to creating greater "surrender-consciousness" among Allied forces, the information program produced evidence of psywar's effectiveness and thus increased the credibility of FELO and PWB. Propagandists explained that in addition to physical and military vulnerabilities, the Japanese also had psychological weaknesses, which psywar units knew how to exploit. I&E officers outlined the propaganda themes employed in the theater and revealed the scope of psywar operations, the numbers of leaflets disseminated, and the locations of leaflet drops and front-line broadcasts. At corps HQ, PWB displayed the leaflets currently in use as well as posters summarizing the reaction of Japanese troops to them on all company bulletin boards.[54] The I&E program did not exaggerate the impact of propaganda but stressed that psywar was designed to achieve long-range rather than immediate objectives. "Leaflets aren't expected to have the Japs waiting on a beach with their arms in the air when a landing is made," stated one pamphlet. "They don't work that way. For the most part, leaflets don't have their effect today—or tomorrow. Their effect is cumulative."[55]

PWB also familiarized Allied troops with the appearance and texts of surrender leaflets disseminated to Japanese troops and provided instructions regarding proper treatment of prisoners. In sectors where Japanese troops had been bombarded with surrender propaganda, Allied troops likewise became the target of leaflets aimed to convince them of the value of taking prisoners. While recognizing the reasons GIs hesitated to take prisoners—"we cannot deny that he has often fought with unnecessary brutality and treachery," said one leaflet—propagandists attributed the "fanatical resistance" of the Japanese to the coercion and regimentation they received as part of their military indoctrination. The message was clear: in order for the Japanese to overcome their fear of surrendering, the Allies must convince Japanese troops that good treatment awaited them. This could be accomplished only by accepting prisoners and treating them in accordance with the rules of the Geneva Convention. "We have promised the Jap, treatment of prisoners that is humane," read one leaflet. "We have told him that his surrender will be honored by you troops who do the capturing. It is up to you."[56]

The I&E campaign undoubtedly achieved some success. One of FELO's weekly publications reported, for example, an incident in which a Japanese soldier emerged from a foxhole waving a surrender leaflet only to be greeted from all directions by shouts of "Don't shoot the bastard." In August 1944 an intelligence report from the Aitape area noted that approximately twenty Japanese prisoners, most of whom possessed surrender leaflets, had been taken during the previous week. The author remarked on the fact that front-line troops had not killed them and stated that this indicated a heightened degree of prisoner-consciousness, which he attributed to "informal talks" to the troops by intelligence personnel.[57] Similarly, a FELO officer attached to the Eighth Army on Leyte reported that "the success of propaganda in these divisions (7th and 77th) has been brought about by the experience the troops now have had, and the realization of the amount of information that we can secure from prisoners who are never security conscious. The greatest check we have had in PW [psychological warfare] is prisoners coming in holding up leaflets and being shot. As troops are being more indoctrinated regarding the value of prisoners, this type of thing is becoming rare."[58]

Personal experience, however, was perhaps a more significant cause of Allied troops' slowly changing attitudes toward Japanese prisoners. Individuals who personally witnessed Japanese soldiers surrendering were thereafter willing to put aside their fears of the enemy's treachery and take prisoners themselves. This trend was often encouraged by commanding officers who responded to enemy surrenders by praising such behavior and pointing out the immediate benefits of the event. For example, after his unit took twenty-six prisoners a commanding officer on Luzon told his men: "Now we know this propaganda works. You men would have had to go into that cave after those Nips. This may have saved your lives." The same officer later remarked that the consensus among his men thereafter was to encourage the enemy to surrender, for they perceived that more Japanese might "come out of those damn caves" willingly once they saw the Allies taking prisoners.[59]

In this regard, length of service became an important factor in determining one's willingness to take prisoners. John R. Sandberg, a pwb officer on detached service with the 308th Bomb Wing, recalled that troop orientation was particularly necessary with new units: "The older infantry units that had been fighting all the way through New Guinea didn't need to be convinced of the benefits of getting them to surrender instead of digging them out. But some of the new divisions just over from the States were all gung ho and going to shoot every Jap they could find, and you had to remind them that wasn't the way it was supposed to be done."[60]

     ■   ■   ■

In a variety of ways pwb attempted to alter attitudes about psychological warfare and the Japanese enemy. While these efforts began relatively late in the war and were met with less than overwhelming success, they nonetheless point to propagandists' awareness of their place in the war effort. The mission of propagandists was to exploit conventional military victories, and they could only succeed by coordinating their operations with those of combat units and convincing senior officers that orienting troops to the value of psywar was worth the effort.

To a considerable degree, the respect given propagandists by Allied officers depended upon the results they obtained. Before amicable working relationships with field commanders could occur, psywar personnel had to prove they had something of value to offer. Thus to some degree Allied propagandists controlled their own fate, and they recognized that in the early months their work was less than satisfactory. Intelligence sources indicated that much of the early propaganda disseminated to the Japanese was not only ineffective but counterproductive. Simplistic propaganda appeals, inappropriate use of the Japanese language, and in some instances statements perceived by enemy troops to be offensive, alienated

Japanese and even stiffened their resistance. Correcting these deficiencies was crucial if psywarriors were to win the confidence of Allied military leaders as well as the attention and respect of the target population.

For psywar to be effective, propagandists must have the audience's attention. To capture and maintain the audience's attention, the propagandist must focus on matters of significance to it, and do so in an agreeable manner. This requires psywar operatives to make informed decisions about the audience's perceptions and predispositions. Propaganda is useless if the target population is not listening, and it is self-defeating if it subscribes to faulty assumptions about that population. Just as lies and contradictions inevitably destroy the credibility of propaganda, so messages that irritate, anger, or demonstrate a lack of sophistication and understanding of the target audience, the situation it faces, its culture, and its language estranges propagandists from the very people they wish to influence.

Because Allied propagandists worked within the framework of a strategy of truth from the beginning, there was no concern over being caught in a web of lies. Allied psywar did, however, suffer early on from a lack of sophistication and understanding of the Japanese. The most common early criticisms of Allied propaganda were that it was simplistic, sometimes to the point of being childlike and naive, and written from a Western perspective rather than appealing to Japanese psychology. Japanese linguists frequently referred to the language as clumsy and foreign-sounding and noted that Allied leaflets were obviously written in English and then translated (sometimes incorrectly) into Japanese, which detracted significantly from the impact of the message.[61]

Such criticisms came from a variety of sources, including linguists attached to ATIS, psywarriors engaged in propaganda against the Japanese in other theaters, and Japanese POWs. The head of ATIS, Col. Sidney F. Mashbir, stated that some of the early propaganda leaflets exhibited malapropisms that rendered the message meaningless and referred to one author who twisted "his Japanese aphorisms as completely as though he had used a Mixmaster." The resulting leaflet, Mashbir said, would have made as much sense to the Japanese as the following statement would to Americans: "Here are some beautiful maple leaves. Therefore you must surrender because a rolling stone is worth two in the bush." In August 1944 the Psychological Warfare Information Review likewise stated that "wrong Japanese phraseology, calligraphy, and mixing various forms of Japanese together, continue to hamper the success of our leaflets."[62]

FMAD agreed with these findings and emphasized that although the content of propaganda messages was very important, *how* those messages were constructed was equally important. In December 1944 FMAD personnel pointed out that the Japanese took words "much more seriously" than did Westerners (especially Americans) and concluded that how one chooses to express an idea might "prejudice its whole utility." FMAD's report noted, for example, that the Japanese were offended by words whose literal translation was "surrender," whereas expressions that meant something akin to "negotiation for resumption of peaceful conditions" were deemed inoffensive. Thus, two phrases that meant almost the same thing to Americans made two very different impressions upon Japanese.[63] Clearly, solutions to problems associated with the Japanese language were most likely to flow from Japanese linguists or, preferably, Japanese themselves. The problem then became finding an adequate number of people well versed in both Japanese language and Japanese culture.

Although there was clearly a consensus among the experts that propagandists failed to employ Japanese properly in the early phases of their work, there was not a consensus on the best way to express propaganda themes in Japanese. Some criticized Allied propaganda for being childlike and naive; others argued that it was written at a level that only well-educated Japanese would understand. It appears that in reaction to the earliest criticisms of propaganda as being simplistic, leaflet writers "corrected" these deficiencies by moving too far in the other direction. Allied propaganda seemed to shift from one extreme to the other.

The first reference to overly sophisticated propaganda occurred in late November 1944, when FMAD reported that more prisoners had criticized Allied leaflets for being too "bookish" or too "involved for those with less than middle-school education to follow easily" than had criticized them for grammatical mistakes or stylistic awkwardness. By the end of 1944 FMAD statistics confirmed that prisoners made fewer and fewer comments about there being actual mistakes in Allied leaflets and mentioned more often the "overly difficult or bookish" style of propaganda. The same report posited the likelihood that the educated linguists who engaged in propaganda composition had "perhaps aimed too exclusively at men of their own intellectual level in the Japanese armed force." The report's authors then suggested that leaflet writers attempt to strike a happy medium by aiming for "expression which is correct and clear but still colloquial."[64]

The difficulties involved in assessing a general trend in the construction of Allied propaganda and enemy reactions to it are immense. Many Allied personnel composed propaganda (some attached to FELO, some to PWB, some to OWI, and still others to ATIS), and a variety of Japanese personalities read or heard the finished product and reacted according to their own individual circumstances and predilections. Japanese prisoners frequently differed on the effectiveness of the same leaflet text or on what constituted the best propaganda themes. What is clear from POW testimony is that Allied propaganda was taken more seriously by Japanese troops and the high command as time passed. As a prisoner captured on Bougainville in November 1944 remarked: "At first leaflets were read but not taken seriously and were thrown away as being propaganda. As time went on, however, the officers and men, weary from their futile struggles, read the leaflets with greater interest and considered their contents reliable."[65] Much of their increasing success was due to propagandists' greater reliance on Nisei (second-generation Japanese Americans) and Japanese POWs in creating propaganda. In addition to the improved quality of propaganda, the quantity of leaflets disseminated to the Japanese increased as well. Finally, the continuing reversals and defeats suffered by the Japanese in SWPA created an audience considerably more receptive to psychological manipulation than in the early years of the war.

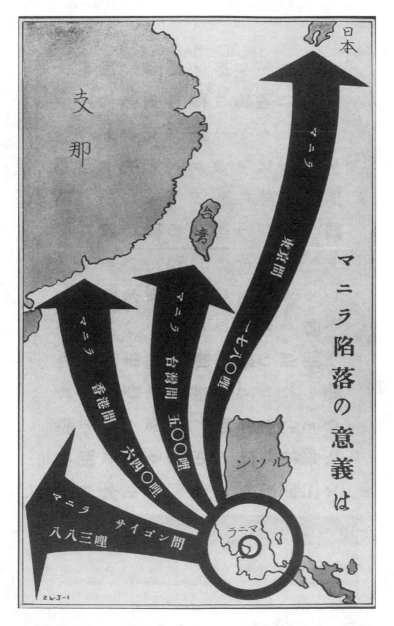

1 "Manila Has Fallen" (PWB, 24-J-1) points to the continued advance of Allied troops toward the Japanese home islands. "With the recapture of the capital city, the American army now dominates the entire Philippines. . . . The American forces, in high morale, are poised for still another strike closer to the homeland." *(Courtesy of the National Archives)*

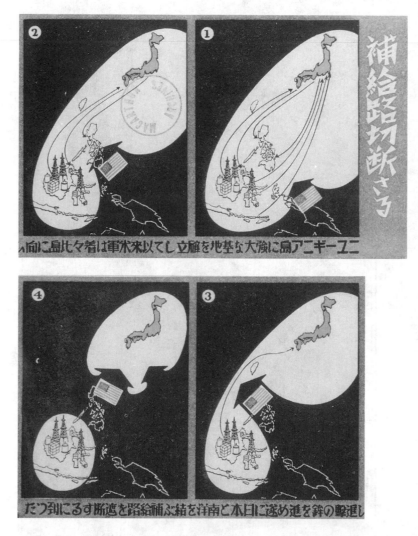

2 "Southern Treasure House" (PWB, 30-J-1) illustrates a prominent feature of the propaganda of despair. A series of sketches shows how Allied advances have cut Japan off from the resource-rich regions of its empire. The "Treasure House of the South Seas" is now useless and Japanese soldiers must fight without adequate supplies. *(Courtesy of the MacArthur Memorial Archives, Norfolk, Virginia)*

3 "Germany Has Capitulated" (FELO, J.262) announced the unconditional surrender of Nazi Germany. "Now that peace has returned to Europe the reconstruction of Germany can begin. Over one million Germans who preserved their lives as prisoners of war, can return home to start a new life. Meantime the armed forces of the Allies, victorious but still soberly determined, are now free to throw their whole strength into the war against the military clique of Japan." News extras such as this were prepared long in advance and intended to demoralize Japanese troops by punctuating the fact that Japan stood alone against the mighty Allied powers. *(Courtesy of the National Archives)*

4 "Peace in Europe" (PWB, 28-J-1) announced the return of peace and the end to the carnage of the "greatest European war in history." It attempted to "create nostalgia in the minds of the Japanese who are continuing to feel the destruction and privation of war" by elaborating upon the joyful homecoming of soldiers, the "great happiness of reunion with their families," the arrival of spring, and the "dawn of a new era." *(Courtesy of the MacArthur Memorial Archives, Norfolk, Virginia)*

5 **"Japan's Hour of Doom"** (PWB, 118-J-1) heightened Japanese despair by vowing to continue the war, which was moving ever closer to the home islands, until the militarists were crushed. "At the beginning of the war, the militarists shouted 'Certain victory!' Now they tell you the choice is between victory and extermination. They are desperate and are trying to put the responsibility on the people." The text also employs an enlightenment theme regarding Allied war aims: "'Unconditional surrender' is a military term meaning the end of the war and the overthrow of the militarists. The warlords are spreading propaganda to the effect that it signifies enslavement of the people and their extermination. This is the last desperate trick of the military, [which seeks] to drive the people to continue useless resistance." *(Courtesy of the MacArthur Memorial Archives, Norfolk, Virginia)*

日海空軍は何處へ行ったのだらうか

6 **"Abandoned"** (PWB, 6-J-1). This divisive propaganda leaflet heightened Japanese despair at the hopelessness of their situation and blamed the navy and air forces for abandoning the ground troops to their fate—a futile death on an isolated island. "Your war eagles [have left] you unprotected against the never-ending bombing of our air force. Also, the Japanese Navy is withdrawing its ships from their bases. . . . you are cut off from supplies and reinforcements and now you cannot even expect to be evacuated." *(Courtesy of the MacArthur Memorial Archives, Norfolk, Virginia)*

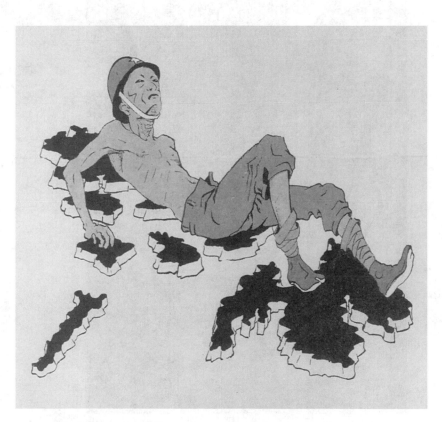

7 "Jap on the Islands" (PWB, 3-J-1) predicted the fate of Japanese soldiers in the Philippines—bombing, starvation, abandonment, exhaustion, suicide, death. "Before you reach this miserable state, which is more than men ought to endure so far from home, we want you to keep something in mind. (It is that) those who choose to come to an honorable understanding with us will find that we treat them as human beings, not as enemies. We shall hold it a duty to see that they have clothing, food, shelter and medical care." Note the leaflet writer's effort to avoid the word *surrender* by urging Japanese to "come to an honorable understanding" with the Americans. *(Courtesy of the National Archives)*

8 **"Type 38 Rifle"** (PWB, 33-J-1). The idea for this leaflet came directly from a Japanese POW interrogation that revealed soldiers' despair at having to fight a well-equipped enemy with antiquated weapons such as the Type 38 Rifle, first used forty years earlier, in the Russo-Japanese War. "Everyone knows that since that time . . . great advances have been made in the development of military equipment. . . . If you had fought with new weapons like the Americans, perhaps tragedies like Leyte might have been avoided. However much of the spiritual strength you may have, how can you expect to tackle a 500-KG bomb from a consolidated bomber with a Type 38 rifle?" *(Courtesy of the Mac-Arthur Memorial Archives, Norfolk, Virginia)*

4 Searching for the Enemy's Weaknesses

> We were taught the importance of willpower in our training. Well, there is much to that, but one cannot fight overwhelming numbers by willpower alone.
>
> Japanese soldier

For men in battle, morale is a key determinant of both physical and psychological stamina. Morale is a state of mind that affects not only an individual's ability to cope with everyday circumstances but his or her perceptions of those circumstances. OWI's Foreign Morale Analysis Division defined morale as the "capacity of a group of men to pull together persistently and consistently in pursuit of a common purpose."[1] As such, morale is both an individual and a group phenomenon, for an individual's outlook often influences that of the group, just as group psychology affects the mind-set of the individual. Realizing the interplay between individuals and the group in wartime, propagandists attacked Japanese morale on both levels.

The IJA, like all armies, was composed of millions of human beings with diverse personalities, character traits, and temperaments. It was also divided into a multitude of units, each with its own peculiar personality based on the nature of the individuals who belonged to it, the character of its leaders, and its wartime experiences. The objective of propagandists was to manipulate the emotional atmosphere of these groups and the perceptions of the human beings who belonged to them.

Before this could be achieved, however, propagandists needed to have a clear understanding of the factors affecting the morale of enemy forces. The sources of high morale discussed in the previous chapter must be offset by the factors that hastened demoralization among Japanese troops, for while it is generally assumed that the Japanese maintained an extremely high state of morale throughout the Pacific War, there is considerable evidence to the contrary.

■ ■ ■

The array of factors affecting Japanese morale can be divided into three groups: material and practical considerations, emotional and spiritual considerations, and personal-profile variables. Although the morale factors in these categories differed, they held one thing in common: the degree to which a specific consideration influenced the state of mind of a Japanese soldier was the product of individual experience. No two Japanese soldiers reacted in precisely the same way to similar circumstances. In part this was because of the obvious fact that no two Japanese soldiers were identical in physical and psychological makeup. Moreover, the wartime experiences of individuals varied greatly depending upon the unit or units one served with, as well as the location and duration of that service. For these reasons, it is difficult to make a general statement about Japanese morale that accurately summarizes the psychological state of affairs in a theater as large as the Southwest Pacific. Nonetheless, it is quite possible to ascertain certain factors that tended to lower the enemy's morale and combined to diminish Japanese faith in their cause and their determination to fight for it.

A soldier's morale is dramatically affected by practical, everyday matters of survival and personal well-being. In wartime the single most prevalent cause of demoralization among troops is defeat in combat.[2] It was fruitless for the Allies to propagandize Japanese while they were winning, but the experience of continued defeats made them susceptible to psychological manipulation. Among Japanese combatants the material and practical aspects of daily life were linked to the emotional and spiritual aspects of their outlook. The battlefield situation was only one, albeit the most important, practical consideration affecting the morale of fighting men. Other material or practical matters such as physical accommodations, the availability of food, ammunition, and other supplies, the quality of the weaponry one depended upon for survival, medical care, relations between officers and enlisted men, and air and naval support were important in either sustaining or eroding troops' determination, confidence, and enthusiasm.

When the morale of Japanese soldiers began to wane due to the prevalence of disagreeable material and practical circumstances, the emotional and spiritual life of those individuals likewise suffered. Most Japanese soldiers entered the Pacific War with a great deal of confidence in the capabilities of the army, its officers, and themselves. They generally had faith that Japan would win the war, that their cause was just, that their training was adequate, and that their spiritual strength was sufficient to overcome all obstacles. Yet this emotional and spiritual aura dissipated and sometimes vanished altogether when the material and practical hardships of the war became too great.

When tangible immediacies reduced a soldier to such depths that he began to lose faith in himself, the army, and ultimate victory, personal-profile factors such as background and personality determined how he responded to crises. Japanese soldiers did not have identical breaking points. Some endured horrific conditions for prolonged periods without losing faith in the cause or confidence in victory. Others fell prey to despair and despondency relatively quickly in the face of less arduous circumstances. Still others were unenthusiastic about military service from the day of their induction and thus had little faith to lose. In short, if it were possible to chart the morale of one thousand Japanese chosen randomly from the ranks of the army at any single point in the war, the likely result would be a continuum ranging from individuals with very low morale to those with very high morale.[3]

Propaganda had little effect on Japanese with exceedingly high levels of morale. For those who entered the army unwillingly and had no desire to take part in Japan's great mission, propagandists had little concern, for when the opportunity arose to extricate themselves from the battlefield, they did so without the prompting of Allied propaganda. Propagandists focused instead on infusing doubts and suspicions into the minds of Japanese troops who fit neither extreme—those whose faith was likely to waver under adverse conditions and whose attitudes were susceptible to manipulation.

Although morale levels varied from individual to individual and from unit to unit, the primary causes of morale loss were of a material and practical nature: battlefield losses, supply shortages, ineffective weapons, nonexistent air and naval support, and officer cruelty. These factors in turn raised in the minds of some Japanese soldiers questions of an emotional and spiritual nature and doubts about the core truths of their military indoctrination. Individuals dealt with these questions and doubts on a personal level and resolved them in accordance with their own personal disposition.

As the Pacific War progressed, the morale of Japanese soldiers declined significantly. Captured Japanese records indicate a higher incidence of courts-martial and desertions and greater friction between officers and men. They also reveal officers' concern that discipline was declining, that troops were subject to "dangerous thoughts," and that fighting spirit was lacking.[4] The great majority of Japanese soldiers remained steadfast in their desire to experience an honorable death on the battlefield; however, many allowed themselves to be captured or chose to surrender. The Japanese army was not composed of men uniformly or irrevocably devoted to the cause of victory. Captured Japanese diaries and prisoner interrogations provide a large body of heretofore neglected evidence that many soldiers experienced not only a crisis in confidence but a collapse of faith in themselves, their leaders, and their nation's ability to achieve victory. The notion, therefore, that the IJA was somehow immune to psychological warfare techniques designed to weaken morale must be examined more thoroughly. That recruits were thoroughly indoctrinated in the longstanding military traditions of Japan cannot be disputed. It does not follow, however, nor does the evidence show, that this indoctrination made the rank and file psychologically invulnerable to morale degeneration.

■ ■ ■

Devotion to the emperor, racial pride, the samurai tradition, belief in Japan's divine mission, and faith in the nation's leaders heightened Japanese military morale. Following Japan's initial battlefield successes, however, these sources of psychological strength were transformed into potential vulnerabilities, with one exception: devotion to the emperor. Wartime intelligence indicated that the deteriorating combat situation was the single most important cause of morale loss, and although the dismal progress of the war induced soldiers to doubt much that they previously had held sacred, their faith in the emperor never wavered. Consequently, in all but one respect the value system of imperial soldiers was open to Allied attack.

The increasing success of Allied military operations left the Japanese army weakened both physically and mentally. MacArthur's island-hopping campaign isolated many troops in areas that could not be reinforced, resupplied, or evacuated by a weakened Imperial Navy. Under these circumstances supply shortages in particular but also intense Allied bombing, officer malfeasance, and the absence of air and naval support, among other factors, eroded Japanese psychological stamina. Battlefield conditions thus exposed Japanese vulnerabilities and created an adversary susceptible to morale operations.

In wartime a soldier's belief in ultimate victory stems from his belief that he is winning now. His perceptions of the current situation depend upon the observable facts upon which he focuses his attention. Once the enemy "begins to doubt that he is winning now," he will come to "doubt victory in the end," wrote Daniel Lerner, a prominent scholar of psychological operations.[5] And so it was with the Japanese. One of the most significant results of the continued battlefield reverses suffered by the Imperial Army was that individual soldiers began to wonder if in fact Japan was winning the war, as they were being told by their officers. For many Japanese the observable facts indicated otherwise. Yet the demoralization that accompanied combat defeats was the result of local battlefield conditions, not the overall military situation. In 1942, for example, Japanese troops being transported from Rabaul to New Guinea were in high spirits, according to one prisoner, because they were unaware of the losses experienced elsewhere in the Pacific. Once in New Guinea, however, they were shocked at the condition of the men they had been sent to reinforce. During the Papuan phase of the New Guinea campaign continued battlefield reverses severely affected Japanese morale. Prisoners taken during the fighting there reported that defeat and disease had succeeded in destroying the stamina and courage of many men. They provided eyewitness accounts of soldiers refusing to follow their officers' orders to attack, troops becoming "completely deteriorated spiritually," and widespread defeatism.[6] A Japanese diarist recorded his reactions to the situation around Lae and Salamaua as follows:

> Being only a platoon leader, I have no knowledge whatever of the general war situation. Nevertheless, all the operations in which I have hitherto taken part have been unfavorable. Our Battalion retreated from Salamaua and Lae. It again evacuated from Finschhafen. Further retreating, it has now taken up garrison duty in its present area. With a force of three divisions at our disposal, we have retreated and retreated. I would like to see, just once, a situation in which the enemy would be pushed back and defeated.[7]

Battlefield reverses also resulted in a crisis in confidence for the Japanese soldier in a strategic sense. If they could be defeated in battle on the tactical level, as Japanese troops soon discovered was true, there was considerably less reason to remain confident in the nation's ability to achieve final victory. As early as 1943 one diarist wrote, "Damages sustained in eastern New Guinea, Madang, Finschhafen, Salamaua, etc., are tremendous. We are fighting a losing battle."[8]

Transcripts of interrogations of Japanese troops captured during the Papuan campaign demonstrate that the most prevalent expressions of dissatisfaction concerned concrete, not abstract, matters. Prisoners made significantly more critical remarks than favorable ones about such issues as supplies, reinforcements, weapons, and battlefield leadership. Conversely, far fewer prisoners expressed loss of faith in concepts of an ideological nature such as ultimate victory, righteousness of the cause, or Japan's "national destiny." The relationship between the local battlefield situation and loss of faith in abstract principles was a causal one that developed over time. Dissatisfaction with tangible factors followed immediately upon the heels of defeat, whereas loss of faith in more exalted concepts emerged gradually as the war continued to go badly for Japan. The cumulative effect of military defeats was evinced by a Japanese prisoner who remarked that in June 1942 he believed the war was practically won. By December of that year he predicted that a Japanese victory would require at least five years. Three months later he had concluded that it would take one hundred years to defeat the Allies.[9]

Ironically, in a number of ways the indoctrination of Japanese soldiers became counterproductive the longer the war continued. As military reversals became more common, many of the fundamental assumptions that had been drilled into recruits were called into question. For example, troops were trained to believe that Japanese victory in the Greater East Asia War was inevitable due to the racial and spiritual superiority of the Japanese, the unparalleled excellence of the Japanese armed forces, and the profound righteousness of the nation's divine mission of uniting East Asia under Japanese rule. Allied battlefield successes, however, caused many Japanese to doubt the accuracy of such rhetoric. Tactical defeat not only reduced Japanese confidence in the nation's ability to achieve victory but also caused individuals to question their own abilities, the expertise of their officers, and the capabilities of the army as a whole. Some soldiers began to wonder privately if there was something wrong with the IJA since for the first time in its history it apparently was experiencing devastating losses. The psychological impact of continual reverses on an army that believed in its own invincibility was much greater than it would have been had its members expected something less than perfection. In short, wartime realities failed to substantiate the rhetoric of military leaders or to fulfill the expectations of the rank and file.

These expectations often included divine guidance. The following excerpt from an inspirational lecture given to troops going into combat is an example of the kind of rhetoric IJA officers frequently employed: "The Imperial Army was always under Divine Protection and assistance, and each man must go into battle with the firm conviction that he would not stop unless the enemy has been completely annihilated. They must show in their conduct the spirit of the Imperial Army's tradition and strive to carry out their duty as warriors. Never should a man hand down to posterity a dishonored name."[10] It was not surprising, then, to find Japanese diarists expressing dismay at discouraging events. One diarist asked, "Isn't God protecting the Imperial Army? Ah, how tragic is this battlefield! Fellow comrades—are you going to let us die? Even the spirits of invincible Japanese soldiers are despondent now."[11]

In addition to the dismal combat situation troops often encountered, they confronted equally onerous difficulties due to lack of supplies. An American Sixth Army report based on the interrogations of fifteen hundred POWs who surrendered on Luzon concluded that hunger, caused by disruption of supply lines, was "the strongest and most effective of the forces which reduced the Japanese morale to the extent that he sought surrender."[12] Japanese prisoners and diarists confirmed that the threat of starvation induced many soldiers to contemplate surrender and some to seek surrender despite the alleged consequences of that act. The examples of hunger-induced surrender are numerous, and many of those captured stated that the prospect of being fed by the Allies was sufficient to overcome their fear of disgrace and possible torture. One prisoner captured on Biak in July 1944 told his interrogators that the soldiers in his unit had agreed that they could not survive much longer in their given circumstances and had determined that "it would not be wrong to surrender" if they would be fed and treated well. Another noted that he and three others from his unit had made a conscious decision to surrender, believing that "it was better to suffer the consequences of surrender rather than to starve."[13] If not complete demoralization, the threat of starvation frequently resulted in the collapse of army discipline, as described by an officer on Bougainville:

> (14 September 1944) It seems that last night somebody came in to steal rations. What disgraceful things can happen in the Japanese Army. It seems that he intended to kill Cpl. Nakashima with a hand grenade and walk off with the rations. . . . At this rate, it's a matter of life and death to be in charge of rations. Even in the Japanese Army old friendships dissolve when men are starving. Each man is always trying to satisfy his own hunger. It's much more frightening than meeting the enemy's assault. There is a vicious war going on within our ranks. Can spiritual power degenerate to this only because battles are lost?[14]

A Japanese prisoner similarly noted that the "food shortage out-did all sources of discontent" and described situations in which food was stolen and officers were hated for eating while the enlisted men starved. He concluded that food was necessary not only for physical strength to fight but for "maintaining spiritual strength" as well.[15] As if to support this prisoner's position on the relationship between food and spiritual strength, the following diary entry describes a complete loss of fortitude due to food shortages: "Who cares about the enemy? How can they be so foolish as to expect us to fight when we are not fed right. . . . What do I care about the war? From today we'll all sleep the afternoon through. Our main object will be rest and wait for the day when we are to be relieved."[16]

An unmailed postcard captured in New Guinea described the hardships the Japanese endured there as "impossible to relate" and stated that the troops ate all manner of insects, tree shoots, and grass to "quell unbearable hunger." The author also bemoaned the prevalence of disease and revealed the degenerative impact of these circumstances by concluding that "to live so as to be able to perform one's duties is even more agonizing and difficult than to die."[17]

An FMAD study on the relationship between lack of food and overall Japanese morale among prisoners taken on New Guinea between November 1942 and June 1944 concluded that Japanese troops who felt their food supplies were inadequate also had considerably less spiritual and emotional resilience. Seventy-eight percent of the prisoners questioned expressed dissatisfaction with the food supply and at the same time exhibited significantly less conviction about the righteousness of the war, less confidence in victory, diminished faith in government and military leaders, less satisfaction with their pay, and a loss of confidence in their weapons.[18] Clearly, the soldier who remarked that food was necessary for spiritual as well as physical strength spoke from experience, and the evidence confirms that as material and physical circumstances deteriorated so too did the mental stamina of many Japanese.

The escalation of Allied air and naval bombardment not only produced demoralization but diminished soldiers' confidence in their military equipment and led to a more pronounced loss of faith in Japanese naval and air power. In addition, Allied advances caused many Japanese to question the validity of their spiritual training and indoctrination. Having been assured that one's spiritual superiority was sufficient to overcome all odds, the discovery that the Allies were indeed a formidable enemy not only in terms of material assets but with regard to strength of character and determination to succeed was a severe blow to Japanese morale.

Firsthand accounts confirmed the devastating impact of bombing on Japanese troops throughout the Southwest Pacific. At Wewak, for example, one soldier noted that "bombing and strafing was so fierce that the men were frequently in a dazed condition and displayed resentment against the Japanese air force for giving no protection." The situation was similar near Hollandia, where, a prisoner noted, "there was complete loss of morale among troops . . . due to constant Allied bombing attacks and lack of Japanese fighter protection." The frequency and intensity of Allied bombing forced Japanese to recognize that the United States had achieved air superiority. Diarists remarked that enemy planes flew "nonchalantly" over Japanese positions and that their own antiaircraft positions, though "desperately active," seemed to have no impact. They noted the "regrettable" situation in New Guinea and Guadalcanal, where American air power had achieved "definite superiority," and stated that incessant air raids gave "everyone a helpless feeling." Other Japanese described the air raids as "unbearable," "fierce," "furious," and "terrifying" or remarked upon the "deathly fear" caused by enemy bombing. The Air Defense Regulations of the Imperial Army's 224th Infantry Regiment asserted that "the loss of fighting spirit is in proportion to air raids, and the lowering of fighting power in this way is remarkable. Experience eloquently verifies the above." Official statements of this sort were confirmed by the rank and file, who asserted that bombing left the men with "no more fighting spirit" or that "physically and mentally we are beginning to feel the effect of the enemy's constant bombings." In a marked repudiation of his spiritual training a soldier on New Guinea remarked, "I won't go so far as to say it is absolutely impossible but I don't think we can win the war with Japanese spirit alone."[19]

Allied air and sea superiority also caused many foot soldiers to lash out at the Japanese air forces and the Imperial Navy. Noting the constant air activity over his unit's position, one diarist began to wonder "when this sky overhead will be ours." Another wrote that while enemy planes "swarmed overhead, there were none of our planes." The Allied air assault against Wewak in February 1944 caused a soldier to write that the situation was far different from "the stories I used to hear in Japan," as "enemy airplanes, contemptuous of our army, fly overhead in large formations" and Japanese aircraft fled. Prisoners recalled that Wewak was entirely cut off from supply by sea, and a Japanese report noted the increasing difficulty in maintaining supplies as a result of Allied control of the sea lanes in the Hollandia area. The Japanese ordnance chief summarized the supply situation at Hollandia in March 1944 as one that "greatly inconvenienced" him in carrying out his duties, noting that thanks to naval failures, the troops had given up all hope of receiving more vehicles or antiaircraft guns. He described the men as feeling "heartbroken" due to their lack of resources and said that "it has come to the point where we cannot endure this indignation."[20]

One prisoner recounted the damage of air and naval bombardment in terms of both physical and material casualties and described the circumstances as extremely "disheartening" as "there were no friendly planes" and "we could do nothing about it." He concluded that the Salamaua front was "tragedy itself" and opined that "had there been friendly planes, in even half the numbers of the enemy aircraft, we should not have gone through such hardships." Other prisoners remarked that since the Allies continually sank their landing craft they suffered from all manner of supply shortages, which produced a sense of despair and hopelessness. Others who had experienced the prolonged hardships of the New Guinea campaign voiced their discontent with the army air force for its failure to support ground troops and went so far as to blame the New Guinea defeat on the inferiority of Japanese air power in both quality and quantity. One prisoner showed his disdain for the air forces, which, in his words, demonstrated "little desire to protect troops," and noted that "many [Japanese soldiers] vowed they had no desire to return to a country that deliberately abandoned them."[21]

Interservice conflict contributed to morale degeneration and led the army to blame the navy and air forces for both battlefield defeats and supply shortages. Demonstrating the schism between the services, one prisoner blamed the New Guinea "disaster" on the Japanese navy, which "completely let down" the army. Another informed his interrogators that he had revised his opinion of the "powerful" Japanese navy. The army had depended on navy personnel for air and sea support as well as for supplies, he said, "but they had failed miserably in both functions."[22] A Japanese army intelligence officer affirmed the presence of animosity between the services: "The relationship between the services is not at all good. There is a great deal of friction between the Army and Navy, and each attempts to blame its failures on some shortcoming of the other. The Navy lives in grand style and has all kinds of supplies and equipment, while the Army has practically nothing. This gives rise to much bitter criticism of the Navy by Army personnel."[23]

In addition to becoming increasingly aware of Japan's inferior capa bilities in the air and at sea, many imperial troops felt disadvantaged by substandard military equipment. Supply problems frequently plagued Japanese units, who faced the enemy with insufficient ammunition and inferior weapons. In New Guinea officers pleaded for "even one more anti-aircraft gun." The Special Warfare Branch of the U.S. Navy's Office of Naval Intelligence (oni) reported that Japanese equipment shortages were such that officers asked discharged soldiers "to consider the seriousness of the situation and for the sake of their country" sell them their pistols and swords before returning to Japan. A Japanese soldier captured in May 1944 remarked: "We were taught the importance of willpower in our training. Well, there is much to that, but one cannot fight overwhelming numbers by willpower alone. We have never lost any battles because of the lack of willpower but we have lost battles because of inferior or inadequate equipment."[24]

Forty-one percent of the prisoners taken in the fighting around Lae and Salamaua expressed a clear dissatisfaction with the quality and quantity of their military equipment. An fmad report issued in September 1944 reviewed the interrogation of seven hundred prisoners and the contents of three hundred captured diaries and concluded that Japanese soldiers in New Guinea showed an utter lack of confidence in their equipment compared with that of the Allies. The study noted that Japanese believed that the principal deficiencies existed, in order of importance, in planes, guns and machinery, manufacturing capacity, and ships and that lack of confidence was most pronounced in New Guinea, followed by New Britain. Excerpts from captured Japanese documents reprinted in the AMF's Weekly Intelligence Review included criticisms of hand grenades, flamethrowers, and grenade dischargers, all of which failed to perform within acceptable standards under battlefield conditions. And although it may be difficult to understand the humor in the story that Japanese soldiers commonly joked about the Type 38 rifle being useful only for purposes of suicide, it clearly demonstrates the disdain with which Japanese soldiers viewed this piece of army issue.[25]

Japanese leaders were similarly concerned about the scarcity of military equipment available to combat troops. Speeches to Japanese civilians were replete with pleas for ever greater production on the home front to compensate for the enemy's material superiority. Despite an unremitting emphasis on the power of the Japanese spirit and the unparalleled bravery of Japanese warriors, by 1944 a not so subtle shift in the rhetoric of Japanese leaders had transpired. In a 1944 speech to the Japanese people Premier General Koiso declared that "material power is helpless when confronted by our traditionally gallant fighting spirit." Yet he went on to rue the absence of adequate material resources, stating that "in spite of the . . . brilliant and dauntless fighting of the officers and men" the overall situation remained unfavorable to Japan. Koiso expressed his sorrow and regret to the heroes of Japan who "had to die for their nation because we did not send them sufficient materials," conceding that "a war is, in one respect, a battle of production and of transportation by our people on the home front against the production power of the United States and Britain," and admitted that Allied material strength was "perhaps ten times greater" than that of Japan. Koiso concluded that it would be difficult for even the formidable imperial forces to win victories unless they were provided with a "minimum amount of weapons and ammunition." Similarly, a Domei News Agency broadcast in May 1945 conceded that spiritual strength had its limitations and that "when material strength fails, spiritual strength will not make up for the lack."[26]

Among the many material and practical considerations that influenced the state of mind of Japanese troops the outcome of combat operations was paramount, followed by the food supply. The intensity and frequency of enemy bombing, the absence of naval or air support, and perceptions of the reliability of their weaponry and equipment likewise affected Japanese confidence, but these factors had a less dramatic effect upon troop morale than did relations between officers and enlisted men. Harsh treatment and cowardly behavior on the part of field officers was the reason most frequently cited by POWs for the collapse of morale and surrender to the enemy among individuals whose confidence was beginning to wane, second only to the threat of starvation.

The criticisms most often leveled against officers were abandonment, greed (specifically with regard to the food supply), incompetence, deliberate falsification of information, and ill-treatment. Tensions between officers and enlisted men led to a decline in discipline, refusal to obey orders, instances of soldiers intentionally killing their own officers, and a great deal of bitterness and resentment, which detracted from unit cohesiveness and morale.

Emperor Meiji's Rescript to Soldiers and Sailors clearly enunciated the responsibilities of Imperial Army officers and their subordinates. It dictated that inferiors regard the orders of their superiors as emanating from the emperor himself and "pay due respect not only to your superiors but also to your seniors" (those with seniority but equal rank and grade). Superiors, on the other hand, "should never treat their inferiors with contempt or arrogance" but should show them consideration and make "kindness their chief aim." Although the rescript declared that official duty might require officers to be "strict and severe," it proclaimed that not only would disrespectful inferiors and harsh superiors destroy the "harmonious cooperation" of the emperor's armed forces but those guilty of such offenses would be viewed as "unpardonable offenders against the State." Nonetheless, the "strict and severe" treatment of enlisted men was the general rule from the time of induction onward.

The attitudes and actions of officers and noncommissioned officers (NCOs) obviously varied, but the abundance of derogatory statements made by POWs and diarists indicates that egregious behavior by imperial officers was widespread. As further proof that the problems between officers and enlisted men were not random or rare, the Japanese high command attempted to put an end to the abuses of army officers by outlawing corporal punishment while at the same time encouraging upright behavior within the officer corps in order to raise troop morale.

That Japanese soldiers most commonly expressed dissatisfaction with the supply situation and the caliber of their commanding officers reaffirms that men in battle concern themselves first and foremost with matters that directly affect their physical well-being. Japanese troops bitterly denounced officers who abandoned them in the field in order to save themselves from further hardships or possible death. The many accounts of such incidents indicate that desertion by officers occurred all too frequently. The reactions of their men varied from despair to a desire for revenge. According to one prisoner, it was common practice for the upper echelons to withdraw talented officers from units that had been "written off." This resulted in extreme demoralization for the troops who were left behind, often under the command of inept replacements.[27]

Soldiers were even more appalled when officers opted to remove themselves from the battlefield, apparently without the permission of higher-ups. Officers who chose this course of action sometimes misled their troops into believing that they too would be evacuated soon. When the alleged evacuation failed to occur, however, the realization that they had been abandoned to either die or surrender was devastating. One prisoner who encountered this situation at Gona stated that if upon returning to Japan he were asked why he had been taken prisoner, he would "demand that they first investigate the desertion of the soldiers by the commanding officers." Another POW recalled that his unit's officers had left the men to die at Hollandia and said that all the men "planned revenge on these officers for the cowardice shown by thinking of themselves and forgetting the men." The most common result of desertion by their officers was a deepened sense of fatalism born of despair. Numerous Japanese diarists commented on the lack of spirit and low morale of soldiers who had been left to fend for themselves.

Many officers also did little to ingratiate themselves with their men when food was scarce. Throughout SWPA, enlisted men grew extremely bitter toward officers who consumed more than an equitable share of the available food and forced the enlisted men to survive on grass, roots, or insects. One prisoner described the behavior of the officers on New Britain, who hid from their men while eating what remained of the food, as "disgraceful." The result, he reported, was that "discipline in New Britain was practically nonexistent" as enlisted men refused to salute, complained openly in the presence of their officers, and prevented the commanding officer from restoring order to the chaos. Another prisoner related an episode at Noemfoor in which the officers confiscated the only food available for their own use. The troops viewed this as "reprehensible conduct," and it became a source of "great dissatisfaction" and "bitter criticism." He also noted that many troops believed that "after the treatment they had had in the Japanese Army it would be a good thing to be taken prisoner." Similarly, a prisoner taken on Bougainville noted that "bad officer-men relations, plus the realization of hopelessness is becoming increasingly conducive to surrender."[28] A corporal in an artillery regiment in the Torokino area recalled that the officers there "filched the rations of the enlisted men" and that the warrant officer was killed by his own men as a result. A prisoner captured near Noemfoor stated that his unit despised the officers for giving the men only potato skins, while they ate the meat of the potatoes. He maintained that the dissatisfaction and bitterness engendered by such incidents was so great that at least two hundred men decided to desert.

The numerous accounts of such incidents reveal widespread dissatisfaction with officers as well as deteriorating unit morale and discipline as the struggle for access to limited stocks of food intensified. In some units military discipline vanished in the face of an almost total obsession with the food shortage. Theft of rations became common, as did hatred of officers who abused the privileges of their rank to gain better provisions for themselves while ignoring the welfare of their subordinates.

In addition to desertion and greed, relations between officers and enlisted men were strained by charges of cowardice, incompetence, and dishonesty. Enlisted men frequently complained that officers ran for cover in the face of even the slightest provocations. Japanese soldiers also grew skeptical of official communiqués concerning the progress of the war and began to doubt the integrity of officers who promised reinforcements that never materialized.

Many soldiers noted that while army officers continued to emphasize the glory of military service and to exhort their men to die gallantly on the battlefield, they failed to live up to the high standards of conduct they espoused. One diarist recounted a lecture given by his commanding officer in which he declared that "it is soldierly to die by a bullet." However, said the diarist, "when it comes to actual bombardment, [the officer in question] would disappear first," and the men were "very unpleasant" about the situation. Captured Japanese soldiers likewise voiced their displeasure with officers who "sought shelter at the slightest occasion" or jumped into a "specially constructed air raid shelter at the first raid warning" or fled for safety despite orders to defend a position until death and without any consideration for their men. Such pusillanimous acts were labeled "beastly and disgraceful," cowardly, and selfish by enlisted men, and they created a great deal of ill-will within units.

Imperial soldiers also accused officers of having poor tactical judgment and blamed their hardships on their superiors' inexperience and incompetence. Prisoners criticized military leaders for wasting Japanese lives unnecessarily, for their heartless attitude toward subordinates, for failure to properly plan supply lines, and for delaying retreat too long. Even the Japanese high command recognized that deficiencies in army leadership presented a growing problem. A secret directive issued to senior officers and captured by the Allies in March 1945 blamed previous military losses on "passive, conservative and thickheaded NCO's and men who were badly commanded and controlled" by division, regimental, and battalion commanders. The directive stated that it was "essential that all officers be rejuvenated" so that they could carry out orders with "daring" and "careful planning" and "encourage leadership in subordinate officers." It dictated that anyone who withdrew rather than defend to the death would be "given the maximum punishment under the penal code" and asserted that in order to elicit the proper fighting spirit from soldiers, officers themselves must be "courageous, active and daring." The directive concluded that "one action is better than a hundred-thousand directives."[29]

The high command responded similarly to reports that Japanese officers sent their troops into combat under the command of NCOs while remaining behind the lines. Junior officers were told that "while advancing to engage the enemy or during battle" every company commander "*must* place himself in front of the company" and deploy his unit only after personally studying the disposition of enemy forces. Several company commanders of the Thirty-third Infantry Regiment on Bougainville were severely disciplined for failing to lead their men into combat. The commanding officer of a unit stationed in New Guinea in July 1943 castigated his subordinate officers for "neglecting their duties; leaving too much work to subordinates without supervision;" and "not being on good terms with their men" and asserted that the "officers' own morale was so low as it was contaminating the other ranks."[30]

A certain degree of grousing by enlisted men is natural, but the high command's concern over the poor performance of its officers indicates a problem that involved more than mere grumbling by a few disgruntled individuals. Part of the problem emanated from the prolonged nature of the Pacific War, for as time passed and casualties mounted, large numbers of inexperienced officers rose to positions of command for which they were unprepared. Although there was little the Imperial Army could do to rectify the situation, ineffective leadership plagued the esprit de corps of army units.

Even more debilitating to the morale of Japanese troops was the harsh treatment meted out to enlisted men in the name of discipline. Leaders of the IJA prided themselves on enforcing high standards of discipline and frequently engaged in what the Japanese called "personal" or "extralegal" punishment. Personal punishment included acts of physical violence inflicted by veteran or senior soldiers on their inferiors. Such violence was outside the established guidelines for military punishment as dictated by the army's Regulations for Minor Punishment and the Army Penal Code. Personal punishment generally took the form of striking inferiors for alleged infractions such as failure to salute, tardiness, imperfect execution of directives, or failure to show proper respect.

Face-slapping was common from the time a recruit entered basic training. Army personnel sometimes remarked on the severity of corporal punishment during basic training. One soldier stated that the most difficult time of his life was the first three months of his military service, when recruits were "kicked and knocked about" not only by NCOs but also by second-year soldiers. He recalled that two soldiers had committed suicide during basic training because of the constant persecution they were forced to endure from their superiors. An American sergeant imprisoned by the Japanese for fifteen months confirmed the ill-effects of corporal punishment. He personally witnessed Japanese soldiers being beaten until they were unconscious by their superiors and noted that "any man who outranks another has the right to administer" such beatings. He reported that recruits were expected to stand at attention while being physically disciplined, and his Japanese captors told him that many recruits committed "honorable harakiri during the training period because they can no longer stand the brutal punishment."[31]

The ill-will engendered by extralegal punishment during basic training was severe, and it became even more pronounced among soldiers who continued to be brutalized by superiors in the field. Given the hardships encountered by Japanese troops in the Pacific War, it is hardly surprising that the brutality of superiors sometimes pushed soldiers beyond the limits of human endurance. One prisoner noted that he had been beaten so severely that he was unable to eat for days. Another recalled that men were slapped with such force that their noses bled. Others reported being struck in the face with rifle butts or "continually beaten at the officer's whim" and that "face-slapping, kicking and beating with boots or wooden clogs were practically everyday occurrences" in the army.[32]

Because personal punishment occurred outside the parameters of official military justice, the attitudes and predilections of those with seniority or rank determined its frequency and severity. Extralegal punishments were generally administered by enlisted men with seniority, NCOs, or officers of lower rank, but it was the commanding officers who played the most important role since it was they who encouraged or discouraged such forms of discipline. One Japanese prisoner remarked that his regiment (the Forty-ninth) was "infamous among Army men for the severity with which its officers and NCO's treated the men"; he recalled that at least one of his fellow soldiers was beaten daily without exception and that he himself had "bruises and bumps on my head the year round." He declared that the Forty-ninth Regiment was so well known for its brutality that there was a saying among Japanese soldiers that "the contour of your face changes when you get into the 49th Infantry Regiment."[33]

Undoubtedly, the Forty-ninth Regiment was an extreme case, yet the deleterious impact of personal punishment on the Imperial Army as a whole was sufficiently well known to incite a movement of sorts to eliminate it. In December 1943 a secret Japanese document intended for officers only summarized the army vice-minister's opinions on the problems caused by the widespread application of personal punishments within the army. He stated that personal punishment weakened the "command and leadership" of the army, destroyed its unity, and was a "primary cause of poor military discipline." The vice-minister asserted that the "old conception" of corporal punishment as a means of strengthening discipline and stiffening morale had been proven faulty by the counterproductive results it had elicited during the Pacific War. Arguing that personal punishment had been used as a substitute for discipline and "misunderstood as exemplifying strong leadership," he made a case for eradicating the practice. Personal punishment, he said, induced Japanese soldiers to desert to the enemy, commit crimes against their superior officers, and become generally undisciplined and demoralized. Referring to the practice as an "unusually vicious custom," the vice-minister declared his intention to eliminate it by informing the army's leadership of its evil consequences and punishing "with particular severity" those leaders who inflicted personal punishment. The document also cites numerous examples of the self-defeating consequences of harsh physical treatment, including hatred of military service and one's superiors, sabotage of military equipment, crimes against officers, including murder, refusal to obey orders, and desertion.[34]

A similar enemy publication captured in June 1944 cautioned veteran soldiers and officers that personal punishment created "antipathy and discontent" among army personnel, declared extralegal punishment to be harmful, and dictated that "under no circumstances is extralegal punishment to be inflicted." Upon a review of punishable offenses within the army, the report concluded that extralegal punishment was the foremost cause of desertion, the greatest cause of crimes against discipline, and the principal cause of crimes against superior officers. It asserted that personal punishment "causes men to lose confidence in their superiors and become recalcitrant. It leads to an estrangement between subordinates and senior officers, and destroys the unity of the organization." The report included an extensive study of the motives for resorting to extralegal punishment and the methods employed in its application in order to devise suitable methods to eliminate the practice altogether. The extirpation of personal punishment, according to the author, hinged upon more thorough training of both officers and enlisted men, constant supervision in the field to ensure that physical punishments were not employed, and the resolute legal punishment of offenders.[35] Despite orders prohibiting personal punishment, the practice continued. And consistent with the army's own assessment, the morale and discipline of soldiers on the receiving end declined. Thus, in addition to the demoralization and antipathy resulting from officer desertion, greed, cowardice, and poor leadership, relations between officers and enlisted men suffered from the resentment induced by the custom of brutal personal punishment, which was never totally eliminated from the IJA.

Japanese soldiers also testified to a loss of faith in their leaders and official communiqués upon hearing optimistic reports that clearly contradicted their personal experience. Japanese officials consciously engaged in the practice of concocting and disseminating false stories or rumors to raise troop morale. Just as officers sometimes promised their men that an evacuation was imminent, they attempted to bolster soldiers' spirits by claiming that reinforcements were forthcoming or that Japan had achieved great victories elsewhere in Asia or the Pacific. Sometimes referred to as "control by rumor," this approach to building morale more often than not led to a loss of trust in those in positions of authority when actual events proved such assurances to be patently false.

As early as August 1943 FELO produced a study showing that Japanese soldiers had very little faith in official communiqués and Japanese radio broadcasts since "Japanese announcements do not reveal the real state of affairs," especially concerning imperial defeats. Prisoners noted the tendency of Japanese reports to "exaggerate victories and minimize losses" in order to lessen the impact of battlefield reverses. Rumors that Japanese troops had landed in Australia were recounted by prisoners taken in both New Guinea and New Britain, who said the stories had been deliberately circulated by their officers and regimental headquarters to cheer up dispirited soldiers. Other prisoners reported being told that the American mainland had been attacked by air or even invaded by Japanese troops. One of FMAD's principal findings regarding Japanese morale was that a large proportion of Japanese soldiers exhibited a decided lack of faith in the accuracy of the news they received. Diarists demonstrated a similar suspicion of reports recounting the situation in the home islands. One private recorded the skepticism evoked by the reassuring letters received from home: "Troops are beginning to doubt whether everything at home is as splendid as it is reported to be. (Surely everything in the garden is not so lovely.)"[36]

Officers also circulated rumors of the impending arrival of reinforcements to hard-pressed troops in an effort to raise morale. Prisoners reported that they were told from time to time that thousands of troops were scheduled to arrive to bolster their positions or that squadrons of aircraft were en route to their area of operations. Officers occasionally convinced their men that their difficulties were due to massive Japanese offensives elsewhere in the Pacific. One prisoner reported, for example, that his unit in New Guinea had been told that it was short of supplies because the navy had been withdrawn in order to support operations in India, where friendly forces had succeeded in capturing Calcutta and advancing two hundred miles inland. In a similar vein, a diary captured on Luzon asserted that the reason for the lack of air support in the Philippines was that six thousand aircraft were being held in Korea.

Japanese reports also contained outrageous claims of the deteriorating condition of the enemy's armed forces. A diarist on New Guinea wrote of the boost in troop morale that resulted from news that 150,000 Americans were starving to death on Guadalcanal. Similarly, other diarists reported hearing that 60 percent of all enemy transports in the Lingayen Gulf had been sunk by the Japanese navy, that 1,500,000 American and British troops had surrendered to Germany in Europe, or that all Allied troops in Western Europe had "surrendered unconditionally."[37] Deception schemes of this sort raised troop morale in the short term, but when reinforcements failed to arrive or soldiers discovered that reports of Japanese success or Allied defeat had been mere concoctions, morale suffered and the ranks lost trust in their superiors. Efforts to enforce discipline and raise morale via disinformation clearly backfired.

Equally distressing to Japanese forces was the lack of any substantive news. As a general rule, only officers had access to shortwave radios, and what written or oral information was imparted to enlisted men was carefully monitored. Not only were personal letters to and from theaters of operation censored but officers received instructions regarding what constituted proper communication with their troops.[38] Restrictions were imposed to prevent military personnel from becoming discouraged over deteriorating conditions both on the battle line and in the home islands. Rather than creating an army oblivious to the reality of the situation, however, attempts to keep the army isolated from disheartening news produced a desire for news bordering on obsession. News was particularly scarce for men in the front lines, and prisoners expressed the opinion that news leaflets disseminated by the Allies were popular because they "provided the only link the troops had with the outside world."[39]

A Domei News Agency correspondent reported that Japanese forces in the Philippines were hungry for news and "eagerly looked forward" to Allied news leaflets, which were "frequently the only source of information available." He also noted that the scarcity of news caused soldiers to swallow the Allied recapitulation of events, which had a "naturally distressing" effect on them. Another journalist for Domei informed his captors that all Japanese reports emanating from theaters of military operations were examined first by the censorship bureaus of the armed services and then by the Ministry of Information, the Propaganda Bureau, and the Bureau of Politics and Economics before publication. He said that the Propaganda Bureau ensured that war reports discussed military reversals on a "very limited basis"; correspondents were required to make military defeats appear to be "spiritual victories" by describing the "heroism of Japanese troops in the face of terrible odds" and to minimize Japan's material and personnel losses while exaggerating enemy casualties.[40]

For units in such perilous straits that defeat could not be disguised, in addition to recounting victories elsewhere, commanding officers attempted to inspire greater dedication from their men. Their pep talks or morale lectures often contained references to the upcoming "decisive battle" of the Greater East Asia War, which would determine the "destiny of Imperial Japan," thereby extracting increased efforts from their men. Even though his unit had received "no proper supplies for the past year" and "in spite of the terrible blows suffered" in the previous attack, the commanding officer of the Japanese Eighteenth Army called upon his men to demonstrate the "truly fine spirit" and "rightly firm loyalty" so characteristic of the "indomitable Imperial Army" in order to fulfill its mission in this time of "national crisis."[41]

In sum, the reality often stood in dramatic juxtaposition to the ideal of perfect harmony and mutual respect between imperial officers and their subordinates envisioned in Emperor Meiji's rescript. The nature of interpersonal relationships within particular units of the Imperial Army varied greatly, and to contend that conflict between individuals of differing rank and grade was the general rule would be an oversimplification of the dynamics of human interaction. Nonetheless, wartime intelligence indicated that the treatment accorded enlisted men during the war was a prominent source of discontent and disillusionment for Japanese troops.

A final material or practical factor affecting the morale of Japanese soldiers was the medical attention they received. When medical supplies were limited, which was generally the case, soldiers suffered from the physical repercussions of diseases such as malaria, beriberi, and dysentery as well as psychological and spiritual ennervation. Medical supply shortages sometimes led to dissension within units as officers and NCOs were attended to first and enlisted men often went without badly needed treatment. Moreover, inadequate medical attention resulted in the needless deaths of many Japanese troops, which bred animosity and a sense of fatalism. The practice of praising soldiers wounded in battle while reprimanding men afflicted with illness or disease likewise produced bitterness among those who, through no fault of their own, became the victims of the sicknesses that ran rampant in the jungles of SWPA.

The practice of killing wounded troops to prevent their capture or to facilitate rapid evacuation also had a negative impact on many soldiers. Although military indoctrination inculcated the belief that the "disposal" of sick and wounded who could not be evacuated was an act of mercy in keeping with the ideal of "death before dishonor," those who witnessed such acts often reacted with revulsion and fear for their own safety should a similar fate befall them. An Imperial General Headquarters report summarizing the lessons of the New Guinea operation berated medical personnel for their inattention to duty, which caused "many patients [to] die without anything being done to save their lives." In the battles for Lae and Salamaua, FMAD found that 89 percent of the

Japanese questioned despaired over their own poor health and 76 percent were demoralized by the medical condition of others in their units. FELO studies of Japanese morale through August 1943 show that sickness was the third most frequently cited cause of Japanese demoralization.[42]

Soldiers suffering from physical ailments often lost the will to survive and sought surrender as an alternative to their misery. One POW remembered just wanting out of the war, so he "deliberately exposed himself to capture." Prisoner interrogations conducted by ATIS recorded a very high incidence of Japanese soldiers captured without resistance or in the act of surrendering because of their weakened physical state.[43]

Japanese troops were also demoralized by the constant presence of dead comrades. To see in the jungle the "skeletons of many men who were once malaria patients" and who were so exhausted that they "fell dead where they were," as one diarist recorded, certainly did little for the morale of the soldiers who remained. In like manner, the abandonment of sick and wounded who were declared obstacles to expeditious withdrawals was disheartening, as indicated by a diarist who described the decision of the platoon commander to leave a sick man behind and without medical aid when the unit evacuated its positions: "It was pitiful, no, it was like cutting my own stomach to leave Ota behind. . . . We finally parted in tears."[44]

Recalling the arrangements made for the sick and wounded in New Guinea, a prisoner stated that hospital accommodations were so primitive that many patients died from "exposure and lack of attention" and that some medications were depleted as early as three days after the unit's arrival. A prisoner captured on Goodenough Island recalled seeing a soldier operated on for a syphilitic sore without anesthetic because those medications were too "valuable to be wasted on anyone who would become diseased from such a cause." He also noted how pitiful it was "to see a grown man crying."[45]

The practice of killing the sick and wounded or providing those who were unfit for evacuation with the means to commit suicide produced mixed emotions among Japanese. On the one hand, some expressed gratitude to their officers for allowing the infirm to die with honor. On the other hand, some soldiers were shot while attempting to save themselves from such mercy killings, and there are eyewitness accounts of others who were clearly dismayed by the events that transpired in medical facilities. One prisoner recalled the "horrible sight" of Japanese medical officers attempting to kill the seriously wounded troops, many of whom "died while walking or were shot running away." Another prisoner noted that his commanding officer ordered his unit to evacuate a position but leave the stretcher cases behind; the incident was "discussed among the troops," who did not view it favorably.[46]

. . .

In some ways Japanese military indoctrination aided the Allies. The Japanese policy of no surrender, for example, meant that soldiers were not told how to behave if they were captured by the enemy. Consequently, Japanese prisoners displayed a surprising willingness to cooperate with their captors and give them pertinent military information, in contrast to soldiers of other nationalities, who were carefully instructed in the proper behavior should they be captured. Having been conditioned to believe that being taken prisoner was the equivalent of losing one's citizenship, Japanese prisoners tended to view themselves as having begun life anew. Many Japanese prisoners thus worked for the Allies as if they had been born again.

Australian intelligence sources reported as early as July 1942 that Japanese troops were not given instructions about divulging military information of use to the enemy should they be captured. Presumably such instruction ran counter to the doctrine of "death before dishonor." FMAD arrived at similar conclusions in its study of Japanese prisoners; according to its findings, they were "psychologically unprepared" to deal with their status as captives and had no formal guidelines for behavior under those conditions. FMAD found Japanese prisoners unusually truthful and willing to discuss "exceedingly useful" military matters, such as the Japanese order of battle and the location of supply depots. Only with respect to their individual identity did Japanese prisoners attempt to deceive their interrogators, since they feared economic and social reprisals on their relatives in Japan.[47]

Japanese sources confirmed that imperial soldiers had internalized the belief that soldiers simply did not surrender. As we have seen, the IJA had a longstanding no-surrender policy. Army regulations dictated that regardless of the circumstances, any officer who surrendered his unit to the enemy would be severely punished, perhaps put to death. Soldiers likewise grew up understanding that to surrender to the enemy was to bring dishonor on oneself and one's unit, as well as one's family and nation. As a result, Japanese officers and enlisted men alike internalized the no-surrender policy and believed that "it was absolutely forbidden in the

Japanese army to withdraw, surrender, or become a prisoner of war."[48] Imperial officers occasionally issued instructions prohibiting their troops from surrendering to the enemy or being taken prisoner. More often, Japanese troops simply assumed that surrender was unacceptable. There was little need for formal statements to that effect since Japanese tradition taught that soldiers never surrendered and the implications for individual behavior in wartime were clear. Prisoners stated, for example, that "surrender is absolutely unrecognizable" or "Japanese don't surrender," but rarely did they recall having been ordered not to give themselves up.[49]

Troops frequently received orders to defend their position to the death, however, and were incessantly reminded of their obligations to the emperor and the nation and of the honor of dying gloriously on the battlefield. It was unusual for Japanese troops to be ordered not to surrender, but military indoctrination made clear the fate of soldiers who dishonored their family and failed to fulfill their responsibilities as loyal Japanese subjects. It was precisely this fate that compelled Japanese prisoners to cooperate fully with their captors. Believing that POW status was the ultimate disgrace, the great majority of men captured by the Allies considered themselves lost to their old lives. Despite the lack of regulations stating that Japanese prisoners were prohibited from returning to their homeland, nearly all captured personnel expressed a fervent desire never to go home. ATIS reported that 88 percent of all POWs questioned about the prospect of returning to Japan after the war stated that they had no wish to do so.[50] They not only feared the likelihood of a court-martial for dishonorable conduct but also expected to be victimized in their communities along with their families, who would be equally disgraced. Prisoners therefore determined that they could never return to Japan and had little choice but to start a new life.

Japanese prisoners almost unanimously requested that no word of their circumstances be sent to relatives, preferring family members to assume that they had died in battle as befit one of their calling. According to one POW, the label "died in action" was immediately applied to those who had not been heard of in three years and they were therefore no longer citizens of Japan. Upon returning to the homeland, he continued, former POWs would be cast out by their friends and family as "dishonorables" and face immediate court-martial, though army regulations declared that "Japan does not recognize prisoners of war."[51]

As for their postwar plans, an Allied intelligence officer declared: "Some prisoners think that after the war they may be able to start afresh in Manchuria or China, from which place they will later be able to revisit Japan with a new identity. Others have the idea of becoming bandits or pirates, as they will not be able to take their old occupations, and by becoming famous in a new career to obliterate the memory that they were once prisoners of war."[52] A Japanese lieutenant maintained that "almost all Japanese prisoners of war have the idea of new life and rebirth," a phenomenon he ascribed in part to the Buddhist doctrine of reincarnation and rebirth. Japanese troops who continued to live after their capture had already "died as a Japanese soldier"; thus "all we prisoners of war have been reborn." He continued, "We all fight against the American Army with all our might before capture, but we ought to be faithful to the American Army when captured. In other words, from that time on we must fulfill our loyalty to America the same as we did to the Emperor before capture. I, after the rebirth, became another Japanese. The only difference from before is that America, who was my enemy, becomes now my very good and kind friend."[53] One might question the honesty of the emotion or suspect that the statement was made under duress or in an effort to please the interrogator. Yet such sentiments were common among Japanese POWs. What is more, the willingness of captive Japanese to participate in the Allied propaganda war against their former compatriots testifies to the authenticity of the born-again phenomenon.[54]

The orthodox attitude toward capture—the perception that one's ties with Japan had been severed forever, that one had for all intents and purposes become dead to his previous life—produced a desire to "make a start on an entirely new life." "I would like to do anything I can for America if you can make use of me," commented one prisoner. "After all, I am not good for anything much anymore. Under such circumstances we are theoretically dead and I don't care whom I work for." In much the same vein, another captive declared that he "now wished to forget about the Army and make an entirely new start." He added that he would like to live and work in Australia as he did not wish to go back to Japan. Yet another internee noted his desire to "make a new life outside Japan after the war," for to return to the homeland would bring disgrace to his family.[55] In Burma a group of prisoners combined efforts to produce a Japanese-language newspaper entitled *New Life* for dissemination to troops still in the field. The following poem from one edition of the paper aptly illustrates the concept of a spiritual rebirth.

NEW PLANT

Taken captive after fighting till the last,
I feel as if transformed and born anew.
I am like the humble shoot of a plant
still covered by the sod.

But wait and see! The surging breath of life
Has filled my body.
Tomorrow, I shall burst forth to build a
Shining Paradise upon the earth.[56]

The desire of most Japanese soldiers to experience a glorious death on the battlefield rather than bear the ignominy of POW status led to other unintended consequences for the Imperial Army. In particular, it became obvious to Japanese commanders in the latter years of the Pacific War that their troops were all too willing to die honorably in the service of the emperor. The propensity of Japanese soldiers to view death as an honorable escape from the hardships of wartime service induced some individuals to commit seppuku or purposely expose themselves to death rather than go on facing adversity. In short, a code of behavior that emphasized "death before dishonor" contributed to self-destructive impulses on the part of some Japanese troops. As one ATIS official put it, "Indoctrination for death has done its work too well." Japanese soldiers sometimes preferred self-destruction to strenuous action in difficult situations. Japanese sources provide numerous examples of men who committed suicide rather than endure the "sufferings of starvation" or as an escape from illness or just a "bad environment." In advancing the notion that "death is lighter than a feather," Emperor Meiji's rescript inadvertently created a fatalistic attitude among Japanese soldiers, some of whom began to regard death as an end in itself rather than a possible consequence of fulfilling one's duties to the nation. This fatalism surfaced in the writings of a soldier who stated that it would be easier to die than to continue to perform one's duties under the agonizing and difficult circumstances the army faced in New Guinea. A diarist in Hollandia expressed a similar attitude, declaring that the men in his unit were determined to "accept inevitable death" rather than remain alive under the "onerous" and "pitiful" conditions of their daily life.[57]

The Japanese command noted with distress that in addition to the fatalistic outlook of some troops, propagating the notion that death in battle was glorious and honorable produced another unfortunate result, namely, a propensity on the part of some men to consciously seek death. Commanding officers thus made every effort to distinguish between "fighting till the end" and "desperate self-destruction." One officer informed his men that "although there is a similarity between fighting till the death and desperate self-destruction, the spiritual interpretations are the exact opposites. The former implies fighting till the end to destroy the enemy. The latter refers to acts of suicide, and are not an expression of true loyalty." A diarist recorded that prior to embarking for the Southwest Pacific his commanding officer issued an order prohibiting the men from using the term *gyokusai* (glorious death) as they needed "to keep fighting to defend the nation." A Japanese official similarly asserted that Japanese troops "must understand thoroughly that what is of value is not death but duty." On Leyte, an officer attempted to curb the "regrettable" number of suicides by issuing an order stating that "retainers of the Empire must not destroy themselves because of personal matters. No compassion can be felt for one who commits suicide. . . . Our philosophy of life is not solved by death, but rather by the degree of success attained in accomplishing a mission." That the willingness to die had been taken to extremes is substantiated by accounts of Japanese forces making reckless assaults with no hope of attaining a military objective. One such source stated that "on several occasions he had seen Japanese leave foxholes well-protected, and well-supplied with grenades, ammunition, and rifles, and charge with nothing but a knife."[58]

Thus, as Japanese officials persevered in attributing to the nation's armed forces a superior spirit and matchless strength of will, battlefield conditions continued to exact a heavy toll on the morale of individual soldiers. The "Japanese spirit" suffered from the hardships that accompanied military defeat. Unrestrained enemy bombing, minimal air and naval support, lack of food and supplies, inferior military equipment, officer malfeasance, and deficient medical attention eroded both the physical and psychological strength of the Imperial Army. Conventional military operations thus exposed Japanese vulnerabilities and paved the way for the Allied propagandists whose job it was to inspire greater doubt, confusion, and despair in the enemy's mind. Armed with weapons as well as words, the Allies set out to destroy not only the ability but the will of the enemy to continue the hopeless struggle for victory.

5 Exploiting the Enemy's Weaknesses

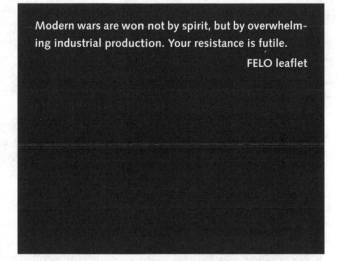

Modern wars are won not by spirit, but by overwhelming industrial production. Your resistance is futile.

FELO leaflet

The propaganda war waged against the Japanese army was designed to exacerbate the ill-effects of battlefield losses and the hardships of combat. Psychological warfare, said Bonner Fellers, "is potent only when one nation is inflicting her physical will upon another."[1] It is an axiom of psychological warfare that battlefield conditions are what create a susceptible target audience. Once the Allies had seized the initiative in the Pacific and their battlefield victories began to mount, the deteriorating combat situation began to have a cumulative effect on Japanese soldiers' state of mind. It was Allied combat successes that gave propagandists the ammunition they needed to attack Japanese morale.

Allied propagandists pursued three main objectives in their campaign to hasten the demoralization of the IJA. First, they sought to undermine morale by providing soldiers with convincing evidence that Japan's military defeat was inevitable and that continued resistance would result in national destruction rather than victory. Second, they aimed to convince enemy troops that the incompetence of the militarists (or military clique, generally referred to in propaganda as *gunbatsu*) had led to this state of affairs. Psywar personnel argued that the *gunbatsu* were not attuned to the will of the emperor in an effort to separate soldiers' loyalty to the emperor, which was firm, from their loyalty to the officer corps and Japan's military leaders, which was more susceptible to erosion. Finally, psywarriors attempted to overcome the mental obstacles that prevented enemy soldiers from surrendering. Given these basic goals and building upon their accumulated knowledge of Japanese attitudes and vulnerabilities, propagandists created a propaganda program that encompassed a number of themes designed to hasten the collapse of Japanese resistance.

The propaganda themes employed in the Southwest Pacific do not easily conform to the categorical divisions espoused by most psywar authorities. Paul Linebarger, for example, lists four types of propaganda: conversionary propaganda, which aims at changing the emotional or practical allegiance of individuals from one group to another; divisive propaganda, which is designed to separate component subgroups of the target population; consolidation propaganda, which is directed toward civilian populations in areas occupied by an armed force and strives to ensure compliance with the policies of the occupying force; and counterpropaganda, which refutes specific points or themes of the enemy's propaganda.[2] If one adheres to these definitions, combat propaganda in swpa employed only divisive and conversionary themes, and then only the latter if one includes in that category propaganda aimed at eliciting the surrender of enemy troops. Daniel Lerner argues that of the five propaganda themes employed during World War I, only enlightenment propaganda and communication designed to induce despair carried forward to World War II.[3] Combat propaganda operations in swpa did indeed revolve around the propaganda of despair, and enlightenment propaganda, though much less prominent, was also a regular feature of psywar. But a thorough examination of the themes employed by FELO and PWB reveals that two other categories of propaganda were central to the war of words, namely, divisive and subversive propaganda. Thus, one can identify four distinct types of combat propaganda at work in swpa, propaganda created to induce despair, division, subversion, and enlightenment. This typology reveals precisely the kinds of messages created by Allied propagandists to manipulate the disposition of Japanese soldiers.

Propaganda of despair sought to dishearten and discourage Japanese soldiers and to inspire in them a sense of hopelessness and defeatism. The dissemination of discouraging war news was a central feature of the propaganda of despair, as was the emphasis on superior Allied material and human resources. Nostalgia leaflets were also designed to induce despair among Japanese troops, as were leaflets that drew attention to Japan's shipping losses and the consequent loss of supplies to men in the field. *Divisive propaganda* aimed to detract from the unity of the enemy by exploiting schisms within the army and between the Japanese army and navy. Within the army, propagandists sought to increase animosity between enlisted men and their officers. They also capitalized on interservice rivalries to convince Japanese ground troops that they had been abandoned by the navy and air forces. The purpose of *subversive propaganda* was to undermine Japanese military ideology, particularly those aspects that were central to army indoctrination, such as the belief in Japanese spiritual superiority, the ideal of "death before dishonor," the image of Japan's military leaders as the instrument of the emperor's will, and the righteousness of the Greater East Asia War. Finally, *enlightenment propaganda* was intended to give Japanese troops a more accurate picture of Allied intentions and capabilities, particularly the magnitude of the coalition's industrial strength, their treatment of prisoners, and in the latter stages of the war the meaning of unconditional surrender.

- - -

Psychological warfare operations must be examined within the context of two extraordinarily important policies governing the propaganda war. First was the strategy of truth. The significance of this policy cannot be overstated, for without it propagandists could not have established and maintained credibility with the target population. The second policy prohibited propagandists from criticizing or attacking the emperor of Japan, and like the strategy of truth, it paid big dividends. These basic policy parameters ensured that Allied propaganda was credible and that it did not alienate the Japanese by attacking the most revered symbol of the Japanese nation.

In his "Basic Military Plan for Psychological Warfare in the Southwest Pacific Area" Fellers cautioned all psywar personnel to "indulge in nothing but the truth," and throughout his tenure as head of PWB he demanded strict adherence to that strategy. In a number of instances Fellers personally rejected propaganda texts that deviated from the truth and thus violated PWB guidelines, which dictated that propagandists must weaken the enemy's will to resist "by disseminating *truth*."[4]

As the basis of all propaganda distributed in SWPA, the strategy of truth imposed limitations on psywar operatives. The benefits that accrued from this policy, however, far outweighed the disadvantages, for the strategy of truth enabled propagandists to establish themselves as a reliable source of information. As one would expect, Japanese soldiers initially rejected the information they received from Allied sources as mere propaganda. However, as the war progressed they became aware that the Allied version of events in Asia and the Pacific more closely resembled reality than did the information provided by their own leaders. The strategy of truth thus had a cumulative effect. It also provided propagandists with a foundation upon which to build a propaganda program that became increasingly damaging to Japanese morale. For example, accurate news bulletins gained the enemy's attention and in time his grudging trust. Thereafter, Japanese were more likely to believe other Allied assertions.

In addition to enhancing the reliability of Allied statements, the strategy of truth conformed to the democratic principles espoused by the British, Dutch, Australians, and Americans. The leaders of totalitarian societies had no qualms about purposely deceiving their own populations as well as those of neutral or enemy nations. The people of the United States, the British Commonwealth, and the Netherlands, however, were accustomed to freedom of expression and resistant to government censorship, which precluded the use of the big-lie approach to propaganda. Policymakers perceived, moreover, that whatever short-term benefits might accrue from departing from the truth would be more than offset by the lasting damage incurred from such a policy. What is more, Allied propagandists realized that once the tide of the Pacific War had turned against the Japanese, there would be little reason to lie; the truth would be sufficiently demoralizing. The strategy of truth thus became the hallmark of Allied propaganda.

Adherence to the strategy of truth required psywar personnel to deal straightforwardly with difficult issues such as the policy of unconditional surrender, announced by President Franklin D. Roosevelt in January 1943. In conforming their propaganda to national policy and the strategy of truth, propagandists were limited in the kind of assurances they could provide to Japanese. In short, the policy of unconditional surrender prevented psywar agencies from making surrender appear more attractive than it really was. Most propagandists criticized the policy of unconditional surrender and argued that it made their task exceedingly difficult. Nevertheless, just as military operations must conform to the objectives dictated by politicians, so must psywar operatives comply with national policy directives.

Roosevelt's public announcement of the Allied policy of unconditional surrender reflected an adherence to the strategy of truth on the highest level. Had the political leadership of the Allied nations chosen instead to deceive the enemy regarding their intentions and promise lenient treatment of the Axis powers, they most certainly would have expedited the war's end. Concealment of the Allies' basic intentions, however, would have precluded a context of overall truth. Since consistency is the mainstay of successful propaganda, the Allies faced a choice between a strategy of truth and a strategy of lies. Allied leaders wisely chose to tell the truth to both their own citizens and the enemy. Whether the unconditional-surrender policy hindered psywar operations or encouraged the enemy to fight on when he otherwise might have given up remains a subject of controversy. Of greater significance for the purposes of this study is how Allied propagandists, in keeping with the strategy of truth, addressed the policy of unconditional surrender.

Propagandists in SWPA promised only that unconditional surrender did not mean extermination of the Japanese population or destruction of the home islands as purported by Japanese leaders. Although Fellers expressed his desire that the Allied governments state in more concrete terms the nature of the peace they anticipated with Japan, no such statement was forthcoming. Fellers nonetheless outlined plans for future propaganda texts should the Allies decide to define publicly the meaning of the term *unconditional surrender* but cautioned that such a program could be implemented only "after these terms are stated by our Government."[5] Since they never were, PWB never defined unconditional surrender except in a negative sense, that is, except to say what it did not mean—destruction of Japan and its people.

This approach was made possible by President Harry S. Truman's news conference of 8 May 1945, during which he elaborated on the meaning of unconditional surrender:

> It means the end of the war.
> It means the termination of the influence of the military leaders who brought Japan to the present brink of disaster.
> It means provision for the return of soldiers and sailors to their families, their farms, and their jobs.

And it means not prolonging the present agony and suffering of the Japanese in the vain hope of victory.

Unconditional surrender does not mean the extermination or enslavement of the Japanese people.[6]

Thereafter, leaflets and loudspeaker addresses to enemy troops outlined President Truman's amplification of the unconditional-surrender policy. PWB also distributed leaflets containing excerpts from a series of radio broadcasts to Japan by Capt. Ellis M. Zacharias. Transmitted between 8 May and 4 August 1945, Zacharias's broadcasts had several objectives, one of which was to explain the meaning of unconditional surrender.[7] Because Zacharias's transmissions "originated with the approval and guidance of top political and diplomatic leaders in the U.S.," PWB approved the creation of a leaflet entitled "Peace with Honor," based upon his radio broadcasts. On the front of the leaflet was a picture of the Japanese goddess of mercy, and the leaflet read, in part:

> The militarists who have brought misfortune upon Japan say the only choice left the Japanese people is victory or extermination.
>
> I am in a position to guarantee with authority that the desperate phrase "victory or extermination" is a deliberate misrepresentation of fact. . . .
>
> I am specifically authorized to reiterate that unconditional surrender is a purely military term, meaning only the yielding of arms. It does not entail enslavement. It does not entail extermination of the Japanese people. These thoughts have been injected by your military leaders as an ignoble device to compel you to continue a hopeless war.
>
> Your future lies in your own hands. You can choose between a useless death for many of your forces or a peace with honor.[8]

Texts such as these were consistent with the bulk of Allied propaganda, which maintained that the Allies held Japanese military authorities, not the Japanese population as a whole, responsible for the war.

The strategy of truth required that propagandists proceed with caution on a number of sensitive issues besides the unconditional-surrender policy. Fellers insisted, for instance, that propaganda not include slogans such as "Philippines for the Filipinos," which he described as "a rather dangerous phrase in that it can be twisted to mean many things." Fellers encouraged PWB to publicize American aid in the reconstruction and rehabilitation of the Philippine Islands but drew the line at making any statements that might be construed as promises to the Filipino people for fear that postwar events would prove them false. Fellers also objected to seemingly innocuous propaganda lines that could be exploited by the Japanese. He strongly advised propagandists to avoid references to the political and economic unity of the United Nations, which Fellers perceived as tenuous. He believed that the political problems of postwar European reconstruction were sufficiently divisive to require that propagandists focus instead on the unity of the Allied military effort to the exclusion of political and economic issues. "If we play up the San Francisco Conference, world peace organizations, and unity in the political and economic order of Europe," he wrote, "I am positive that the whole mess will explode in our lap. It will discredit our fine record for absolute accuracy." Citing the "different purposes" of the United States, England, and the Soviet Union in the occupation of Germany, for example, Fellers concluded that "there is no reason we should be sucked into the complications which exist in Europe. We have nothing to gain but everything to lose."[9]

MacArthur's military secretary wished to eliminate propaganda lines that could be construed as false and thus cause enemy or neutral populations to doubt the veracity of PWB output. In response to a weekly military plan that referred to freedom of the press as practiced by the United Nations, Fellers noted that such a statement "throws us wide open for criticism." He denied the existence of a world free press among the United Nations and argued that a free press "exists neither in India nor in Russia. . . . nor does it exist in the Balkans." Fellers therefore instructed PWB to eradicate that propaganda line from its plans.[10]

Another major issue affecting propaganda output concerned the Japanese emperor. The fundamental policy question was whether Allied propaganda should indict the person of the emperor for the actions that had plunged Japan into the Pacific War or picture him as an unwitting victim of the militarists' manipulations along with the rest of the Japanese people. In February 1943 MacArthur's chief intelligence officer, Charles A. Willoughby, expressed the view that the Japanese emperor was "thoroughly a party to and an instigator of this war" and that to suggest that the war had been forced upon Japan by the "militaristic clique" would be contrary to fact. In November Gen. George C. Kenney concurred with Willoughby's assessment, adding that "the strongest weapon of the Jap is his faith and belief" in the emperor. "If we take away that faith," Kenney argued, "he will no longer be so anxious to die for his Emperor."[11] Adherents to this school of thought believed that the emperor should be a target of Allied propaganda precisely because he was of fundamental importance to the Japanese belief system. Moreover, for those who believed that the emperor had actively contributed to the decisions that had engulfed Asia in war, as did Willoughby, to disregard the role of the emperor by describing him as a pawn of the militarists violated the strategy of truth.

Willoughby and Kenney were, however, a minority in the debate regarding the proper policy for dealing with the emperor. Japanese experts working in conjunction with OWI, FELO, ATIS, and PWB argued that written attacks upon the emperor or the imperial institution would be harmful. Propagandists concerned themselves with two aspects of the question. On the one hand, they debated whether it was wise to attack the imperial institution in an effort to weaken or destroy a pillar of Japanese morale. In other words, *should* Allied propaganda attempt to discredit the emperor? On the other hand, social scientists turned propagandists questioned whether it was even possible, given the means available, to weaken Japanese faith in the emperor. That is, *could* Allied propaganda discredit the emperor? Far East specialists, after lengthy consideration, replied negatively to both questions. They argued that even if propaganda could cause the Japanese to lose faith in the emperor and all that he symbolized (which was highly unlikely), such a course of action would have detrimental consequences.

Propagandists and Far East specialists agreed that little could be done to denigrate the emperor in the eyes of his subjects. As director of FMAD, Alexander H. Leighton analyzed a vast quantity of information about the Japanese, their traditions, and institutions. He concluded that even if the Allied powers wished to destroy popular loyalty to the imperial institution, there was little reason to believe it could be done. The emperor, said Leighton, served as "a point of religious focus, a symbol of national pride and self-respect and the symbol of a protective secular authority intimately part of the whole Japanese system of human relations." In his view, the chances that "persuasion or argument or critical discussion" might alter Japanese perceptions of so exalted a figure were extremely remote. "The religious aspect alone is a formidable one," he wrote, in addition to which one must consider the factors of national pride and self-respect. Leighton argued that history recorded few instances in which the religious beliefs of a people have been changed by either the persuasiveness or the military forces of an enemy. "The type of belief which the

Japanese have regarding the emperor," he said, "is not open to dissolution by such means as are at our disposal now."[12]

Propagandists agreed that the collapse of Japanese faith in the emperor would "no doubt speed the end of the war." They maintained, however, that attacks on the imperial institution would have far-reaching and largely negative consequences. Such a policy would destroy the credibility of the one authority figure to whom all Japanese paid allegiance and leave a power vacuum of monstrous proportions in a postwar Japan plagued by all manner of political, military, economic, and social instability. Leighton warned that in criticizing the emperor the "United Nations would lose more than they would gain due to the postwar difficulties of dealing with a country of multiple competing leaders, in a state of economic and moral collapse, and full of civil wars, *ronins* [masterless samurai], pretenders to the throne, nests of resistance and underground movements."[13] Furthermore, there was a consensus among owi, felo, atis, and pwb personnel that of all the authority figures in Japan only the emperor commanded sufficient respect to ensure compliance with a declaration of surrender. If a Japanese surrender prior to complete annihilation could be achieved only through an imperial rescript, then attempts to destroy the emperor's credibility would be foolish.

atis was nevertheless asked to assess sample propaganda leaflets attacking the emperor. The ten atis officers who participated in the survey (who had lived in Japan an average of twenty-nine years) unanimously and independently disapproved of the proposed leaflets. The head of atis, Col. Sidney F. Mashbir, summarized the reactions of his officers: "It is the unanimous opinion of qualified officers in this section that the use of this line of propaganda would do as much to unite the Japanese as Pearl Harbor did to unite the U.S." Mashbir declared that propaganda attacks upon the person of the emperor "would arouse a feeling of unreasoning fury even greater than the effect upon Christians of an attack upon the Vatican or upon Mohammedans of an attack upon Mecca." Propaganda disrespectful of the emperor was "highly dangerous," insisted Mashbir, and would likely have "costly consequences." When asked their opinion of propaganda texts critical of the emperor, Japanese prisoners concurred. Japanese subjects perceived the emperor as "all things to all men," said the pows, and personal attacks against him would only increase soldiers' determination to defeat the Allies.[14]

Allied policymakers, unable or unwilling to arrive at a solution to the problem of the emperor's disposition, gave propagandists no guidance on how to approach this sensitive issue except to avoid it altogether. For want of a more thoroughgoing policy, the Allied Political Warfare Committee (AWPC) declared in April 1942 that psywar units should simply "avoid any mention of the person of the Emperor" and focus instead on propagating the notion that Japan's military leaders were using the imperial institution to serve their own ends rather than to implement the will of the emperor.[15] The political leadership's failure to make a decision concerning the postwar status of the emperor tied the hands of propagandists. Although U.S. policy clearly stated that unconditional surrender meant the removal of Japan's military leaders from positions of authority, the fate of the imperial institution remained a mystery. To distribute propaganda equating the emperor with the militarists would foreshadow a similar fate for the emperor. Propaganda that attacked the emperor would communicate a policy decision that had not been made by the proper authorities.

PWB's "Basic Military Plan" clearly instructed propagandists to "ignore rather than attack the Emperor." In a cross-cultural comparison similar to Mashbir's, Fellers asserted that to hang the emperor would be analogous to Christ's crucifixion. To state that the emperor had erred "would be as blasphemous as for a Catholic to question the faithfulness of the Virgin."[16] Thus, Fellers remained consistent in his opinion (voiced as early as 1935 in his study of Japanese military psychology) that the emperor should not be attacked by outsiders in wartime and that the imperial institution could and should be used to further peaceful initiatives.

By 1944 the consensus was that since no official decision had been made concerning the postwar fate of the imperial institution and since the Japanese people harbored a seemingly irreversible reverence for him, propagandists should never attack the emperor. They chose instead to portray him as a victim of the military clique whose policies were leading Japan to destruction. In combination with the strategy of truth, the decision to refrain from making statements critical of the emperor constituted the guiding principles of psywar in SWPA. Together, these guidelines set the parameters for a propaganda program that was credible because it was truthful and inoffensive because it did not attack the most sacred symbol of the Japanese people and nation.

. . .

Next to knowing the enemy, the most crucial task for propagandists was to establish the credibility of their output. Adherence to the strategy of truth facilitated the process of gaining the enemy's trust in the accuracy of Allied information, but establishing credibility was a long-term process. Only with the passing of time and considerable contact with Allied propaganda did Japanese soldiers place greater credence in the words of their enemies. Initially rejected out of hand as mere propaganda, Allied communications slowly began to wear away the natural aversion of Japanese troops to anything originating from within the enemy camp. Because Allied news reports tended to confirm what Japanese soldiers experienced firsthand, they were credible and hastened the process of demoralization. News was a prominent weapon in the propaganda war.

News as Propaganda

Propagandists, aware of the cumulative nature of their work, devised a three-step approach to creating a susceptible target audience. As taught by FELO and carried on by PWB, the first step toward gaining the enemy's attention called for an almost total emphasis on the distribution of news. This proved to be an effective policy for two reasons. First, Japanese soldiers were hungry for news since they heard very little of it. Second, news reports, unlike ideological appeals or promises of good treatment to prisoners, could be confirmed by facts observable to troops in the field. A soldier captured on Bougainville, for example, reported that his company commander encouraged troops to collect news leaflets as the "officers and men alike look forward to the leaflets as a means of keeping posted." He also noted that leaflets were read but not taken seriously at first. "As time went on, however, the officers and men, weary from their futile struggles, read the leaflets with greater interest and considered their contents reliable." Another POW stated that the men in his unit accepted Allied news leaflets "without question" and considered them more accurate than the news reports distributed by their own headquarters. Other prisoners reported that they developed a grudging respect for Allied news coverage since it "was frequently confirmed to be true later" or was "supported by their own experience." POWs often stated that because the "facts were born out by actual conditions" they were "rather difficult to deny." One prisoner was especially impressed with an Allied news bulletin that reported the Japanese advance across the Owen Stanley Mountains, which convinced him of the truth of the rest of the report.[17]

Indeed, news coverage was so integral to the overall effort that until 1944 psywar units employed few other propaganda devices. FELO reported that it relied on news leaflets almost exclusively until early 1944. PWB similarly allocated a considerable portion of its resources and attention to the compilation and distribution of accurate news. In his directions to PWB personnel, Fellers noted that "before we can succeed in any campaign, we must first establish belief in our leaflets—not only in the accuracy of their factual contents but also in our sincerity." To establish the credibility of their output was thus a major objective of PWB, and Fellers maintained that the regular dissemination of news sheets was the best way to accomplish that task.[18]

FELO and PWB assembled several news publications for regular distribution to Japanese troops. They also printed brief news sheets from time to time that summarized recent trends or developments in the Pacific War, and they used news extras to announce major events such as the Allied landing in the Philippines, the collapse of resistance on Leyte, the fall of Manila, or the surrender of Nazi Germany (plate 1). FELO issued three regular newspapers: the *Weekly War News,* the *South Pacific News Bulletin,* and the *Pictorial News.* PWB's news publications included *News from Home, News of the Week, Jijitsu Shimpo* (Factual news account), and the *Rakkasan News.* Besides keeping Japanese troops informed of the war's progress, these publications aimed to convince enemy soldiers that an honest appraisal of events showed that Japanese defeat was inevitable. Fellers argued that the quickest way to establish credibility was to concentrate in the early phases of a campaign on matters already known to Japanese combatants. Gradually propagandists inserted information theretofore unknown to the enemy but relatively easily confirmed by him. Finally, newspapers reported events that Japanese readers undoubtedly would have rejected as outlandish at an earlier date but now, having been "softened up" by previous exposure to Allied propaganda, would find more believable.[19]

News publications continued to be a mainstay of the Allied psywar program throughout the war, but by 1944 both FELO and PWB were diversifying their operations by targeting specific Japanese units with made-to-order leaflets. Throughout, propagandists searched for ways to exploit psychological vulnerabilities exhibited by Japanese soldiers. Psywarriors did not *create* animosity between enlisted men and officers;

they merely *exploited* a weakness that already existed. Intelligence sources revealed that the relationship between officers and their men frequently caused dissension, and propagandists created leaflets based on such intelligence. Likewise, Allied propaganda did not originate the question whether Japanese spiritual strength was sufficient to achieve victory but played on doubts voiced by Japanese soldiers themselves.

Propaganda of Despair

One of the principal goals of newspapers was to convince Japanese combatants that victory was impossible. As such, "news" was a form of despair-invoking propaganda. Propaganda of despair focused the audience's attention on disagreeable practical and material conditions in order to discourage the enemy. Texts that illustrated Allied superiority in material and human resources sought to evoke a sense of hopelessness in the Japanese. Some leaflets concentrated on Japan's inadequate air power:

> "Even one more plane."
> With this slogan, the gunbatsu is encouraging plane production. But "one more plane" is not enough. The reason why is that the United States is producing a plane every five minutes, day and night. Since the attack on Pearl Harbor, the U.S. has produced 171,000 planes. This is a ratio of seven U.S. planes to one Japanese plane. This is only the U.S. Our allies, Russia and England, produce many thousands more.
> How can Japan meet this production?[20]

A FELO leaflet noted that the United States had produced 33 million tons of shipping since it entered the Pacific War. Capitalizing on the shortage of supplies experienced by much of the Japanese army, it continued: "You who are on this island know how little shipping Japan has. . . . Modern wars are won not by spirit, but by overwhelming industrial production. Your resistance is futile."[21] Not only did the propaganda of despair provide proof of the Allies' awesome material strength but it demonstrated how that power translated into daily misery for Japanese soldiers. Using the words of Japanese leaders, propagandists repeatedly pointed out the importance of the resource-rich southern regions to Japan's war effort and played up Allied advances in the South Pacific that cut Japan off from this lifeline (plate 2).

Propagandists also attempted to foster defeatist attitudes within the IJA by employing a "Japan Stands Alone" theme in the aftermath of Germany's capitulation. "Full Strength Instead of Ten Per Cent" was the caption of a FELO leaflet that remarked that even before the surrender of Germany the Allies had penetrated Japan's inner defensive perimeter. "Now the war in Europe is over," it continued, "and for the first time we can concentrate our overwhelming strength entirely against Japan. Now we no longer divide our forces and supplies, and all our resources, rather than a mere 10%, will be thrown into battle against you. You failed to stop us earlier. Do you think you will stop us now? The day of Japan's defeat draws nearer and nearer."[22] Admittedly, Japan received little material assistance from Germany, and the Japanese were aware of their inferior productivity and lack of mineral resources long before V-E Day. The realization that it would now face a coalition of mighty enemies concentrated solely on the defeat of Japan, however, could not but inspire concern among Japan's armed forces (plate 3).

In addition to propaganda emphasizing Japan's deteriorating military position and Allied material superiority, nostalgia themes provided a means to inspire despair in the enemy. Although Allied propagandists disagreed over their value, nostalgia leaflets sought to cause uneasiness about conditions on the home islands and increase war weariness. Beneath a photograph of Mount Fuji, one nostalgia leaflet recalled to soldiers' minds that "now is the season of beauty in your homeland. Your parents and wives await you, and your dear children wonder whether they will see you again. But you are here on a miserable island, awaiting only our overwhelming force of men and machines. Your military leaders grow fat at home as they continue to mislead your people" (plate 4).[23]

Nostalgia themes were the only form of the propaganda of despair that did not focus on specific material and practical considerations. With this one exception, the output of Allied propagandists revealed their belief that the immediate circumstances confronting soldiers in the field provided the best ammunition for reducing the enemy to a state of despondency. Because battlefield reverses were the single greatest cause of demoralization, propagandists went to great lengths to exploit military setbacks. Propaganda of this type not only struck at the heart of troop morale but enabled psywarriors to pursue directly the goal of convincing the Japanese that defeat was inevitable. PWB's "One Stride after Another," for example, attempted to achieve these goals by recounting the Allies' progress in the Southwest Pacific from New Guinea to the reoccupation of the Philippine Islands: "The fact that the war is drawing nearer and nearer to the Homeland of Japan, is also clear from the bombings of the Homeland by the B-29 bombers, and the capture of Iwo Jima. Is it not true that no matter what you do, nothing can affect the war's progress toward the Homeland?"[24]

FELO also attempted to weaken Japanese resistance by arguing that "American might is too great to be resisted successfully." One of its leaflets recalled Adm. Nakamura Ryozo's definition of Japan's vital defense line as the Marianas, Yap, and the Palaus. "Even while his brush was still wet," the leaflet reads,

> Saipan fell, followed rapidly by an occupation of Tinian and Guam.
>
> Thus your inner defense is steadily being penetrated as overwhelming American forces, aided by tremendous quantities of equipment, drive on toward Japan.
>
> Your resistance will gain you nothing. Your navy cannot match the great numbers of our fleet; your wild eagles are driven from the skies by our vast air armadas; your war plants in Japan and Manchuria are being smashed by our new giant bombers. You can't fight our unlimited forces and equipment with your bare bodies.
>
> Don't throw away your lives in vain![25]

PWB likewise employed the words of a Japanese leader in leaflets targeting Japanese troops on Luzon. The text quoted a speech made by Premier Koiso Kuniaki on 21 November 1944 in which he said that "the rise and fall of Japan depends on the Leyte battle." The leaflet then described the battle as the "biggest disaster in the history of the Japanese army" and expressed wonder that the Japanese should believe they could hold Luzon when they had failed in Leyte even though it had been considered crucial to the Japanese war effort.[26]

This genre of leaflets resembled news reports in that they contained information describing recent events. Yet propaganda texts of this sort went beyond simple news accounts to include a larger message, namely, that the military advances of the Allies portended ultimate defeat for Japan and therefore continued resistance was futile. While straightforward news reporting aimed to demoralize enemy troops, it allowed readers to draw their own conclusions about Japan's future. Leaflets akin to "One Stride after Another," on the other hand, were much more blatant. Regardless of the tack taken or the specific theme used, propaganda of despair sought to convince the Japanese army that despite its gallant efforts the war was lost. And as a general rule the chief motive behind such propaganda was to force Japanese troops to think about the dismal circumstances they found themselves in (plate 5).

Divisive Propaganda

Divisive propaganda was designed to exacerbate tensions and schisms among the constituent elements of the Japanese armed forces. It fed on problems internal to the Japanese military system. By contrast, propaganda of despair manipulated factors that were largely external to the institutional dynamics of the Imperial Army, such as the availability of shipping, industrial output, or the collapse of Italian and German resistance.

Divisive propaganda had two principal aims: to discredit Japanese military leaders and by so doing alienate enlisted men from their officers, and field personnel from the *gunbatsu,* who controlled the Japanese government; and to heighten interservice rivalries. Attempts to destroy the credibility of Japanese military leaders took three forms. First, propagandists told enlisted men that their officers were liars and could not be trusted. Second, they nurtured soldiers' suspicions of their officers by blaming them for failures in operational planning and execution and the lack of medical and logistical support and charging them with basic incompetence, greed, and cowardice. Finally, they argued that although the *gunbatsu* portrayed themselves as the handmaidens of the emperor, in fact they were not operating in accordance with the emperor's wishes. The militarists, said the propagandists, were destroying the nation in a relentless pursuit of war aims that were bound to result in defeat.

A significant part of the Allied effort to discredit Japan's military leaders consisted in publicizing their lies. Responding to an October 1944 speech in which a Japanese naval officer claimed that Japanese forces had inflicted tremendous damage (including the sinking of American carriers) upon the U.S. Navy in operations off the coast of Formosa, FELO published a series of three leaflets under the title "Your Leaders Are Liars!" The texts announced that the bombing raids currently being inflicted upon Japanese troops originated from precisely the same carriers allegedly sunk in October. "These leaflets and the bombs which accompany them," stated one leaflet, "are the answers from these same carriers to the lies of Japan's leaders." Japanese leaders "think they can throw dust in your eyes," another leaflet in the series asserted, but "our bombers tell you that not one carrier was sunk off Taiwan during October."[27] pwb similarly discounted Japanese leaders' claims of great victories over the enemy when there were none. One leaflet began by asking whether Japanese troops doubted the truth of their leaders' claims:

> For example, the number of heavy American warships shown in the Pictorial Weekly's chart as sunk or badly damaged turns out to be far greater than the total number America possessed at that time.
>
> Suppose that the Americans really had lost this enormous number of ships! Then how could they have gone on step by step to retake most of New Guinea, and the islands of Saipan, Guam, Palau, Morotai, etc? Whatever one's productive capacity, one can't do one's fighting with paper warships.
>
> Or to take a more recent example: Again great war results were announced for the sea battle off Formosa. . . . But strange as it may seem, just 5 days later the American forces landed on the Philippines!
>
> Why is it that every time that these great war results are announced, the American forces get closer and closer to the Homeland of Japan, while your plight in battle gets more desperate?[28]

Using the words of Japanese leaders, propagandists cultivated the growing awareness among enlisted men that what they were being told did not correspond to reality. In so doing, they encouraged Japanese fighting forces to question the veracity of their leaders and at the same time eroded their morale by revealing that the war was not going as well as they once thought.

Divisive propaganda also sowed suspicion about Japanese commanders' competence. Psywarriors played on the known grievances of the rank and file against their superiors. For example, a Japanese prisoner wrote a leaflet expounding on the callous attitude of some officers toward their men. He conceded the existence of a few kind officers but questioned whether they constituted a majority. "There are some officers, extremely inconsiderate ones," he wrote, "hoarding several months' rations for their own use, while giving only one *go* or two *go* of *Sac-Sac* to the patients, without any seasoning at all. Is it necessary for you to follow those inferior commanders?"[29] Another pow wrote a leaflet recounting the hardships endured by the men in his unit—meat only once a month, ever-decreasing size of the daily rice ration, inadequate tobacco allotments—who were "slaved from daybreak to dusk." "What have the Officers? All the best food, the best tobacco, sake, beer, and dances, on top of their high pay. They have no regard for the men whatsoever, and when the American bullets come flying, you can't find them."[30]

Japanese soldiers who noted with dismay the apparent ease with which commanders sacrificed the lives of their men prompted propagandists to write leaflets such as one entitled "Makibi" (Thinning out). Its purpose was to convince enemy troops that their officers' incompetence produced excessive and unnecessary casualties. Other leaflets blamed all manner of miseries on inept Japanese commanders. A Japanese officer who surrendered on Cebu designed a leaflet attributing the military defeats at Guadalcanal, New Guinea, Bougainville, and the Philippines to deficient military leadership. He noted that American air power was daily attacking industrial centers in Japan and that the parents of Japanese soldiers suffered from lack of food. "Why did the Japanese Army bring forth this misery?" he asked. "I believe it is due to government leaders in misinforming the people of National Power and the obstinacy of military leaders."[31]

Propagandists attempted to provoke the ire of Japanese troops in the Philippines by drawing their attention to the large concentrations of men in southern regions of the theater who had been "outmaneuvered, immobilized and rendered useless" to the war effort. They concluded by describing this state of affairs as simply "another blunder on the part of your military leaders who, by blunder after blunder, have brought Japan to the very brink of disaster."[32]

Gen. Yamashita Tomoyuki, commander of the IJA in the Philippines, was a particularly popular target of divisive propaganda designed to demonstrate that Japanese officers were unequal to the challenge presented by MacArthur. One leaflet attacked Yamashita for his failure to defend Leyte even though it had been clear to Japanese military leaders for two years prior to the landing that the "advance of General MacArthur's American forces has been directed towards the Philippines." Yamashita had nonetheless been "caught unprepared and his desperate, last-minute defensive strategy was ineffective, resulting in an enormous sacrifice of human life." Not only had MacArthur consistently outmaneuvered Yamashita and other Imperial officers, the leaflet stated, but "he has achieved these successes *with a minimum of casualties!*" Japan's military leaders, it concluded, must accept the blame for the loss of hundreds of thousands of valuable lives.[33]

Propaganda also compared Yamashita unfavorably with General Nogi, whose exploits during the Russo-Japanese War were legendary. Under

General Nogi's leadership the Japanese had suffered heavy casualties during the battle for Port Arthur, and Nogi consequently had determined that duty compelled him to commit suicide. The emperor, however, had strictly forbidden him to do so, saying that the "General could serve the country far better by living than by dying." In dramatic contrast to General Nogi, a pwb leaflet noted, Yamashita had accepted none of the blame for the blunders on Leyte, which had "caused useless death to more than 100,000 men." He had sought instead to place the blame on others.

> To cover his own failures he forced his officers and men to needless sacrifice in the name of "Gyokusai" (glorious death). He remained quite undisturbed as he looked on these vast numbers of sacrifices.
>
> It would seem that the difference between the splendid spirit of Gen. Nogi, and the base attitude of the military leaders of today, represented by Yamashita, is like that difference between clouds and mud.[34]

A leaflet entitled "One General Gains Fame While Tens of Thousands Die" accused Yamashita of adopting a "wild and unsound" strategy that served only to pile up a "mound of human sacrifices," thus demonstrating that the lives of his men were of "no concern to him whatsoever." Moreover, Yamashita refused to accept the "obligation of the warrior's code" (i.e., honorable suicide). Why, then, should soldiers follow in the path of their comrades in the Solomons and New Guinea who had died a "lonely dog's death in a distant land just because of such incompetence and irresponsibility"? the leaflet asked.[35] In February 1945 Yamashita stated that he had been chasing General MacArthur "all over the southern seas area" without success but that "this time it will be different." Propagandists responded by asking Japanese troops who was chasing whom. "Japan itself seems to be the next logical place for Yamashita to chase MacArthur," the leaflet predicted with sarcasm.[36]

Propagandists also called attention to the poor medical care Japanese troops received. FELO produced a series of leaflets pointing to the dismal circumstances confronted by troops on bypassed islands. One emphasized the lack of food, which resulted in the slow starvation of many men. Another merely asked a series of questions: "Are many of your soldiers dying as a result of illness? Are many of you ill at the present time? What kind of medicine are you getting? Is your situation grave?" It concluded by announcing that medical treatment and food would be theirs behind Allied lines.[37]

The practice of killing the sick and wounded was the target of other propaganda created to show the futility of continued resistance. Leaflet writers quoted an order emanating from the Fifty-eighth Independent Mixed Brigade stating that in areas where there was danger of enemy penetration, "you will dispose of all sick and wounded soldiers." Allied propagandists declared this to be a death sentence for Japanese troops, who were left with only two options: they could die a useless death by continuing to fight a superior enemy or "if you don't continue to fight, you are to be killed by the order of your direct superiors."[38]

Divisive propaganda also sought to use soldiers' loyalty to the emperor to cultivate distrust of Japanese military leaders at home. Propagandists denounced the *gunbatsu* as excessively ambitious men whose actions were leading Japan to disaster. In commemoration of Empire Day a Japanese prisoner appealed to his former army colleagues to think of the future of the nation. He described the *gunbatsu* as "sinister clouds obscuring the will of the Emperor" and, recalling the fateful outcome of events directed by similarly power-hungry men in Japanese history, asserted that "devouring ambition leads to military downfall." He went on to say that Japan's current leaders, who "talk always of loyalty and patriotism," were at the same time "perverting the Emperor's true will."[39]

In a variety of ways divisive propaganda worked to loosen the ties that bound the army together as an effective fighting force. It also fostered dissension between the service branches, encouraged internecine squabbling, and increased army doubts about the effectiveness of the navy and air forces. Propagandists capitalized on Allied control of the sea and air by arguing that Japanese troops could expect no air support, supplies, or reinforcements, thus amplifying army suspicions of the naval and air services. Inspired by Japanese leaders' penchant for portraying defeats as great victories, a FELO leaflet entitled "Open Your Eyes!" declared that the magnificent Japanese navy, which was to be the spearhead of Japanese victory, continued to flee from the American navy "even in its own waters." Likewise, Japan's "wild eagles . . . are obviously too few and too weak to protect you."[40] Japanese troops on Luzon were bombarded with propaganda stating that neither the air forces nor the navy had demonstrated the capability or the willingness to make its presence felt against the mighty Allied armed forces. It noted that despite navy claims that it would destroy the U.S. fleet and assertions that the army's air forces would come to their assistance, Japanese soldiers could see for themselves that neither had come to their defense.[41] The navy was the target of a leaflet entitled "Where is the Japanese Fleet?" which notified troops in the Philippines that the Imperial Navy had made "almost no attacks" on the American fleet during landing operations in the Lingayen Gulf even though the convoy had been discovered a full four days prior to the operation. "This shows that you can no longer count on the Japanese fleet," the leaflet said (plate 6).[42]

Divisive propaganda continually accused the navy of abandoning ground troops. The theme of abandonment found expression in propaganda that simply listed islands where soldiers had been left to their fate. One such leaflet reads, "Your navy abandoned your troops at Makin; it abandoned them at Tarawa; it abandoned them at Kwajalein; it abandoned them at Saipan, Tinian and Guam. It has now abandoned you!"[43] In a similar vein, propagandists asked Japanese soldiers: "Does Japan have two codes of bushido: One for the navy and one for the army? The navy runs away to save itself, but the army, abandoned and cut off from all aid, is expected to remain and die a useless death. . . . You cannot win alone" (plate 7).[44] Finally, Allied propaganda attempted to widen the cleavage between the Japanese army and navy by drawing attention to the disparities in the treatment accorded personnel in the two services. "The Navy men are accustomed to good food, wine, and comfortable living conditions," stated one leaflet, "while the Army men have been trained to bear the brunt of American firepower, to forage for food, and to sacrifice their lives for their leaders. Is this situation fair?"[45]

Subversive Propaganda

In contrast to divisive propaganda, which made use of practical circumstances and material deficiencies to incite discord and spread antagonism between the services, subversive propaganda attacked Japanese morale by chipping away at attitudes of a more spiritual or emotional nature. Army indoctrination taught soldiers that the Greater East Asia War would liberate Asian peoples from the domination of the Western powers, that it was Japan's national destiny to unite Asia under Japanese leadership. In response, propagandists tried to impress upon the enemy that they were not, in fact, fighting for a righteous cause. Psywarriors also pointed out that regardless of what they had been told in training, spiritual force was not sufficient to overcome the material and industrial superiority of the United Nations. The notion that Japanese soldiers must experience "death before dishonor" to fulfill their duty came under attack as well. Propaganda suggested that to preserve one's life and continue to serve the nation in the postwar era showed greater loyalty than did dying uselessly for a lost cause. Leaflets also produced evidence that Japanese soldiers did indeed surrender and assured readers that prisoners were well treated, in contrast to what their officers told them.

Intelligence revealed that the indigenous peoples of occupied areas in Asia and the Pacific generally were not favorably disposed toward their Japanese "liberators." Propagandists used this information to convince Japanese soldiers that their so-called righteous cause was not perceived as such by the very people who were purported to benefit from the war. A captured Japanese soldier wrote a leaflet reminding his former buddies in the army that the Greater East Asia War was "being fought for the happiness of all Asiatic people." Nonetheless, he said, the "Filipino people are everywhere alienated from us" and the war had failed to bring happiness to the people of Asia.⁴⁶ Another leaflet disputed the claim that Japan was fighting a sacred war by pointing to the immoral conduct of some Japanese. It recounted the "cowardly" and "barbaric" acts of the Japanese forces in Manila and noted with contempt that officers who ordered the killing of innocent civilians and defenseless women and children "dare to do such things as these, while at the same time telling those under them to be god-like soldiers!"⁴⁷

Subversive propaganda aimed at destroying the enemy's faith in *Yamato damashii* was most often inserted into texts that emphasized Allied industrial and material might. The goal was to demonstrate in practical terms what Japanese soldiers were discovering for themselves, namely, that "war cannot be won by courage alone." Leaflets seeking to cultivate despair by contrasting the industrial output of Japan with that of the United States, for example, sometimes included direct references to Japanese confidence in their peculiar spirituality. One such leaflet declared: "Modern wars are won not by spirit, but by overwhelming industrial production." Leaflets belittling the Type 38 rifle asserted that however much spiritual strength one may possess, antiquated weapons cannot fend off the attacks of an enemy well equipped with modern weaponry. Another propagandist asserted simply, "You can't fight our unlimited forces and equipment with your bare bodies."⁴⁸

Leafleters also made a concerted effort to destroy the death-before-dishonor mentality. Propaganda texts repeatedly discussed the futility of continued resistance, which they equated with seeking death. Propagandists suggested that rather than die uselessly in a war Japan was destined to lose, soldiers should preserve their lives in order to continue their loyal service to Japan after the war. Propagandists insisted that loyal subjects had a responsibility to both their ancestors and their progeny to survive the war and devote their lives to rebuilding the homeland. One leaflet noted that the process of reconstruction would require a great deal of manpower. "The greatest loyalty that you could show," it asserted, "would be to avoid useless death, to surrender and to prepare to work for your people after the war." A group of prisoners confessed in a leaflet they wrote to their former compatriots that "we found it useless to continue as it was clear that our duty lay in preserving our lives in order to work for Japan after the war." Rather than come to an "untimely and inglorious end," leafleters said, Japanese soldiers should arrive at an "honorable understanding" with the Allies in order to preserve their honor and better serve their emperor and nation "by living to help build a greater Japan when the war is over."[49]

Propaganda also sought to undermine the belief that Japanese troops do not surrender by proving that a significant number of Japanese prisoners were in Allied hands. Propaganda leaflets dropped on northern Luzon stated that on Okinawa alone more than seven thousand Japanese soldiers had surrendered to Allied forces. Meanwhile, the leaflet continued, "hundreds are surrendering daily" in northern Luzon.[50] Propagandists also adopted the technique of using historical examples to demonstrate that Japanese had surrendered to enemies in the past—that POWs had not always been disgraced. "In olden days, before Japan became a powerful nation, citizens were forbidden to visit other countries. If they returned to Japan after such a visit, they were put to death. With [the] enlightened rule of the Emperor Meiji, such practices were abolished. After the Russo-Japanese war, more than 2,000 Japanese soldiers taken prisoner by the Russians returned to Japan. Some of these men hold important positions in Japan today."[51] Aware of the difficulty of persuading Japanese soldiers that many of their comrades lived comfortably in Allied captivity, propagandists believed that the best way to prove the truth of their statements was to disseminate photographs of Japanese prisoners. Consequently, surrender passes and leaflets promising good treatment to soldiers who gave themselves up generally displayed photos of men engaging in the everyday activities of life as a POW. Prisoners also wrote leaflets and gave loudspeaker broadcasts, which served as further proof that at least some members of the Japanese army considered the concept of "death before dishonor" outmoded.

Subversive propaganda struck at the heart of several tenets of Japanese military indoctrination. It focused on refuting the myths that strengthened soldiers' spiritual and emotional life and thus stood as pillars of Japanese morale. Whereas propaganda devoted to the creation of despair and divisiveness pointed to the desperate circumstances caused by material and practical hardships, subversive propaganda attacked Japanese beliefs and values. The ultimate objective, however, of all three propaganda devices was to create doubts and uncertainties not only about Japan's chances for survival and victory but about the fundamental tenets of the Imperial Army's military indoctrination.

Propaganda of Enlightenment

The intent of enlightenment propaganda, which sought to destroy misconceptions the Japanese held about their enemies, resembled that of subversive propaganda. Enlightenment propaganda, however, attacked Japanese perceptions of their enemies rather than of themselves. Specifically, Allied propagandists sought to clarify the meaning of the unconditional-surrender policy, to enlighten the Japanese about Western society in general, to reveal the magnitude of Allied industrial production, and to inform the enemy of Western attitudes toward POWs. The theme of material superiority was thus the most pervasive element of the Allied combat propaganda campaign. It played a prominent role in leaflets designed to inspire despair as well as in divisive propaganda intended to promote schisms between Japan's armed services. It also appeared in subversive propaganda that undermined the Imperial Army's confidence in the power of the "Japanese spirit." Thus, Allied industrial might was the only theme employed in every aspect of the propaganda war.

Leaflet writers addressed the Allied policy of unconditional surrender under the rubric of enlightenment propaganda. As discussed earlier, the most difficult aspect of this issue for propagandists was adhering to the strategy of truth and at the same time assuring the Japanese that the phrase *unconditional surrender* did not portend the horror they imagined. In the end, enlightenment propaganda dealt with this very delicate issue by assuring Japanese soldiers that the demand for unconditional surrender simply meant the termination of military hostilities and the overthrow of the militarists who had initiated the war. As President Truman explained it, "Unconditional surrender does not mean the extermination or enslavement of the Japanese people," and these were precisely the terms propagandists employed in their leaflets.

The other two foci of enlightenment propaganda became blurred over time, as discussions of "Occidental character" inevitably degenerated into pronouncements on how the Allied nations perceived and dealt with POWs. Nonetheless, propagandists did cite America's humanitarian aid to Japan following the 1923 earthquake as evidence of Allied humanity and aversion to suffering. "Americans are kind-hearted people," stated one leaflet, "the same people who rushed to the aid of stricken people of Tokyo with food, clothing and medical supplies after the great earthquake of 1923." More common, however, were leaflets and broadcasts announcing that the Allies looked upon POWs differently than the Japanese did. "In spite of the fact that POWs are enemies," noted one propagandist, "Americans never look down upon them like Japanese do. Rather they respect the Japanese soldier who surrenders, as a brave soldier who fought to the very last and survived."[52]

Japanese POWs wrote leaflets refuting Japanese claims that the Allies tortured prisoners. One POW wrote: "Our fear of ill treatment and torture has completely vanished. We are convinced that the tales of American cruelty were all false propaganda."[53] Another former Japanese soldier composed a leaflet to assure Japanese troops still in the field that the Allies "are not trying to kill all the Japanese soldiers, even though they are trying to win the war. They are not thinking about killing the Japanese one by one. Our thinking about the U.S. forces is entirely wrong. They are not angry with us, when we are captured. They show their friendliness like fellow comrades."[54]

· ■ ■

These propaganda themes were part and parcel of an extended psywar campaign. Beginning with newspapers, which initiated the softening-up process, propagandists moved on to propaganda intended to induce despair, doubts, and disunity among enemy combatants. The final assault in the Allied propaganda campaign came in the form of the direct surrender appeal. Having established credibility with the enemy through the strategy of truth and accurate news reporting, inspired despair, promoted divisiveness, subverted beliefs, and enlightened the audience about the predilections of the United Nations, the final step for propagandists was to encourage Japanese soldiers to lay down their weapons and surrender. Propagandists attempted to accomplish this using direct surrender appeals, which commonly described the military situation as hopeless, declared that further resistance was futile, and stated that Japanese combatants had only three options. They could continue to fight, in which case they would inevitably die of starvation, disease, or battle wounds; commit suicide; or cease resistance and live to assist in the reconstruction of postwar Japan.

Psywar operations thus passed through three phases, distinguished by the propagandists' intentions. In the first phase psywarriors sought to gain the audience's trust. In the next phase they focused on eroding enemy morale by undermining Japanese confidence and raising the Imperial Army's consciousness of Allied capabilities and intentions. The final phase was devoted to eliciting enemy surrenders. The objectives of psywar and the broadly conceived propaganda themes employed to achieve them remained constant. Likewise, the strategy of truth and the decision to blame the militarists for the war and all its attendant miseries remained cornerstones of Allied psywar operations. Yet the propaganda war did change over time, adapting to new circumstances and responding to current intelligence assessments. Through a process of trial and error, Allied propagandists became more proficient as the war progressed.

9 Surrender leaflet layout. The first step in the production of the standard surrender leaflet. *(U.S. Army Signal Corps photo, courtesy of the MacArthur Memorial Archives, Norfolk, Virginia)*

10 Target area. At a forward command post of the Twenty-fifth Division officers pinpoint the area where the surrender leaflets are to be dropped. *(U.S. Army Signal Corps photo, courtesy of the MacArthur Memorial Archives, Norfolk, Virginia)*

11 Briefing. The Seventeenth Reconnaissance Squadron being briefed on the area of the Cagayan Valley (Philippines) where bombs and the surrender leaflets are to be dropped. *(U.S. Army Signal Corps photo, courtesy of the MacArthur Memorial Archives, Norfolk, Virginia)*

12 The payoff. A platoon of the Twenty-fifth Division captures a group of Japanese who came out of the brush waving surrender leaflets over their heads. *(U.S. Army Signal Corps photo, courtesy of the MacArthur Memorial Archives, Norfolk, Virginia)*

13 Nisei searching prisoners of war.
(U.S. Army Signal Corps photo, courtesy of the MacArthur Memorial Archives, Norfolk, Virginia)

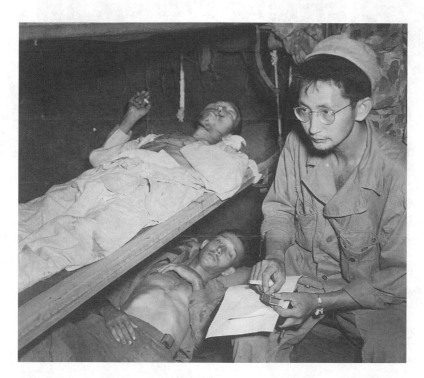

14 American interpreter with wounded Japanese prisoners on New Britain. *(U.S. Army Signal Corps photo, courtesy of the MacArthur Memorial Archives, Norfolk, Virginia)*

15 American interpreter *(second from left)* interrogates Japanese soldiers captured during the Buna Campaign on New Guinea. *(U.S. Army Signal Corps photo, courtesy of the MacArthur Memorial Archives, Norfolk, Virginia)*

16 American interpreter *(second from left)* discussing surrender terms with a Japanese general east of Manila in 1945. *(U.S. Army Signal Corps photo, courtesy of the MacArthur Memorial Archives, Norfolk, Virginia)*

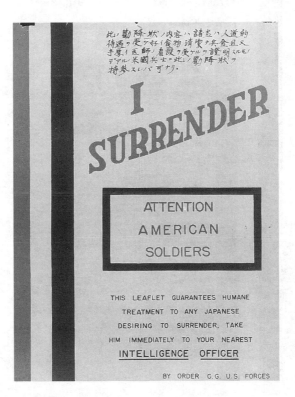

17 The standard PWB surrender leaflet until early 1945, when the words "I Surrender" were eliminated from the leaflet front at the urging of Japanese prisoners. *(Courtesy of the MacArthur Memorial Archives, Norfolk, Virginia)*

18 The new PWB leaflet used the phrase "I Cease Resistance," which was less offensive to Japanese troops than "I Surrender." Notice the masks still in place over the eyes of the pictured prisoners. Originally designed to protect their identity, the policy was later changed. *(Courtesy of the MacArthur Memorial Archives, Norfolk, Virginia)*

6 Fine-tuning the Mechanism and the Message

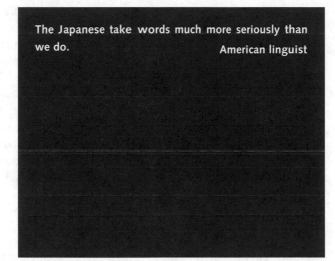

The Japanese take words much more seriously than we do.

American linguist

An effective psychological warfare campaign requires the coordinated interplay of several factors. It builds on the successes of field armies. It depends on accurate intelligence about the enemy's situation and state of mind. It entails the development of logical objectives based on one's perceptions of that enemy. It demands accurate use of the enemy's language and cultural symbols. To borrow from the propaganda leaflet illustrating the Allies' continuous advance toward the home islands and ultimate victory, propagandists made "one stride after another" in devising more effective means of waging war on enemy morale. The outbreak of war in the Pacific caught Japan's enemies unprepared in terms of both conventional armaments and psywar capabilities. As a result, psywar operations got off to a slow start. Not only did the Allies have to create new organizations to conduct morale operations but they had to find personnel with the skills to carry them out. Linguists were in particularly high demand not only for the creation of accurate and apt propaganda texts but as intelligence operatives who could analyze captured documents and interrogate POWs. Through a process of trial and error, self-criticism, and the advice of POWs and propagandists operating throughout Asia and the Pacific, FELO and PWB discovered ways to improve their techniques as they fine-tuned their message.

. . .

ATIS was the single most important source of intelligence for combat propagandists in the Southwest Pacific. Established at the direction of GHQ, SWPA on 19 September 1942, ATIS had as its mission translation of captured enemy documents, interrogation of POWs, and collation and distribution of the results of their work to Allied military forces in the theater.[1] Originally ATIS was composed of thirty-five Australian linguists, but the heavy responsibilities entrusted to it soon demanded a dramatic expansion. By the end of the war this intelligence organization employed nearly four thousand linguists, had interrogated more than fourteen thousand POWs, had scanned, summarized, or translated 2 million documents, and had distributed more than 20 million pages of intelligence on the Japanese.

From October 1942 through June 1945 ATIS was headquartered in Brisbane, Australia. Referred to as Base ATIS, its headquarters comprised the Translation, Examination, Information, Production, and Training Sections. After successful Allied counteroffensives in SWPA and the forward movement of MacArthur's headquarters to Hollandia, New Guinea, ATIS created an advanced unit, ADVATIS, in September 1944. This "miniature ATIS" was designed to "service immediate requirements at the forward base" in Hollandia. As MacArthur's forward headquarters advanced toward the Japanese home islands, ATIS personnel went with it. ADVATIS accompanied MacArthur to Manila in May 1945, then made its final move in October 1945, when it began operations in Tokyo to assist MacArthur (now supreme commander, Allied powers) during the occupation. Meanwhile, beginning in January 1943 ATIS created a number of advanced echelons, each of which typically employed fifteen linguists and five nonlinguists, to provide translation and interrogation services to Allied forces in the field. Below the corps level, advanced echelons detached linguists to serve with tactical units, where they were known simply as ATIS detachments or language units. These language units accompanied Allied combat forces on every significant landing in the theater, from Papua to the Philippines, conducting preliminary translations of captured documents and interrogating POWs.[2]

ATIS produced and distributed hundreds of publications to the Allies during the war. For purposes of psychological warfare the most useful reports were those pertaining to the interrogation of prisoners. ATIS interrogation reports gave propagandists much-needed feedback on the quality of their output by recording the reaction of Japanese troops to Allied propaganda. They also served as a source of negative evidence, for POWs who had had no contact with Allied propaganda indicated that propagandists had failed to disseminate their material in sufficient quantities or with sufficient accuracy.

In addition to interrogation reports, propagandists relied on ATIS's Current Translations, which exposed trends in enemy morale as displayed in diaries or official communications between field commanders and the higher echelons of the IJA. ATIS also circulated a series of Enemy Publications, which were verbatim translations of Japanese military manuals, intelligence reports, and operational orders. The bulk of these were technical in nature and thus were not always applicable to propaganda work. Yet a number of these reports showed the institutional practices and problems plaguing the IJA. Numbers 80 and 82, for example, were transcripts of morale lectures given by Japanese officers to their men, revealing the nature of ongoing military indoctrination. In addition to interservice rivalries, declining discipline and morale, strained relations between officers and enlisted men, and supply shortages, this series revealed the IJA's concern over Japanese soldiers who upon returning to the homeland gave an honest appraisal of the declining military situation and thus spread discontent among civilians. They also discussed the IJA's use of extralegal punishment, which by its own admission had a decidedly negative impact on morale.

ATIS also compiled research reports on specialized topics. FELO and PWB found these studies helpful in writing propaganda that accurately portrayed life in the Japanese army. ATIS research reports confirmed the antagonistic relationships between officers and men, IJA efforts to manipulate the morale of enlisted men by circulating false rumors, and the practice of killing sick and wounded troops. They also described the psychological impact of Allied bombing on Japanese troops and the lack of amenities available to them. Between April 1944 and February 1945 ATIS compiled a particularly useful research report "intended to give a rounded and documented exposition of Japanese military psychology." The five-part report, nearly two hundred pages in length, gave propagandists a wealth of information on the Japanese army's history, traditions, and methods of indoctrination. It revealed both the historical roots of the custom of self-immolation and the reasons for its continued practice. It also assessed the role of the "emperor cult" in Japanese military psychology, revealing how the emperor was used to motivate combatants during the Pacific War.[3]

FMAD was another important source of information for propagandists. In contrast to ATIS, which processed data on a multitude of subjects, FMAD concerned itself almost exclusively with measuring enemy morale. Established in early 1944, FMAD was made up of persons trained chiefly in psychiatry, anthropology, history, and sociology. In addition to Alexander H. Leighton, who served as chief of the division (and went on to participate in the U.S. Strategic Bombing Survey in Japan after the war), other prominent members of FMAD included George E. Taylor, Clyde Kluckhohn, Ruth Benedict, John Embree, Herman Spitzer, Owen Lattimore, and John M. Maki, many of whom continued to distinguish themselves as academicians after the war. FMAD's research was based on "prisoner of war interrogation reports; captured diaries, letters and official documents; reports from neutral observers in Japan; smuggled Japanese newspapers and periodicals; and radio broadcasts."[4] Using these resources, FMAD pinpointed how specific factors and circumstances influenced troop morale and the impact of propaganda (among other things) on enemy combatants.

In addition to studying general trends in enemy morale, FMAD sought to ascertain variations in morale resulting from differing backgrounds and experiences. It concluded, for example, that morale was higher among navy personnel than among their army counterparts, that soldiers from rural areas had higher morale than city-dwellers, and that "less sophisticated" (i.e., less educated) Japanese were more inclined toward optimism and confidence than were "intellectuals." FMAD also compiled special reports on such topics as the principle of self-sacrifice and Japan's no-surrender policy, the role of the emperor in Japanese society, and general characteristics of the "Japanese Fighting Man." The division also wrote several reports analyzing the effect of Allied propaganda on Japanese morale and offering suggestions for improvement. In sum, ATIS and FMAD were instrumental in helping propagandists understand enemy soldiers, the military exigencies they faced, and the reasons they continued to fight.[5]

PWB's Collation Section applied the information derived from ATIS and FMAD to ongoing morale operations. The Collation Section's primary functions were to collect intelligence of use to propagandists, analyze it for evidence of specific enemy weaknesses, and make detailed recommendations to planning and production personnel about how the data should be used to achieve PWB goals.[6] The process depended on Daily Collation Summaries, worksheets of a sort that classified pertinent intelligence data according to specific goals. For example, an ATIS bulletin contained the following entry from a captured Japanese diary dated 18 June 1944: "We have no food and we are in a difficult plight. The enemy soldier is not to be feared greatly, but over against our rifles and machine guns, he has naval guns, air bombardment, artillery, and tanks which pile up casualties in great numbers. The annihilation of our unit is imminent." The Collation Section determined that this information could be used to weaken the enemy's faith in the power of the "Japanese spirit." Consequently, collators filed this bulletin under the PWB objective of "challenging the adequacy of Japanese spiritual force" and advised planners to "point out that it will take more than Japanese spirit alone to overcome the tremendous material advantages and fighting ability of Allied forces."[7]

ATIS's role in the process of propaganda creation is revealed through a chain of events that began with an ATIS interrogation report in which a Japanese POW stated:

> The Government is trying to create the impression among the men that because they are Japanese and therefore possess the Yamato spirit they cannot lose battles and cannot be destroyed. They shipped us to distant lands—to New Guinea and Guadalcanal—and expected us to win the war with Type 38 Rifles and the Yamato spirit, but without food or airplane protection. Are they expecting five feet of Yamato spirit to overwhelm 500 kg bombs from Consolidated B-24s? This is absurd.

Inspired by this report, the Collation Section recommended a series of leaflets portraying the "one-sided character of the present struggle" and demonstrating the war's futility. The process culminated with a leaflet describing both the history of the Type 38 rifle (which was first used in the Russo-Japanese War) and the advancements made in military technology since then. The leaflet read, in part, "Why then do you have to fight against automatic rifles with rifles of the bolt-action type? . . . However much spiritual strength you may have, how can you expect to tackle a 500-KG bomb from a Consolidated bomber with a Type 38 rifle?" (plate 8).[8] Allied propagandists thus seized an opportunity born of the enemy's own words to heighten Japanese despair.

Using data amassed by intelligence agencies throughout Asia and the

Pacific, the Collation Section created extensive files of documentation organized according to nineteen narrowly defined PWB goals.[9] The material thus arranged was analyzed and translated into propaganda texts by PWB planners and production personnel. The Collation Section gave planners the wherewithal to translate raw material (data on enemy morale) into the finished product (demoralizing propaganda texts). PWB's stated goals are listed below, arranged by the four propaganda themes employed in SWPA, as defined in chapter 5. Asterisks indicate propaganda objectives that were included in PWB's list of stated goals but rarely pursued in practice. Note that these objectives do not fit readily under the four themes, just as they did not fit harmoniously into the general pattern of psywar operations in SWPA.

Propaganda of Despair
Create realization that Japan stands alone.
Plant doubt concerning adequacy of shipping.
Instill fear by outlining future military operations.
Cause uneasiness about conditions at home.
*Attempt to create hysteria by picturing defeat, devastation of air
   raids, and natural phenomena.
*Create confusion and surprise at unexpected events.

Divisive Propaganda
Plant doubt concerning truth of communiqués.
Plant doubt concerning effectiveness of fleet.
Plant doubt concerning effectiveness of air force.
Spread antagonism between army, navy, and air force.
Plant suspicion of leadership.

Subversive Propaganda
Plant doubt concerning righteousness of cause.
Challenge adequacy of spiritual force alone.
Show futility of soldiers' seeking death.
Show how military gangsters have betrayed the emperor.
*Exploit superstition.

Enlightenment Propaganda
Reduce Japanese ignorance of Occidental character.
Reduce Japanese ignorance of Occidental industrial strength.
Reduce Japanese ignorance concerning Allied treatment of POWs.

Many propaganda leaflets accomplished more than one goal at a time, just as some of PWB's stated goals fall under more than one heading. Subversive propaganda leaflets designed to convince the enemy that spiritual force alone could not achieve victory, for example, would simultaneously cause despair and were often written in such a way as to convince Japanese of Allied material superiority, a prominent feature of enlightenment propaganda. Similarly, divisive propaganda illustrating that Japan's military leaders consistently lied about the war also cast doubt on their other claims (e.g., about the righteousness of the cause or the notion that they were merely implementing the will of the emperor) and thus became subversive propaganda as well.

The Collation Section also produced a series of reports summarizing significant trends and developments in enemy morale. Its Review of Significant Trends Discerned in Daily Collation Summaries, first issued in September 1944, drew attention to objectives worthy of immediate attention. The October 1944 issue stated that challenging the adequacy of spiritual force alone was an especially effective propaganda activity. According to the Collation Section's reading of the latest intelligence, Japanese were becoming more vulnerable to suggestions that their spiritual force was no match for American military and industrial strength. It then supplied evidence extrapolated from intelligence sources to support its assertions. The Review of Significant Trends thus enabled planners to concentrate on enemy susceptibilities as they became more pronounced.[10]

The Collation Section produced two other regular publications, Patterns, Trends, and Prospective Developments Offering Opportunities for Exploitation and Implementation of Basic Military Plan and Japanese Trends of Psychological Significance, which likewise provided guidance on the timely preparation of propaganda texts.[11] Finally, Psychological Warfare Reactions and Developments, also compiled by PWB's Collation Section, gave propagandists immediate and continuous feedback on the consequences of their operations. Reactions and Developments reprinted excerpts from interrogation reports and captured enemy documents showing Japanese responses to Allied propaganda, and passed along information about techniques that had proven valuable in other theaters.

The creation of good propaganda depended first and foremost on successful combat operations that produced dispirited Japanese soldiers. Intelligence agencies substantiated the demoralization caused by battlefield conditions, among other things. The Collation Section reorganized the available intelligence, highlighting specific enemy vulnerabilities and furnishing ideas for propaganda texts. In the event, psywar planners depended upon a complex network of people to lay the groundwork and provide the wherewithal for assaults against the enemy's mind. Although the interplay between these forces was slow to develop, they proved to be mutually reinforcing. PWB constructed a propaganda campaign on the foundations laid by combat troops in pursuit of a goal held in common with those troops—the collapse of Japanese resistance (plates 9–16).

.   .   .

Pinpointing the psychological vulnerabilities of Japanese soldiers did not automatically lead to the writing of effective propaganda. Regardless of the brilliance of Allied military and naval campaigns, the efficiency of intelligence gathering, and the astuteness of the Collation Section's perceptions of the enemy's state of mind, ultimately somebody had to translate these assets into real words, and then into Japanese that was accurate, convincing, and powerful enough to influence the thoughts of enemy soldiers. Allied propagandists struggled throughout the war to improve their output by refining techniques, eliminating inaccuracies, and adopting new approaches to old problems.

A number of valuable improvements resulted from suggestions made by propagandists operating in other theaters. A Japanese linguist working for OWI's China Division in early 1945, for example, prepared a lengthy analysis of forty SWPA leaflets. He criticized the leaflets for being too tentative and for lacking bold conclusions. He also recommended that leaflets encouraging Japanese soldiers to surrender include reassurances that the Allies would not send prisoners' names or pictures to their relatives in Japan, thus allaying soldiers' fears of shaming their families. In reference to a series of PWB leaflets stating that the Allies observed the rules of the Geneva Convention respecting POWs, he surmised that the average soldier would not understand the meaning of such statements. This OWI linguist also pointed out that references to "Nazis" might confuse Japanese troops and suggested that propagandists refer instead to "Germans" when discussing events in Europe. Moreover, he advised propagandists to limit their coverage of the ETO and concentrate on events in the Pacific, which were of much greater concern to Japanese.

Despite his criticisms, OWI's analyst concluded that the leaflets produced in SWPA were better than those prepared in other areas of the Pacific, particularly in terms of "employment of the enemy's words and the unmasking of the enemy's painful spots." Yet he asserted that the "common deficiency of these leaflets is the numerous mistakes in writing." About one PWB news bulletin he said, "The mistakes in grammar, wrong words, and senseless writing in this newspaper are terrible. Besides, the letters are so small that they are hard to read. They are almost of little value as propaganda." The author offered two solutions: first, have Japanese prisoners examine all propaganda before distribution to ensure that the language was correct and the contents inoffensive; second, make use of POWs who were willing to write leaflets. "We ourselves have so far put this into practice in North China with brilliant results," he said.[12]

Other propagandists in the China-Burma-India (CBI) theater went a step further in their analysis of Japanese-language propaganda and the utility of Japanese prisoners. According to a report issued by the Propaganda Committee in Yenan, one of the cardinal rules of the production process was to "check the effectiveness of leaflets with POWs" and accept their opinion without question. Yenan's Propaganda Committee also regarded POW interrogation reports as the best source of material for propaganda. Thus, in the CBI theater POWs were vital to the propaganda war. Long experience in China had proven that "effective propaganda against the enemy can only be done by Japanese" as the enemy forces are "more receptive to propaganda sent to them by Japanese." Furthermore, noted Yenan propagandists, distributing propaganda written by prisoners was the only way to prove that Japanese troops were not killed upon capture.

The Propaganda Committee adhered to the motto "One good leaflet is more effective than 10 mediocre leaflets." It insisted that the only way to produce good texts was to write them, rewrite them, and rewrite them again. Its leaflets were revised anywhere from three to seven times before dissemination. Reviewing and rewriting propaganda material was also the best way to develop good leaflet writers. The rigorous process of creating acceptable propaganda texts should not end once a leaflet had been approved for distribution, the committee reported; "periodic study of old leaflets is necessary for improving the work of leaflet writers." In short, the mechanics of propaganda dictated by the Propaganda Committee in Yenan required the input of Japanese prisoners and continuous attention to detail in the form of review and revision.[13]

Although these suggestions were so reasonable as to preclude debate, psywar operatives often disagreed over what constituted good propaganda. The China Division of OWI criticized SWPA propagandists for failing to state their conclusions with sufficient force. Yet AIB recommended that leaflet writers allow readers to employ their "powers of inference" to determine the meaning of Allied propaganda. As head of PWB, General Fellers preferred that the audience draw its own conclusions. He stated that psywar methods must not employ high-pressure salesmanship tactics; rather they should provide the Japanese with irrefutable information that would lead them to draw the desired conclusions through their reasoning. "The result must come from within" enemy troops, not be forced upon them by outside forces, said Fellers.[14]

Leafleters also disagreed about the wisdom of stressing Allied material superiority. ONI's Special Warfare Branch urged propagandists not to rely heavily on the theme of American material strength since Japanese were contemptuous of American dependence on material factors in wartime. Use of that propaganda line, said ONI analysts, would play directly into the hands of Japanese propagandists, who stereotyped Americans as being obsessed with material things and spiritually vacuous. FMAD similarly noted that the stress placed on Allied material dominance might cause Japanese troops to fight more stubbornly in order to demonstrate their spiritual prowess.[15] Given the pervasiveness of this theme in FELO and PWB leaflets, however, it is clear that propagandists in the Southwest Pacific rejected the advice of those who cautioned against overemphasizing Allied material strength. In fact, PWB employed this propaganda line in every aspect of its campaign: enlightenment propaganda included the objective of reducing Japanese "ignorance of Occidental industrial strength"; propaganda of despair sought to increase Japanese doubts about their shipping capacity; divisive propaganda asserted that Japan's naval and air power were no match for that of the Allies; and subversive propaganda themes designed to undermine the enemy's belief in the power of his spiritual force invariably argued that no amount of willpower could overcome an enemy with the material advantages the Allies possessed.

In some instances psywar operatives were prevented from implementing suggested propaganda lines for reasons other than philosophical disagreements. FMAD stated, for example, that it would be good propaganda to state that the conditions for Japanese surrender would require the Japanese government to accept returning Japanese prisoners without reprisal. This approach would "result in a great increase in surrenders and marked diminution in the fierceness of resistance," said FMAD. Ruth

Benedict, a senior analyst for owi, also suggested that "every effort be made to have a Commission set up for consideration of the settlement of Japanese pows after Japan's capitulation in order that we may say to them that provision is being made for their future." Benedict argued that such a policy would "literally make it possible for [the typical Japanese soldier] to 'think' about the alternative of giving himself up," an alternative that was unthinkable to most Japanese soldiers. Another owi analyst similarly maintained that a White House pronouncement that Japanese troops taken prisoner "would have the opportunity to work out their personal destiny" and that stipulations regarding the return of prisoners "would be a part of our terms of unconditional surrender" would be "of the greatest use" to propagandists.[16]

But Allied policymakers chose not to clarify the terms of the unconditional-surrender policy in this manner. Without the assurances of civilian leaders that the fate of Japanese pows would be addressed at the time of Japan's surrender, propagandists were prevented from using a propaganda line that might have elicited the surrender of more enemy soldiers. The strategy of truth stopped propagandists from reassuring Japanese soldiers that if they surrendered, their postwar fate would not be as distasteful as they imagined. Despite the wisdom of some suggestions, then, the strategy of truth and ill-defined political policies prevented the adoption of propaganda lines that might well have proven valuable.

Even so, propagandists and social scientists actively engaged in the war against Japan developed valuable connections that resulted in the widespread adoption of proven techniques. Having their work analyzed by outside reviewers gave propagandists the chance to learn from their own mistakes as well as others' and gave rise to new ideas when existing methods proved ineffective. Nonetheless, consistent with owi's experiences in North China, pows, rather than other propaganda teams, proved to be the most valuable source of critical analysis for pwb.

▪ ▪ ▪

Japanese prisoners improved the Allied propaganda war in several ways.[17] During interrogation, for instance, pows gave their impressions of enemy propaganda and offered suggestions for its improvement. Many of these ideas were subsequently adopted. In an attempt to prove not only that imperial soldiers did surrender but that they were not tortured, the Allies featured pictures of Japanese captives in surrender propaganda. Some POWs assumed a more active role in the analysis, creation, or delivery of propaganda messages. And on a few occasions, "reborn" prisoners returned to Japanese lines to confirm the truth of Allied promises of good treatment in hopes of convincing others to surrender. Japanese prisoners thus became a valuable commodity and an integral part of the propaganda machine.

As a general rule, ATIS interrogators questioned prisoners about their own morale and the morale of their units. PWB's Collation Section used this information to determine trends in enemy morale. POW critiques of Allied propaganda texts were even more valuable, although their comments were diverse and often contradictory. Some prisoners noticed details, such as a Japanese character used improperly in a particular leaflet; others pointed out deficiencies in the overall propaganda campaign. All in all, it was unusual for two prisoners to react to the same leaflet in exactly the same way.[18]

Nevertheless, interrogation reports showed that Japanese prisoners were in fundamental agreement on some issues. Almost to a man, for example, they stated that propaganda should include maps showing the strategic juggernaut created by the Allied forces in the Pacific, as well as local-situation maps pointing to the adverse tactical conditions confronting enemy troops. Prisoners also agreed that news leaflets were well-received by Japanese troops and that over time they had established the credibility of Allied propagandists. In this regard, however, many POWs suggested that news leaflets focus keenly on developments in the Pacific and in the home islands since those events were of immediate concern to soldiers. World news, they maintained, was of little interest to troops engaged in the Greater East Asia War. Japanese prisoners were also united in the belief that the Allies ought to increase the quantity of leaflets dropped to ensure greater saturation of targeted areas and soldiers' more frequent contact with a variety of leaflet themes.

Prisoners similarly agreed on a number of ways to improve surrender leaflets. They were unanimous in the view that leaflet writers should be more vociferous in their assurances that prisoners were well treated. They insisted that since the Japanese fear of Allied torture was often the biggest obstacle to surrender, propagandists should exert every effort to assuage this fear. They also maintained, however, that Japanese troops found it very difficult to believe Allied promises of good treatment no matter how sincere or how insistent. Most prisoners confessed that they had had little faith in such reassurances until they discovered firsthand the truth of Allied claims. They therefore encouraged greater emphasis on the theme of good treatment but could not guarantee that it would produce any more prisoners than previous efforts.

Captured Japanese soldiers offered concrete advice on surrender leaflets that referred to international laws pertaining to the treatment of prisoners. Most POWs stated that neither they nor their commanding officers had any knowledge of the Geneva Convention or international laws respecting POWs. They urged Allied propagandists to inform Japanese not only of the existence of such international conventions but of their precise terms. In response to their urging, an ATIS translator suggested that a propaganda leaflet containing a "translation of relevant passages of the Geneva Convention" be created immediately. His memorandum recounted an interrogation in which one prisoner stated that he and the seven men who had surrendered with him had not been convinced by Allied promises of good treatment and believed "there was a possibility of their being killed." Nevertheless, all eight men had decided to surrender "since prolonged hardship in the mountains would mean eventual death anyway." The prisoner assured his interrogator "that most high ranking Japanese officers, who would have influence in persuading their men to surrender, were ignorant of the rules of the Geneva Convention and actually believed that prisoners of war were executed legally upon capture."[19] Upon discovering this shortcoming, propagandists produced precisely the kind of leaflet envisioned by POWs and ATIS.

Prisoners also pointed out that surrender leaflets were not always clear about exactly how and where Japanese troops should surrender. Therefore, propagandists began to provide enemy soldiers with explicit instructions about when to surrender (during daylight), how to surrender (by clearly displaying a white flag or surrender leaflet while advancing slowly toward the Allied lines, preferably stripped to the waist), and where to surrender (at designated points in the Allied lines where military personnel had been told to expect such activity). Once they had more detailed instructions, more Japanese were willing to test the truth of Allied promises of good treatment. In one rather humorous incident on Bougainville a FELO officer reported that "a Japanese on his way in was seen to be displaying no less than six surrender leaflets—one in each hand, one in each ear, one in his mouth, and one tucked in a grass band tied around his waist!"[20]

Prisoners also told their captors that Japanese soldiers had concerns about what life as a POW would be like. Besides assurances that they would be well fed, would receive immediate medical attention, and would not be mistreated, surrender appeals said little about how POWs spent their time. Several Japanese soldiers remarked that repeated assurances of the good treatment awaiting prisoners made the idea of surrendering seem more cowardly than if troops had been told they would have to earn their keep.[21] Propagandists responded with leaflets stating that prisoners who wanted to work would be allowed to do so, or, more often, they simply showed photographs of prisoners engaged in productive pursuits.

The legality of photographing POWs for propaganda purposes became an issue soon after psywar operations began. Japanese POWs often stated that surrender appeals would be more persuasive if they included pictures of soldiers already in captivity. They thought that leaflets depicting the condition of Japanese troops at the time of their capture and showing the same men after they had regained their health would be particularly effective. They also suggested that pictures show a large number of prisoners so that they would not appear to have been staged. Group photographs would also demonstrate that the Allies had taken many Japanese prisoners, thereby allaying soldiers' fears that they would live an isolated life in captivity.

In August 1943 the State Department responded to a War Department query whether photographing POWs for propaganda purposes violated international law. A State Department official replied that "in the opinion of this Department the proposal does not contravene any international commitments of this Government."[22] Nevertheless, until March 1945 the CCS required that all photographs of prisoners be "masked," that is, that the eyes of the subjects be covered. (These masks are shown on the "I Cease Resistance" leaflet shown in plate 18.) The CCS justified this policy on the grounds that "the possession of such photographs by the enemy authorities would lead to identification, to reprisals against the prisoners' families, and to a decrease in future surrenders."

Upon further investigation, however, the CCS determined that in the opinion of "interested agencies" (including OWI, the British Political Warfare Executive, and the State Department) the precautionary measures (i.e., the masks) should be removed. The change in policy was predicated on the dictates of the Geneva Convention, which required the United States to notify the Japanese government of all prisoners taken. Whether or not the prisoners depicted were identifiable, the information was available to Japanese authorities. Moreover, the "interested agencies" argued that altered photographs produced suspicions about their authenticity and made it difficult to tell not only whether the prisoners depicted were in fact prisoners but also whether they were Japanese. Consequently, the ccs lifted the ban on unadulterated photos and declared that the use of such pictures be left to the discretion of theater commanders and the "local and expert personnel actually in charge of the surrender propaganda." The directive did recommend, however, that the prisoners' names not be used in propaganda without their free consent and that "in all such cases of use, the fact of [their] consent shall plainly by made known."[23] Thereafter the practice of masking pictures of Japanese pows used on propaganda appeals was discontinued.

A final and rather dramatic adaptation to the surrender program initiated at the suggestion of Japanese prisoners concerned the language emblazoned on pwb's standard surrender leaflet. The Anglo-American Outline Plan for Psychological Warfare against Japan, approved by both the jcs and the ccs, recommended that combat propaganda avoid the "use of the word 'surrender' *(kosan, kofuku)* or other words which the Japanese associate with dishonor." Yet this document did not become official until May 1944, by which time propagandists had discovered for themselves that Japanese soldiers strenuously objected to the use of such terms. Following felo's example, pwb tried not to offend its audience by using terms that meant "surrender" in Japanese. It relied instead on phrases suggesting that Japanese troops "come to an honorable understanding with the Americans."

pwb's surrender appeals, however, were printed on the flip side of a leaflet bearing the English words "I Surrender" printed in large letters (plate 17). This leaflet, which became pwb's standard surrender leaflet, was first created by a field unit detached to the Sixth Army shortly after the establishment of pwb. In early September 1944 the Sixth Army's propagandists requested that pwb print five hundred thousand copies of the leaflet for general distribution in the Sixth Army's area of operations. pwb's leaflet section fulfilled the request despite its concern that the English portion of the text would be "intelligible to a fair proportion of Japanese troops."[24] Fellers suggested that his executive officer, Col. J. Woodall Greene, discuss the matter further with the Sixth Army's intelligence officer. Greene subsequently reported to Fellers that the Sixth Army wished to retain the English text. The Sixth Army's intelligence officer justified the wording on the grounds that "a great many Japs who have attempted to surrender have been killed" and argued that the inclusion of the words "I Surrender" would have a greater impact on American troops than any other phrase. Thus, the use of the word *surrender* on PWB leaflets was for the benefit of *American* soldiers. The leaflet section's prediction that Japanese troops would understand the meaning of the word, however, was accurate, for propagandists operating in SWPA noted that "the word 'surrender' was objected to by nearly all prisoners." Consequently, at least one field unit stopped using the leaflet.[25]

Shortly thereafter PWB decided to eliminate the word *surrender* from its standard surrender appeal. Greene explained that the decision, made in January 1945, resulted from two developments. First, criticisms of the leaflet from both intelligence officers and ATIS interrogators were occurring more frequently. Second, Greene said that "at the time it was designed the primary concern was to interest the American troops in taking prisoners" but subsequently the situation had changed. He credited the "educational campaign" launched by PWB and I&E with making American troops more conscious of the value of taking prisoners and familiarizing GIs with the surrender campaign undertaken against Japanese units. Greene concluded that "the time has come to change our 'Surrender' leaflet to make the strongest appeal possible to the Japanese."[26] By early March the new surrender leaflets had been distributed to all PWB field units. In place of the words "I Surrender" the new leaflet displayed the words "I Cease Resistance" above a photograph of a group of Japanese prisoners (plate 18).

In addition to offering criticisms of Allied propaganda texts and techniques, Japanese POWs sometimes played a more active role in psywar operations. OWI's Psychological Warfare Team in the India-Burma area asserted that the most effective way to convince Japanese troops that POWs actually existed was to show evidence of them in propaganda leaflets.[27] Most prisoners concurred and argued that promises of good treatment would be more effective if they were relayed by Japanese soldiers who had surrendered and were thus living proof of Allied claims. PWB provided that proof in one of two ways. First, as just described, they disseminated leaflets with photographs of prisoners. Second, and more persuasive, they had POWs write leaflets or address their former comrades directly over loudspeakers.

The first recorded use of prisoner-created propaganda in SWPA occurred at Aitape. In September 1944 FELO reported that a Japanese prisoner wrote a "special surrender leaflet . . . addressed to his former comrades." Although the report did not describe the contents of the message, it did note that a minimum of ten soldiers surrendered with this leaflet in their possession. It also disclosed that several other soldiers confessed that they had pretended to be asleep when their units retreated in hopes of being captured.[28]

Only a month later, in October 1944, Colonel Greene had to convince General Fellers that POWs were crucial to the propaganda war. In response to FELO's decision to return two prisoners who were working on propaganda texts to a prison camp, Greene wrote to Fellers: "These two boys have been of great value in helping with the Japanese leaflets we completed and are working on those now in production. Personally, I don't see how we can get along without them or someone of similar ability." The same letter revealed that in previous discussions on this topic Fellers had "discouraged the idea," but, said Greene, "there does not seem to be any other way, if we are to continue to produce Japanese leaflets." Within ten days Greene received Fellers's approval, "secured a place for the prisoners of war," and convinced OWI to provide funds to pay for their subsistence.[29]

Greene encountered another obstacle to using Japanese POWs in psywar operations in February 1945 when he requested official approval to retain custody of a Japanese prisoner turned over to him by ATIS. Although he followed the established procedure and received the "usual 'no objections'" from the proper authority, MacArthur's chief intelligence officer, Charles A. Willoughby, intervened. Greene, fearing that Willoughby's actions would result in the prisoner's return to a POW camp, informed Fellers that "Willoughby seems to be under the impression that this is the first time a [prisoner of war] has been used for Psychological Warfare." Greene asked Fellers to explain to Willoughby that POWs "have been used for some time" in this line of work and inform him that FELO was employing two at that very moment and PWB was working with three others. There is no record of Fellers's discussion with Willoughby, but neither is there any indication that Greene had further difficulties in retaining the services of prisoners wishing to assist PWB. By May 1945 PWB was employing the services of nineteen POWs.[30]

Japanese prisoners wrote a significant number of leaflets. Most of these leaflets focused on persuading Japanese forces that the Allies did indeed treat prisoners according to the provisions of international law. Others commented on the abundance of Allied war material and told Japanese troops that it was time they realized that the war was lost and continued resistance would only lead to national destruction. POW leaflets achieved better results primarily because they were written by Japanese and thus contained none of the errors so characteristic of propaganda authored by Westerners. Leaflets created by prisoners also convinced some troops in the field that Japanese soldiers did surrender and that the credo of "death before dishonor" was not adhered to universally.

Throughout Asia and the Pacific, Japanese prisoners contributed to psychological warfare operations. The OWI Psychological Warfare Team in Assam assembled a group of six POWs who had expressed interest in doing propaganda work. They began working on a full-time basis in August 1944. The Assam team advised other psywar units interested in devising a similar arrangement that the best-suited candidates were men who had had contact with Allied propaganda and had discussed the material with their associates before being captured. The Assam team also noted that the prisoners must be compatible, that one or more of them must speak English, and that the group functioned best under the direction of Nisei who knew Japanese psychology and language.

In Burma, prisoners wrote a newsletter for distribution to their former comrades in arms. Entitled *New Life,* it first appeared in March 1945; its aim was to convince Japanese troops that they had a responsibility to survive the war and build a new Japan. This group of POWs said they were working for Japan's future even in captivity and were destined to "arm ourselves once again to serve our country as the arrowhead of Japanese reconstruction." In SWPA, prisoners undertook a similar project in the form of the *Rakkasan News.* The first issue was written in the Philippines and appeared in March 1945. Its purpose was to weaken Japanese morale by informing Japanese troops of the "true picture of the war." Distributed on a weekly basis, *Rakkasan News* focused almost exclusively on the progress of the Pacific War and current developments in Japan.[31]

In addition to helping with leaflets and newsletters, POWs made front-line loudspeaker addresses to Japanese troops and occasionally returned to the field to convince others to surrender. A 6 March 1945 surrender broadcast to Japanese troops trapped in a cave in the Zambales Mountains on Luzon resulted in the surrender of one man, who then volunteered to speak over the loudspeaker. He exhorted those still in hiding to give themselves up, promised they would be well cared for, and concluded with the statement that "an honorable surrender is preferable to certain death." Clearly some IJA soldiers had become remarkably familiar with the major propaganda themes employed in the theater.[32]

One of the more dramatic results of front-line broadcasting occurred on Luzon, where two Japanese medical officers surrendered to the Eleventh Corps after a series of public-address-system appeals spanning several days. These two officers then volunteered to lead American troops into a cave concealing more Japanese who wished to give themselves up. In the process, the medical officers persuaded twenty-four soldiers to surrender. On other occasions prisoners were allowed to return alone to Japanese lines for the purpose of gaining additional prisoners. During September 1944 such an attempt was made by both Japanese and Formosan prisoners near Noemfoor. The operation resulted in the return of all the prisoners who were released for this purpose as well as the surrender of several Japanese soldiers and more than two hundred Formosans. A similar operation on Morotai in July 1945 ended in failure, however, when two of the six prisoners sent out to obtain the surrender of other Japanese failed to make contact with any Japanese units. Two were captured by the indigenous population, and two others were forced to escape into the jungle when they encountered an armed native patrol (the latter two were subsequently recovered by the Allies unharmed).[33]

■ ■ ■

Well before POWs began to contribute to the propaganda war, Nisei proved themselves indispensable to psychological warfare operations in SWPA. Thousands of Americans of Japanese ancestry served in the Pacific during the war; most served as translators and interrogators with ATIS (or with the Southeast Asia Translation and Interrogation Center [SEATIC] or the Joint Intelligence Center, Pacific Ocean Areas), but many also worked with various psywar units. Nisei who volunteered for service in the Pacific took inordinate personal risks since most were still considered Japanese citizens under Japanese law and would thus be considered traitors to the emperor if captured and likely tortured to death. Nisei also risked being mistaken for the enemy since they looked Japanese. Many cases of mistaken identity have been documented. In one instance Chinese soldiers in Burma "captured" a Nisei translator and forced him to march barefoot for hours, to the American lines, whereupon the Chinese were finally convinced of their error. Nevertheless, many Nisei looked upon military service as a means to prove their loyalty to the United States, despite the American government's misbegotten policy of imprisoning their loved ones on the U.S. mainland in relocation centers.

Already in September 1943 ATIS reported that the "supply of Australian Japanese linguists is now about exhausted." Because of this shortage, the report continued, "Nisei must be used." ATIS noted, furthermore, that while non-Japanese could be trained to read, write, and speak Japanese, the process took several years, and even then "white men . . . will not have the background and 'native feel' for the language that the Nisei have inherited."[34] The paucity of qualified linguists was a most vexing problem for both ATIS and psywar detachments. The problem was never adequately solved, though it was mitigated by the influx of newly trained linguists from the United States Army's Military Intelligence Service Language School at Camp Savage and then Fort Snelling, Minnesota.[35] The services of these linguists, the majority of whom were Nisei, were indispensable to Allied intelligence and morale operations. Regrettably, in contrast to the amount of scholarly attention paid to the treatment of Japanese Americans in the United States during the war and the well-deserved praise for the accomplishments of the 442nd Regimental Combat Team in Italy and France, the distinguished service of Nisei language specialists in the Pacific War has not received adequate recognition. This is undoubtedly one of the few aspects of the Pacific War that deserves more scholarly attention.

Although the vast majority of linguists (Nisei and white alike) in SWPA were assigned to ATIS, small teams of translators were attached to ATIS advanced echelons throughout the theater. At its peak, ATIS employed the services of three thousand Nisei, most of whom received their training at the Military Intelligence Service Language School. Since PWB and FELO personnel were similarly detached to army units and served under the direction of intelligence officers and in close association with ATIS linguists, propagandists quickly came to rely on the advice and expertise of these translators. PWB itself employed many Nisei who devoted their attention fully to propaganda work.

As a result of their knowledge of Japanese culture and their intensive language training, Nisei propagandists devised improved methods of presentation and were better at communicating directly with the enemy by means of front-line broadcasts. Nisei linguists thus contributed to psywar operations the same kind of knowledge and skills that were in such demand from Japanese prisoners. The efforts of Americans of Japanese ancestry, however, were made on behalf of their devotion to the war effort as American citizens and at considerable personal risk.

·   ·   ·

Psywar operations suffered early in the war due to the absence of a long-standing tradition in support of such efforts, an ad hoc organizational structure, and a dearth of both trained propagandists and Japanese linguists. The work of ATIS and FMAD, however, improved psywarriors' understanding of the enemy's culture and history as well as his military indoctrination. PWB's Collation Section enabled propagandists to ascertain trends in enemy morale and devise appropriate means to exploit Japanese psychological vulnerabilities, which became more pronounced as the Allies advanced closer to the Japanese homeland and left behind an enemy army suffering from the demoralization that inevitably accompanies military defeat.

The interchange of advice and experiences between propagandists operating in different theaters of the war accelerated the process of developing effective propaganda techniques, as did the age-old process of trial and error. Of even greater value were Nisei, who were a vital part of Allied psywar. Japanese POWs, who provided much needed feedback on the impact of Allied propaganda, likewise became indispensable to the development of more effective morale operations. All of these factors enhanced the quality of Allied propaganda, though some of them emerged late in the war and thus had only a short time to prove their worth. The extent to which the improved methods of propagandists produced a truly effective psywar campaign, however, is a more difficult question.

7 Assessing the Results

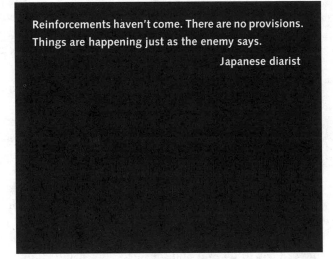

Reinforcements haven't come. There are no provisions.
Things are happening just as the enemy says.

Japanese diarist

The greatest difficulty in studying psychological warfare is assessing its effectiveness. The purpose of combat propaganda in the Southwest Pacific was to hasten the collapse of Japanese resistance by contributing to the demoralization of enemy combatants. That imperial Japan surrendered on 15 August 1945, however, does not prove that psychological warfare succeeded in achieving its goals. Japan surrendered because of military defeat. The success of psychological operations is much more difficult to determine than that of conventional operations, for as General Fellers put it, "There are too many intangibles and indeterminates to permit an abstract, definable assessment."[1] In some cases the evidence is clear and the conclusions are obvious: Allied propaganda techniques improved over time. In other instances definitive judgments are not so easy to make. It is impossible to know, for example, exactly how many Japanese were influenced by Allied propaganda, and to what degree, or exactly how Japanese soldiers responded to it, if only because no two Japanese soldiers had identical experiences or reactions. Each responded as an individual to the totality of his wartime experiences, only one of which may have been contact with enemy propaganda. In short, although one can draw many firm conclusions based on "hard" evidence, some aspects of psychological warfare require speculation based on more limited evidence.

■ ■ ■

It is useful to begin by stating what psychological warfare did not do. First, combat propaganda did not cause Japan's surrender. Japanese troops did not rise up en masse and demand an end to hostilities or a change of government. Second, not only did Japanese soldiers not openly revolt against their officers but the vast majority remained with their units and continued to fight up to the time they received word that an imperial rescript had ended the war. Where Allied propaganda proved effective the results were more subtle than mass surrenders (with a few notable exceptions) or open rebellion. But that propagandists' successes were not as conspicuous as battlefield victories does not mean that they were not substantive. In fact, Fellers concluded that propaganda operations produced a host of substantive results. The head of PWB asserted that the psywar campaign had saved American lives, increased the two belligerents' understanding of each other, raised Allied troop morale, reduced battle casualties, furthered deception operations, influenced friendly peoples, lowered enemy morale, induced enemy surrenders, hastened the enemy's decision to sue for peace, and facilitated the military occupation of Japan.

The evidence supports Fellers's assertions. But regardless of how much or how little the propaganda war contributed to Japan's defeat, it was an effort that had to be made and there was never any question that it would be made. Had the Allies not launched a bona fide propaganda campaign against Japan, one might be forced to agree with postwar scholars who argue that Americans were motivated by racial hatred and sought only to exterminate the Japanese enemy to a man. Without a genuine propaganda campaign against Japan the Allies would have been criticized legitimately for failing to pursue all avenues toward a quicker resolution of the conflict. For the Allies to have waged psychological warfare only against Germans and Italians without making an equivalent attempt to persuade Japanese to give up the fight would lend credence to claims that in the Pacific War the enemy was regarded as subhuman, beyond rationality, and worthy only of a kill-or-be-killed approach. But that was not the case. For a great many Allied intelligence officers, linguists, and propagandists the Japanese were simply a different kind of enemy—an enemy whose code of conduct they thought peculiar (and detestable), to be sure, but an enemy who had a psychological breaking point like any other.

To analyze the successes of Allied psywar operations requires a set of criteria that indicate the extent to which propaganda demoralized enemy soldiers. First, what were the reactions of Japanese soldiers? Did propagandists convince Japanese soldiers that Japan could not win the war? Did they persuade Japanese enlisted men that it was in the best interests of Japan to preserve their own lives in order to rebuild their nation after the war? Did Allied propaganda, by exploiting military victories, provoke such a sense of despair among enemy armed forces that their fighting effectiveness declined? In short, one must determine whether combat propaganda operations altered the enemy's state of mind in ways that furthered the Allied war effort.

Second, what were the attitudes and actions of Japanese field officers and the Japanese high command? Were Japan's military authorities convinced that Allied propaganda adversely affected soldiers' morale? Did Japanese military leaders make a concerted effort to raise troop morale, thus indicating that demoralization had become a significant problem among the rank and file? Did Japanese officers refute Allied propaganda or prevent their men from reading material distributed by their enemies?

Finally, did propagandists effectively use all available means to achieve their objectives? Did they come to know the enemy well enough to accurately pinpoint his psychological frailties? If so, did they devise appropriate methods to exploit those vulnerabilities? Or did propagandists fail to attack specific aspects of enemy morale that may have proven susceptible to erosion?

The best evidence to support the contention that combat propaganda produced positive results is the responses of the target audience and of those concerned with isolating that audience from dangerous influences. Since defeat in battle was the most demoralizing factor for combatants, and since Allied propaganda sought to capitalize on such defeats, it is difficult to discern where the demoralization induced by battlefield defeats left off and where the demoralization induced by propaganda in support of military operations began. Yet many captured enemy documents and statements of Japanese troops deal specifically with Japanese perceptions of and reactions to Allied propaganda.

Propaganda's effect on the attitudes of enemy soldiers depended on a variety of factors. In almost all cases propaganda failed unless the target population had been softened up by physical hardships. Japanese troops who were physically weakened by lack of food or disease, who suffered continuous military reversals, who had few supplies and inferior equipment, or who had been treated poorly by their officers were susceptible targets. The extent of an individual's contact with enemy propaganda also determined its effectiveness. Propaganda had a cumulative effect. Only occasional contact with enemy leaflets had little impact. On the other hand, an intensive propaganda barrage over a period of weeks or months was likely to be influential. Individual predispositions also affected soldiers' reactions to enemy propaganda; some simply succumbed more readily than others. Finally, propaganda that confirmed the target's own experiences was considerably more persuasive than propaganda that described events or circumstances foreign to the audience. Thus, successful propaganda depended on adversity in the target audience, intensive campaigns of long duration, the predisposition of individuals who came into contact with it, and the degree to which it conformed to individuals' experiences.

Combat propaganda did influence enemy soldiers. Some Japanese troops openly admitted that they had been influenced by combat propaganda, and many conceded that over time they had come to believe the propaganda contained in enemy leaflets. One Japanese soldier captured in the Philippine Islands stated that he had been suffering from low morale when he received a news sheet announcing the Allied landings on Okinawa, which shattered what remained of his fighting spirit. This piece of news convinced him that "no last stand of his or his companions could prevent the defeat of Japan," so he decided to surrender.[2]

Numerous POWs admitted that they and their comrades had not only read enemy leaflets, although most were forbidden to do so, but discussed them with other soldiers. One prisoner reported that the information contained in leaflets announcing the fall of the Solomons and Japanese failures in New Guinea had "made troops angry, as it told of their failures and was the truth, which hurt." Several other prisoners recalled that the men in their units had looked forward to reading enemy propaganda, that many believed the contents, and that they had been particularly impressed by propaganda that "confirmed their own bitter experiences." Soldiers in "full vigour" had merely laughed at enemy leaflets, but those "with weak spirits were influenced by them," confessed another prisoner. And certainly as the war progressed the number of Japanese combatants in "full vigour" plummeted. By some estimates, as many as two-thirds of Japan's total military deaths resulted from illness or starvation. It is thus logical to conclude that more and more Japanese became susceptible to the war of words as time passed and conditions worsened.[3]

Allied agencies responsible for gauging enemy morale concluded that propaganda became increasingly influential in 1944–45. According to an FMAD report issued in December 1944, at least 16 percent of Japanese prisoners had indicated that they had been affected by propaganda in ways favorable to the Allies. The numbers rose as the months passed. FELO reported in January 1945 that 75 out of 227 prisoners had reported being influenced by Allied leaflets and that of the 3,056 Japanese personnel captured following the Allied landings at Aitape and Hollandia 614 were known to have surrendered as the result of leaflet propaganda. Later studies showed that by March 1945, 46 percent of the POWs taken in the Philippines in 1945 had been "unmistakeably influenced" by Allied propaganda.[4] FMAD contended that even if propaganda caused only a small percentage of the enemy "to show visible signs of their weakened resolve and faith, this in itself will be a powerful item in psychological warfare since it will probably affect other men. . . . even if the first to be influenced are only those who are weak in morale, it may well be that their example will influence a wider circle of those on the border line and finally draw in more and more of those who were previously resistant."[5]

Japanese prisoners generally estimated that 50–60 percent of the men in their units had responded favorably to propaganda. One soldier noted that "only half of [the men in his unit] believed the 'good treatment' promises" in leaflets. Yet, considering the intensive indoctrination designed to convince all Japanese soldiers that the Allies tortured and murdered prisoners, for half the men in a given unit to believe the Allies' promise of good treatment would be a significant propaganda victory.[6]

By the end of September 1944 FELO reported that on average 21 percent of the enemy soldiers captured in Dutch New Guinea had surrendered as the result of leaflet propaganda. The percentages were particularly high at Noemfoor and Sansapor, where 38 percent of POWs stated that Allied propaganda had convinced them to surrender. There is little archival material pertaining to propaganda operations in the Sansapor area; however, events on Noemfoor Island are more fully documented. According to a FELO report, between 2 July and 16 September 1944, 212 Japanese surrendered along with 590 Formosans. Four of these soldiers wrote their own "letter of surrender" to the commanding general of the

Allied army on the back of a propaganda leaflet and turned themselves in. The letter listed the names and ranks of the four individuals and stated, "The above four persons hereby surrender to your Army's invitation. Please be kind enough to spare our lives. We swear to obey your orders absolutely."[7]

A subsequent FELO report contained the account of another soldier who had surrendered on Noemfoor Island. He recalled that on 22 July 1944 a concentration of approximately 1,500 Japanese troops had discovered 300–400 leaflets near their positions and proceeded to read them and pass them "from hand to hand." The prisoner estimated that the leaflets had been read by half of the men before the officers intervened and ordered them burned. "After reading these leaflets," the soldier continued, "the dissatisfaction which they already felt became more evident, and everyone talked about deserting and wondered whether it was true they would not be killed, as claimed in the leaflets." About half of the men had believed the leaflets' claims, and some had stated frankly that after the treatment accorded them in the IJA "it would be a good thing to be taken prisoner." In the end, the Japanese command had ordered a general retreat and groups of men from a number of different units had deliberately separated themselves from the main body of troops so that they could surrender to the Allies. The prisoner concluded that such "wholesale desertions" would not have occurred had it not been for the Allied leaflets.[8]

In December 1944 OWI reported that 256 Japanese troops had surrendered on Noemfoor at the end of September. That these men arrived at the Allied lines in groups of about 30 men each substantiates the prisoner's account that the deserters had deliberately split up into small groups the better to effect their surrender. During follow-up interrogations the Noemfoor deserters accused their officers of "reprehensible conduct" for having confiscated all the food for themselves.[9] In this instance, as in most, Allied propaganda exacerbated the unease of already disillusioned Japanese soldiers. The general retreat ordered by the officers merely provided soldiers with the opportunity to desert.

A number of other mass surrenders occurred in SWPA as a result of Allied propaganda campaigns. On 3 May 1945 the First Independent Mixed Brigade, led by the unit's commanding officer, his adjutant, and 2 other officers, surrendered to Australian forces in the Aitape sector of British New Guinea. This was the first recorded incident of the surrender of an entire Japanese combat unit. The 42 men who participated used Allied leaflets to effect their surrender. The commanding officer who had precipitated the mass surrender (a professional soldier with twenty years' service) stated simply that the situation was hopeless and he "agreed with the contents of the leaflets that it was futile to continue fighting," so he "decided to save the lives of his men."[10]

On Luzon, in addition to the 24 Japanese soldiers who surrendered to Allied forces in May 1945 at the prodding of 2 Japanese medical officers (see chapter 6), between 3 and 9 June 1945, 215 Japanese troops turned themselves over to the U.S. Army. This was the largest group surrender in the Southwest Pacific. There is little additional information on the circumstances of this group surrender, but Sixth Army intelligence sources did report that the majority of these 215 prisoners "admitted that they had been directly influenced by American psychological warfare activities."[11]

During late February and early March 1945 enemy soldiers surrendered to American forces in the Philippines in response to a series of loudspeaker addresses. The target of the operation was a group of Japanese soldiers located in the Legislative, Finance, and Agricultural Buildings of Manila, the last area of resistance in the city. Beginning on 25 February and continuing through 1 March, the Fourteenth Corps PWB field unit broadcast a series of surrender appeals to Japanese forces located in the compound. The operation resulted in the surrender of 29 soldiers, all of whom stated that their actions had been a direct consequence of the propaganda appeals. The final loudspeaker address, delivered by a Nisei member of the PWB field party, produced 22 prisoners. Interrogations of these prisoners disclosed that most of the Japanese still trapped in these buildings wished to surrender but were prevented from doing so by their officers. In a contrasting instance, an NCO in charge of a squad of 8 men surrendered and stated that he wished to surrender his entire squad but wanted American assurances that his wounded men would receive medical attention. Upon receiving such a guarantee, he returned to his position and brought back all of his men but one, who preferred to commit suicide rather than surrender.[12] The attitudes of Japanese officers thus often determined whether Japanese soldiers had the opportunity to surrender.

Leaflet barrages and loudspeaker appeals occasionally inspired Japanese soldiers to surrender in large groups. Much more common, however, were instances in which Japanese surrendered as individuals or in small groups. Most officers prevented their men from giving themselves up en masse, holding them in check with threats of physical reprisals or ostracization. Many diarists recorded their intention to surrender at the first opportunity, but many soldiers never had that chance. Often POWs confessed that they had made up their minds to surrender months before they had an opportunity to do so safely.

As the war entered its last bloody year, more Japanese soldiers found their way into the hands of the Allies. As the battle for the Philippines intensified and propaganda operations there reached a crescendo, the number of prisoners taken and the circumstances surrounding their capture reflected the positive impact of psychological warfare. A Twenty-fourth Corps report revealed that of the 278 Japanese prisoners the unit had taken as of 11 January 1945 a majority had surrendered with leaflets in their hands or as a direct result of Allied propaganda. An FMAD study of 251 prisoners captured in the Philippines between January and March 1945 revealed that 38 men had surrendered willingly, 23 of whom were NCOs or officers. Only 29 of those captured were physically incapacitated at the time and thus unable to resist, and perhaps most significantly, only 18 of the 251 resisted capture with every available means. Officers and NCOs accounted for 97 of the 227 prisoners for whom rank was recorded.[13]

By May and June a variety of intelligence sources revealed that prisoners were entering the Allied lines more regularly and in larger groups. In one three-day period, from 6 to 8 May, 207 Japanese troops surrendered in the Infanta and Dingalan Bay areas and the Cagayan Valley, all waving surrender leaflets. On 8 May 66 enemy troops surrendered en masse with leaflets in hand. During the first week of June in the Dingalan Bay area, of 149 prisoners interrogated 129 confessed to having read and "given consideration" to enemy propaganda. "It looks like this is a beginning of the mass surrender that we have been waiting for," concluded the intelligence summary.[14] The conclusion proved premature, yet such incidents indicated that the complexion of the war had changed dramatically, not only with respect to Japanese willingness to surrender but also in terms of the attitude of Allied officers who earlier in the war had had to be convinced that even a single imperial soldier would surrender.

Between 4 and 11 June Sixth Army units in the Philippines took 748 POWs, most of whom possessed surrender leaflets. In several instances they surrendered in groups of more than 50. Thus the total number of prisoners and the size of the groups were increasing. Allied analysts attributed the growing numbers to several factors, most prominently the ill-trained, badly equipped, and malnourished character of the IJA in the Philippines. But observers did not discount the increasing intensity of propaganda operations in the Philippines. The number of leaflets distributed on Luzon between 25 January and 15 February represented a 75 percent increase over the number distributed in the first 115 days of the campaign. The Allies dropped 25 million leaflets on enemy troop concentrations on Luzon alone.

By the end of the campaign the U.S. Sixth Army had captured 7,297 Japanese prisoners on Luzon and reported that "almost 70% of all prisoners surrendering made use of surrender passes or followed exactly the instructions contained in them." The Sixth Army concluded that its most effective psywar campaign of the war had been waged on Luzon and that the results "demonstrated the power of propaganda as a tactical weapon."[15] Table 1 illustrates the increasing effectiveness of the propaganda war in the Philippines.

TABLE 1. Philippine Campaign, 20 October 1944–4 July 1945

Period	Leaflets	POWS	Enemy Dead	Ratio of POWS to Dead[a]
20 Oct.–1 Dec. 44	200,000	93	9,345	1:100
2 Dec. 44–1 Jan. 45	500,000	241	15, 026	1:62
2 Jan.–1 Feb. 45	3,500,000	859	52, 290	1:60
2 Feb.–1 Mar. 45	6,500,000	906	61,129	1:68
2 Mar.–1 Apr. 45	10,000,000	714	46,594	1:65
2 Apr.–1 May 45	8,500,000	1,230	37,180	1:30
2 May–1 June 45	12,000,000	1,777	34,180	1:19
2 June–1 July 45	13,000,000	4,397	33,093	1:8
2–4 July 45	1,000,000	276	1,851	1:7
TOTAL	55,200,000	10,493	290,318	

Source: Bonner F. Fellers, "Report on Psychological Warfare in the Southwest Pacific Area, 1944–1945" (Washington DC: U.S. Army Center of Military History, Historical Records Division, 1946), annex 21.
[a] The numbers of dead have been rounded off to the nearest whole number.

The figures for the remaining weeks of the Philippine campaign are sketchy. PWB reported that 79,476,560 leaflets were disseminated in the Philippines; this number apparently includes those intended for Filipino civilians as well as those intended for Japanese troops. Fellers reported that by the end of the Philippine campaign 12,181 Japanese had surrendered. Since 314,387 Japanese troops were killed in the Philippines, the total ratio of POWs to those killed in action was 1:26 (1:25.81) for the entire campaign. Extrapolating from these statistics, Fellers figured that since the Philippine liberation resulted in 59,510 American casualties, for every 5.3 Japanese combatants killed the American forces sustained one casualty. Had the Allies had to kill each of the 12,181 Japanese prisoners taken in the Philippines, they would have suffered an additional 2,300 casualties.[16]

Clearly the incidence of Japanese surrender increased as the war continued. A close approximation of the numbers of Japanese captured annually in SWPA indicates that 1,167 POWs were taken in 1942, 1,064 in 1943, 5,122 in 1944, and 12,194 in 1945. According to figures compiled by the Australian Military Forces and FELO, 4,610 military prisoners were captured in areas where FELO operated. Of these, 951, or 20.63 percent, surrendered as a "direct result of FELO propaganda activities."[17] Although exact figures are difficult to obtain, the Allies captured at least 19,500 Japanese soldiers in the Southwest Pacific. This figure is decidedly minuscule compared with the hundreds of thousands of German and Italian troops who surrendered during World War II. During the Russo-Japanese War, however, the Russians took only 2,000 Japanese prisoners. In comparison with prisoners in the ETO, then, Japanese prisoners were a rarity. When considered in light of Japanese history, however, that 19,500 prisoners were taken in SWPA alone defies the stereotype of the Japanese soldier as invulnerable to psychological warfare.

There is an understandable, albeit misleading, tendency to gauge the success of psychological warfare simply by counting prisoners, and by devoting considerable discussion to those numbers I do not mean to exaggerate their significance. Propagandists in SWPA consistently argued that provoking the enemy to surrender was not their primary goal: they sought to demoralize the enemy above all else. If, in the process, Japanese soldiers surrendered in greater numbers, so much the better. To psywar operatives, POWs were a much welcomed indication that their operations were working, not the sole arbiter of success. The "Basic Sixth Army Plan for Psychological Warfare," for instance, stated that the objectives of propaganda operations were to "create a receptive attitude toward leaflets" as a source of reliable news, to "develop confidence in our truthfulness," and to weaken enemy morale in order to make the enemy's defeat easier. Only "after defeat," continued the report, "the main objective will be to encourage surrenders to decrease the cost of mopping up."[18] One FELO operative even went so far as to claim that FELO took fully as many prisoners as it wanted. "These [surrender] leaflets had a profound effect upon the Japanese troops," wrote H. N. Walker, "and, although surrenders were rarely spectacular, they became steady and regular and, in fact, quite as numerous as we wished them to be. All that we wanted were sufficient Japanese who could give information about troop dispositions and the strength of their opposing us. We were not particularly interested in securing large numbers of Japanese, for we would have been obliged to feed, guard, clothe and transport them."[19]

Although POW statistics are one useful assessment of the impact of Allied combat propaganda, they do not provide any insight into less tangible results of psywar operations. They do not, for instance, shed any light on the number of Japanese troops who deserted or committed suicide because of propaganda. Such numbers are all the more difficult to obtain because Japanese statistics on army desertions are inherently unreliable. In the official view of the IJA a missing soldier was presumed dead; a member of the armed forces was classified as a deserter only if he was subsequently recaptured by Japanese authorities.[20]

Whereas most Japanese soldiers refused to consider surrender a viable option, desertion was a more palatable course of action. Tenth Corps propagandists concluded that "desertion is frequently regarded as more acceptable to the Bushido-trained Jap than outright surrender. It gives the cornered Jap an opportunity to rationalize his position without too much loss of face." In January 1945 PWB reported "an increasing trend toward desertion in the Japanese Army." It cited, among other sources, a Japanese document captured on Leyte warning that "the *ceaseless desertions* in the field in recent times will seriously affect the fate of the Empire, and under war conditions it is extremely alarming."[21] Even though military authorities failed to keep accurate records of the desertion rates, many Japanese officers expressed dismay at their escalation.

Imperial officers also found it necessary to inform their men that acts of suicide "are not an expression of true loyalty," evidence that soldiers resorted to such acts too often and that it had a detrimental effect on fighting effectiveness. Although the epitome of Japanese military indoctrination may be found in the statement "Bushido is found in death," the officer corps found it necessary to make a distinction between "fighting till the end" and "desperate self-destruction." Death was not always "lighter than a feather." The expression of true loyalty was "duty to the point of death," as one officer stated, "not death unto itself."[22]

Not only is there little evidence of the number of Japanese troops who committed suicide in SWPA but there is no way of knowing how often such acts were prompted by Allied propaganda. Nevertheless, Japanese combatants did attest to the demoralization wrought by propaganda. Although most Japanese troops had no access to radios, one soldier wrote in a letter (later captured) dated 2 July 1944, "Each night I listen to enemy propaganda and feel depressed." Another wrote that Allied propaganda describing Japanese defeats and the growing strength of the Allies made him "completely war weary." Prisoners often said that reasonable human beings had to admit the truth of Allied leaflets defining the Japanese position as hopeless. "Fighting without weapons and supplies is impossible," one said, "no man can doubt this."[23]

Japanese diarists helped reveal the impact of Allied propaganda. The first reference to Allied leaflets found in captured enemy documents occurred in a diary. On 5 December 1942 a diarist at Buna simply noted that the enemy had dropped leaflets on the Japanese positions. Japanese often copied the entire texts of leaflets into their diaries. In nearly every case the reproduced leaflets pertained to local circumstances, not sweeping ideological issues. Those leaflets were generally summarized by diarists in a sentence or two. Sometimes soldiers did not recall Allied propaganda until circumstances turned sour. In October 1943 Allied forces began to inflict devastating blows on the Japanese forces on the Huon Peninsula. In the midst of the ordeal one soldier was reminded of the words of a leaflet, which he then entered in his diary: "New Guinea will be your grave." Another diarist described his situation in March 1943: "Reinforcements haven't come. There are no provisions. Things are happening just as the enemy says." Because his unit's lines of communication had been severed, another Japanese wrote that he had received no news from home and was lonely. As a consequence, he said, "I could even believe enemy propaganda leaflets."[24] A diary captured on Luzon in May 1945 included the following entry:

> The enemy is encountering trouble in penetrating our firmly entrenched positions, has resorted to psychological warfare and is dropping propaganda

leaflets. We are generally stirred by "Parachute News" and the skillfully written propaganda, however, we are more than ever determined to destroy the enemy. Those who are weak spiritually are moved but whether the others are shaken or not is difficult for me to say. Brave warriors of Japan do not have blind faith in enemy words![25]

Other captured documents reveal a growing concern among Japanese officers about the "dangerous thoughts" implanted in the minds of their men by enemy propagandists. The attitudes and actions of IJA officers show that they were not convinced that the emperor's soldiers were impervious to the ill-effects of the propaganda war. On the contrary, military leaders made a concerted effort to prevent enlisted men from coming into contact with Allied propaganda and to devise measures to combat its influence. In light of a report issued by Imperial Army Headquarters on 17 August 1943 stating that "the spiritual strength of an army is the first consideration," one must conclude that Allied efforts to erode that spiritual strength would be interpreted as a serious threat. IJA Headquarters, noting Allied efforts to place the blame for the Pacific War at the feet of the "militarists," asserted that "it is earnestly desired that all troops observe the trend of the enemy's ideological warfare with composure and that at the proper time positive defensive measures be devised."[26]

Until positive measures were devised, however, Japanese authorities resorted to negative ones. Although the practice was not universal, most commanding officers issued orders to their men to refrain from reading Allied leaflets and to turn them in to military police units or other designated authorities. In some units possession of enemy propaganda leaflets was a military offense punishable by death, as reported by two soldiers who admitted they had carried leaflets for six months "although it meant death to be caught with one." IJA officers in New Guinea received orders to confiscate and destroy all leaflets in their areas of operations. The high command also initiated an "intensive counterpropaganda campaign . . . not only to counter the effect of propaganda on the natives but also on their own troops." A Japanese document captured near Wewak dated 1 March 1944 demanded that all leaflets found in the area be taken immediately to headquarters, adding that it was "strictly forbidden" for army personnel to "use them."[27] In western New Britain, army headquarters issued a pamphlet on security regulations dated 1 February 1943. It dealt at length with the subject of propaganda:

Instructions should be given to the effect that any native or soldier who has discovered enemy propaganda leaflets, etc, will immediately report this to the nearest MP [Military Police] unit or to the force to which the soldier belongs.

At such a time, officers will give such guidance to the finder that the latter will not be led astray by the enemy's propaganda, and that the contents of the above-mentioned propaganda will not give rise to rumours.

Furthermore, all forces will make an effort to forestall the above by picking up, as far as possible, all propaganda leaflets which have been scattered. They will immediately submit these to Group Headquarters.[28]

One POW recalled that his commanding officer had confiscated leaflets from his men and warned them to turn in all similar material to officers as the information contained in them was "incorrect." Even so, prisoners disclosed that most enlisted men either read the leaflets before surrendering them to their superiors or simply never turned in the material. In a search of one thousand dead Japanese, Allied troops discovered that more than nine hundred had at least one leaflet on their person, and one had what amounted to a bundle of more than twenty-five. FELO did concede, however, that "positive evidence was seen on various abandoned camp sites that FELO leaflets had been put to unofficial uses."[29]

In their attempts to prevent soldiers from reading Allied propaganda officers occasionally went so far as to claim that enemy leaflets were contaminated. Soldiers at Rabaul were told that "leaflets were contaminated with dangerous bacteria," according to one prisoner. In another attempt to prevent their men from being influenced by enemy propaganda, Japanese officers on Leyte ordered their units to retreat out of listening range of front-line propaganda broadcasts. Prisoners later reported that troops in the area had shown considerable interest in the Allied message despite being permitted to hear only the first portion.[30]

The Japanese high command acknowledged in a variety of ways that Allied propaganda had undesirable effects. On several occasions officers grudgingly admitted the existence of Japanese POWs. The first known admission by Japanese authorities that the Allies had taken Japanese prisoners came in Burma in March 1944. In an official order to his troops the commanding general of the Fifty-fifth Division told his men that imperial troops had been captured and declared it to be "the crowning disgrace" of a Japanese soldier. He then instructed his officers to warn every soldier in their command to stand by their principles and "not to give capture a thought." He continued, "If by any chance a man, while unconscious, falls into the enemy's hands, no word must be spoken regarding our forces, their organization, armament, strength or dispositions, and no action which could profit the enemy may be undertaken whatever punishment, or kind treatment may be received."[31] The commanding general had to preface his instructions about how soldiers should behave if captured with a statement that allowed for such an eventuality only in instances when they were rendered unconscious. In this way he avoided the dilemma of contradicting military indoctrination, which insisted that Japanese soldiers never became prisoners.

A Japanese intelligence report captured in May 1945 revealed growing concern over the security of military information. The "enemy is gaining extremely detailed intelligence reports," it declared, and in a "great number of instances" Japanese POWs were the source of the information. The report advised "complete spiritual indoctrination" of troops with regard to proper behavior in the event of capture. Although there is no evidence that this kind of "spiritual indoctrination" occurred, Japanese military authorities had acknowledged the existence and significance of Japanese POWs.[32]

An officer's diary captured on Morotai addressed the issue of Japanese prisoners. "It appears," he wrote in February 1945, "that there are considerable numbers of prisoners in enemy hands. . . . The balance of the men are either missing, dead, starved, captured or committed suicide." In a slightly different way another Japanese officer admitted the existence of POWs. Upon reading a propaganda leaflet written by a Japanese prisoner he exclaimed to his men, "One of our men wrote this. These men that are getting lost and being reported missing are over there with the Americans getting fed!"[33]

Captured Japanese documents indicate an increasing concern over the detrimental effects of Allied propaganda and its skillful exploitation of Japanese weaknesses. In July 1943 a commanding officer on New Guinea noted a growing tendency on the part of his men to harbor "dangerous thoughts," making them more likely "to be affected by enemy propaganda." Another captured document, dated 3 July 1943, instructed all units to compile a "list of personnel of different types likely to be affected by enemy propaganda" so that those men might be watched more closely in view of the Allies' "persistent" psywar campaign. A Japanese report on counterespionage activities expressed concern over the ill-effects of enemy propaganda and instructed officers in all areas where the Allies dropped propaganda leaflets to "watch for any minute change in conditions, and keep rumors strictly under control."[34]

Japanese authorities were particularly irritated by Allied propaganda capitalizing on tensions between the Japanese army and navy. The Japanese Navy Ministry issued a report in October 1943 stating that because of shipping shortages, forward outposts were not receiving adequate supplies. Consequently, there was a "marked difference" between the standard of living of navy personnel and that of army personnel. Not only had this situation led to ill-feeling on the part of the army, the report warned, but Allied propagandists had begun to exploit the interservice hostility. "An immediate and thorough investigation is therefore felt to be imperative," the report concluded.[35]

While concern over Allied use of the army-navy rift mounted, Japanese leaders complimented Allied propaganda and attempted to devise methods to check its influence. Because of the Allies' "constant use of skillful psychological warfare," in the words of one captured document, enlisted men and their superior officers were ordered to "trust and cooperate with each other to their utmost." Such orders were logical responses to divisive propaganda aimed at creating distrust between soldiers and their officers. The Domei News Agency described the Allied psywar campaign in the Philippines as "extremely well-planned." It reported that Allied propaganda was "extremely realistic,"with an "aura of truth and credulity surrounding it," and was done in a "very fresh and interesting manner."[36]

In response to an inquiry concerning the state of military discipline in the 115th Infantry Regiment a Japanese officer noted that offenses against military discipline "both in the realm of ideas and through corrupt practices" had increased. "Moreover," he said, "enemy propaganda technique is getting more and more pertinacious—recently to the extent of taking a provocative attitude. It is essential to see that they are not led astray by enemy propaganda." The "they" referred to in the report included soldiers with "subversive ideas" or "peculiar family affairs," those who "complain habitually," and "old offenders." A report emanating from the Fifty-third Infantry Regiment reflected similar apprehensions concerning the potential and real problems caused by enemy propaganda. Among other things it stated that "recently, the stratagem of psychological warfare has been more frequently used by the Americans and Australians. They have become very active in broadcasting false propaganda and dropping propaganda leaflets. Consequently, each unit commander will improve the alertness of all officers and soldiers of the Imperial Army so that they will not believe even minute items of false propaganda."[37]

Japanese authorities clearly expressed the need to prevent the spread of "dangerous thoughts" inspired by Allied propaganda. Even though they only reluctantly admitted its influence, military leaders implemented countermeasures, albeit of an ad hoc nature. Japanese Military Police units were given the task of "defending against enemy propaganda," and military leaders stressed the need for "speedy and complete countering of enemy propaganda" by the officer corps. "Although enemy propaganda may be ineffective," declared a Japanese manual on counterpropaganda, "it is important that precautions be taken, as constant repetition may make the men believe it." The document also rued the fact that the rapid dissemination of Allied propaganda gave them "no time to establish counter-measures. It tries to divert our attention to other items and exhaust us by making it necessary but impossible to establish frequent counter-measures." A Japanese leader similarly noted that "the war of thought is as important as that of armed might or economy. In a protracted war, spiritual strength is important . . . successful thought war must be encouraged [as at present there is] too much questioning of thought."[38]

Japanese countermeasures designed to mitigate against the dangerous influence of Allied propaganda consisted in prohibiting the armed forces from reading leaflets, refuting Allied claims with counterpropaganda, and lifting the spirits of Japanese troops through frequent morale lectures that included exhortations not to succumb to the enemy's war of words. "To combat enemy propaganda," instructed one set of Japanese orders, "we must discover and destroy its sources, check its spread, and counter it by making our own propaganda faultless." One POW remarked, however, that the Japanese high command had been alarmed by the consistent improvement of Allied propaganda primarily because its own propaganda was "worthless." A Domei correspondent on Mindanao commented on the need to "minimize the effects of food propaganda on Japanese soldiers" because it made a definite impression on troops suffering from short rations. Apparently the only countermeasure devised in this instance, however, was to take leaflets away from Japanese soldiers since they "caused definite unrest."[39]

Efforts to isolate troops from Allied propaganda were the most common Japanese countermeasure. One file of daily orders captured on New Guinea instructed officers not only to "prohibit personal possession" of leaflets but also to "endeavor to gather propaganda pamphlets dispersed as quickly as possible, so that no damage will be done." Japanese authorities realized that they had to satisfy the curiosity of their troops about the current state of affairs in the Pacific. Otherwise, said the report, they would read Allied propaganda, which would "confuse their minds."[40]

Yet, increasingly Japanese soldiers turned to Allied propaganda for news of the Pacific War. According to the Japanese Military Police manual, "The main requisites for defence against enemy propaganda are to understand the true purpose of our war, to uplift the morale of the entire army, and together with them advance boldly on the road of loyalty, bravery, and victory." In addition, "when enemy propaganda concerning our troops is anticipated, a thorough understanding of the facts should immediately be passed on to the officers and men."[41] Morale lectures became a staple in the Imperial Army. A staff intelligence report issued to commanders in the Hollandia area read, in part:

> Recently the objective of the enemy has been to lower the fighting spirit and discipline of units in this area. In regard to their extensive use of propaganda, firm control of units under your command should be maintained. Endeavor to augment unit solidarity and elevate morale. Awaken the spirit of vengeance and annihilation of the enemy and exploit the sterling qualities of the Imperial Army in this crisis so that troops will not be influenced by propaganda.[42]

At Cape Gloucester similar instructions were given to officers of the 141st Infantry Regiment. A bulletin dated 14 December 1944 noted that the enemy "has suddenly become active with an unscrupulous form of psychological warfare." Accordingly, it said, "all unit commanders will imbue all ranks under their command with a fuller realization of the fact that they are soldiers of the Imperial Army, so that they will not be misled by enemy propaganda." In another instance the commanding general of the Seventeenth Army attempted to counteract Allied propaganda by reproducing an Allied leaflet and distributing it to his men down to the company level. Attached to the Allied leaflet was a paragraph explaining to troops that this was the nature of Allied propaganda claims and warning them "not to permit oneself to be swayed by same."[43]

With the possible exception of efforts to collect Allied leaflets in order to "avoid regrettable results" and countless morale lectures to raise the spirits of the armed forces, the IJA devised no effective measures to counter Allied propaganda. Nonetheless, the evidence reveals a real concern on the part of the officer corps and the high command that Allied psychological warfare was taking a toll on troop morale.

．　．　．

Allied propagandists in the Southwest Pacific achieved remarkable successes. Perhaps most notable, given the lack of knowledge and expertise at the beginning of the war, they developed a clear understanding of the "inscrutable" Japanese enemy. Despite the plethora of postwar accounts describing the war against Japan as a brutal war of racial annihilation, there were hundreds of men within the Allied camp who struggled daily to find a way to bring the war to a close short of killing the enemy to a man. Allied propagandists sifted through voluminous studies and reports on Japanese history, culture, and military traditions and kept abreast of the latest intelligence in an effort to discern what motivated the Japanese fighting man. They never lost sight of the fact that no two individuals are identical and thus recognized the many variations that existed within that mass of men referred to as the Imperial Japanese Army. By late 1944 propagandists had differentiated several personality types prevalent among enemy soldiers and could offer a list of factors that tended to produce either higher or lower morale, as well as the circumstances that produced soldiers most susceptible to propaganda. Through careful analysis of POW interrogations, captured diaries, and the insight provided by a variety of budding experts on Japanese culture and military morale, propagandists learned, for example, that the most ardent Japanese enlisted men were relatively young, from rural backgrounds, with limited education and relatively short terms of military service.

An FMAD study of captured Japanese diaries concluded that "in the case of Japanese as in American society, there are many different personality types," and it classified those personality types into five groups. Only a small minority—10 percent—of the Japanese diarists qualified as "sons of heaven," that is, exhibited the stereotypical characteristics of the fanatical Japanese samurai, a "ruthless, fierce, tough, strongly indoctrinated fighter." (A study of German prisoners captured in Western Europe produced similar results. The ardent Nazis, the "hard core," made up only 10–15 percent of the Wehrmacht. These findings challenge the prevalent assumption, both then and now, that the Japanese were uniformly fanatical whereas German soldiers were at least rational, civilized human beings.) Of the remaining 90 percent of the Japanese diarists in the FMAD study 15 percent were described as "men of action," who "accept the circumstances of war as a matter of course" and neither demonstrated great patriotic fervor nor complained excessively about the conditions under which they served. Another 15 percent were classified as "dissatisfied soldiers," soldiers who were "once thought to be non-existent in the Japanese Army." These men were chronic complainers who frequently vented their sense of hopelessness and frustration on the pages of their diaries. Twenty-five percent of the diarists in the study were classified as "intellectuals," who realized that Japan was likely to be defeated and were aware of the imminence of their own personal destruction. Finally, the remaining 35 percent of the diarists were "men of feeling and emotion," that is, men who, according to FMAD analysts, were keenly conscious of the loss of life and the destruction of the natural world caused by the war. FMAD's report cautioned against generalizing too broadly from the findings; nonetheless, it argued that it was "instructive to see the range of personality which the diaries exhibit and to enter into the experience of Japanese individuals in this manner."[44]

Without disregarding the range of individual experience and personality, propagandists succeeded in identifying a number of significant trends. PWB and FELO discovered sources of the Japanese army's strength of spirit but also identified the most significant causes of demoralization among its constituent members. Devotion to the emperor, racial pride, a powerful warrior tradition, confidence in the nation's military leaders, and faith in Japan's divine mission and national destiny proved to be powerful forces for sustaining Japanese will. Conversely, Japanese troops' morale deteriorated because of battlefield defeats, supply shortages, inferior and inadequate equipment, fractious relations between officers and enlisted men, substandard medical care, lack of accurate news, and interservice rivalries. FMAD studies of Japanese morale informed propagandists that throughout the war three factors had a consistently positive influence on Japanese morale. Faith in the emperor never diminished (the only factor of which this could be said). Belief in the purpose of the war—to defend Japan from economic enslavement and protect Asians from Western imperialists—was the second most constant factor in sustaining troop morale. Finally, Japanese soldiers' faith that the home front would remain strong rarely wavered. On the other hand, even FMAD's earliest data revealed that Japanese morale was continually eroded due to inadequate supplies of food and matériel as well as doubts regarding the truth of the "news" they received. FMAD's research indicated that most situational factors affecting Japanese morale were not constant forces for either sustaining or diminishing morale; rather, they changed as the fortunes of war shifted. As the Japanese military machine ground to a halt Japanese soldiers' faith in victory, the high command, political leaders, their associates and immediate superiors, their own training, and interservice cooperation diminished. In the end, it was clear that "the Japanese are not supermen with invincible and unchanging morale. Japanese morale, like that of all peoples, is not a constant, but definitely 'expendable.'"[45]

The Allied propaganda campaign emerged from propagandists' conclusions about Japanese military morale and was founded on three fundamental policies that ensured its subsequent successes: tell the truth, don't blame the emperor, and build on the foundations laid by combat forces. The strategy of truth enabled propagandists to capture the audience's attention and establish the credibility of their output. By refusing to hold the emperor responsible for the debacle of the Pacific War, the Allies avoided antagonizing Japanese soldiers. This policy simultaneously offered another avenue of attack on the militarists, who were painted as traitors to the emperor and nation, having distorted the imperial will and led the nation to destruction.

SWPA propagandists' success must also be credited to their willingness to serve as the handmaiden of combat forces. Psychological warfare sought to exploit the favorable situation created by conventional armaments. It capitalized and built on the fact that Allied military victories had left Japanese troops both physically weakened and psychologically vulnerable. To his credit, Gen. Bonner Fellers remained cognizant that "psychological warfare can proceed no faster than winning armies" and instructed propagandists to plan and time their operations as dictated by battlefield developments.

After the Allies seized the initiative and began to inflict repeated defeats on the Japanese army, FELO and PWB succeeded in creating a propaganda campaign organized around rational objectives and specific enemy weaknesses. Propagandists defined nineteen propaganda objectives, which included deepening Japanese troops' doubt about the effectiveness of their navy and air forces, the truth of their leaders, that spiritual force was sufficient to achieve victory, that their cause was righteous, that the militarists were true representatives of the imperial will, and so on (see chapter 6). I have categorized the leaflets produced in pursuit of these objectives according to the four general responses propagandists hoped to elicit from the enemy, namely, despair, increased divisiveness, subverted fundamental beliefs, and enlightenment. Of the four, propaganda of despair was the most successful chiefly because Allied military victories so effectively prepared the way for the propaganda war. Conventional military operations were the single greatest cause of Japanese demoralization, but, said FMAD, "the effects of military power may be importantly supplemented by psychological warfare." Allied propagandists excelled at focusing the enemy's attention on Japan's dismal battlefield losses and poor logistical performance and thus encouraged a sense of gloom and doom among Japanese soldiers.

Allied propagandists succeeded in convincing large numbers of enemy troops that Allied material superiority was probably too great to overcome even with "Japanese spirit." By 1945 many Japanese had concluded that they could not win the Greater East Asia War. In an FMAD study of prisoners taken in the Philippines in early 1945 more than 50 percent conceded that they had lost their faith in ultimate Japanese victory. Such findings were unprecedented. And of the 147 prisoners questioned about their unit's morale, 72 described it as "bad" and only 39 thought it was "good" (21 said unit morale was declining and 15 gave no clear response). "At no time in the past," FMAD emphasized, "have Japanese prisoners been willing to concede in a proportion of more than two to one that the morale of their units was unsatisfactory."[46]

In their campaign to spread despair Allied propagandists also exploited the Japanese hunger for news. A great many leaflets, as well as the *Rakkasan News*, were designed to present a realistic, albeit demoralizing, picture of the war. Propagandists took advantage of the fact that enemy forces were so hungry for news that they would devour any and all that was provided, even by the enemy. One Japanese prisoner recounted his metamorphosis after reading various leaflets and the *Rakkasan News* over a two-month span. According to the Allied interrogation report, he originally discounted Allied leaflets and news sheets as "merely propaganda nonsense," but as the situation became more and more unfavorable for the Jap troops and his unit gradually decreased in strength PW [prisoner of war] began to change his views and came to look upon the so-called propaganda as a messenger of the truth and an accurate description of the present day situation. About the middle of May, PW made up his mind to surrender to U.S. troops at the first opportunity."[47]

Propagandists also made effective use of divisive propaganda themes. Japan's performance during the Pacific War became a case study of the debilitating consequences of uncontrolled interservice rivalries. Allied propaganda adeptly capitalized on the animosities between land, sea, and air forces. Divisive propaganda targeted relations between officers and enlisted men as well; in units led by officers who displayed little or no concern for the lives and well-being of their men propagandists found a ready audience.

Allied propagandists encountered significant obstacles, however, in achieving the goals of subversive and enlightenment propaganda. Subversive propaganda sought to undermine basic tenets of Japanese indoctrination, including the inevitability of Japanese victory, the superior spiritual qualities of Japanese warriors, that the Greater East Asia War was a righteous cause, and that to sacrifice one's life in service to the emperor and nation was the highest honor. The Japanese soldier's belief in the righteousness of the Greater East Asia War proved to be one of the strongest pillars of his morale, second only to his faith in the emperor. In spite of Allied efforts to convince enemy soldiers that the cause for which they were fighting was more a fabrication of a manipulative military clique than a true reflection of national policy, most Japanese soldiers continued to perceive the war as Japan's national mission, for which they were willing to fight and die. Most soldiers also continued to believe that "Japanese spirit" made them superior warriors. Their confidence that spiritual prowess was adequate to ensure victory, however, diminished as the war continued. Certainly the strength of Allied conventional military arms was the factor most responsible for shaking this pillar of Japanese faith, but propagandists magnified the impact of battlefield defeats and forced Japanese combatants to confront the personal and strategic implications of continued combat reversals.

One might argue that propaganda designed to convince Japanese soldiers of the futility of dying on the battlefield for a lost cause succeeded only in those cases where Japanese soldiers formally surrendered. Yet the IJA experienced a surge in the number of desertions, diminished enthusiasm for the war, discipline problems, "dangerous thoughts," and a great deal of fatalism. The degree to which propaganda exacerbated these tendencies cannot be determined with precision or summarized in a statistical table. Nonetheless, as 1945 wore on, the frequent and favorable remarks made by Japanese diarists and prisoners regarding the credible and persuasive nature of Allied propaganda, combined with the high command's attempts to prevent Japanese troops from falling prey to the "dangerous thoughts" inspired by this "treacherous tactic," provide evidence that Allied propaganda had a decided impact on Japanese morale.

Surrender constituted merely one way dispirited troops might respond to abysmal circumstances, and it was a response largely conditioned by cultural factors. For the Japanese, surrender was the equivalent of dishonor. For German soldiers, in contrast, there were "conditions under which surrender could be honorably performed." In the Wehrmacht surrender was tolerated provided it was done in accordance with accepted patterns of conduct. A German soldier might offer token resistance, for example, or purposely allow his position to be overrun, or determine that his situation was clearly hopeless and no military benefit could be achieved by further resistance, at which point he could effect an "honorable" surrender under the German military code of conduct.[48] For Japanese soldiers, however, surrender was not an acceptable option. Thus, they often sought what seemed to Westerners less obvious or less rational alternatives, ones that produced no military advantage but met Japanese standards for honorable conduct: desertion, suicide, or desperate acts of self-destruction. That these acts are much more difficult to quantify does not make them any less an indication of demoralization.

Unfortunately, and probably unavoidably, propaganda of enlightenment failed in its primary goal of persuading enemy soldiers that the Allies did not torture and murder Japanese prisoners. Despite the use of prisoner photographs, the dissemination of millions of good-treatment leaflets (many of which were written by POWs), and the pronouncements on Allied adherence to the Geneva Convention, the majority of Japanese troops were never convinced of the truth of these claims. Nevertheless, given the alternatives, many soldiers decided to risk their lives to verify the truth of Allied assertions. But even the majority of Japanese who surrendered to the Allies expected to be either tortured or killed. Likewise, most did not accept propagandists' benign explanations of the meaning of unconditional surrender. Japanese remained convinced and fearful that losing the Greater East Asia War would bring devastation on their homeland.

Again, in contrast, German soldiers found Allied promises of good treatment to be the single most effective weapon in the propaganda war waged against them and were "convinced that the law-abiding British and Americans would not in most situations harm them upon capture." And few believed that if Germany capitulated the Allies would wreak havoc on the civilian population or destroy the German nation as they knew it. A survey of German POWs indicated that "only a small minority ever expressed fears of the consequences of an Anglo-American occupation," and never more than 20 percent believed the Allies would take revenge against the German people after the war.[49]

It bears repeating that cross-cultural comparisons are often misleading. Germany and Japan had very different histories and cultures. The training and indoctrination of their armies were conditioned by their respective cultures. Imperial Japanese soldiers adhered to different rules of engagement and retained unique ideas about what constituted acceptable conduct in wartime. Their expectations regarding the intentions and capabilities of their enemies were likewise conditioned by cultural biases. An enemy's cultural predispositions must be considered not only in evaluating its conduct during wartime but also in judging its response to psywar operations. It is incumbent upon scholars to recognize the impact a given nation's rules of engagement will have on the success of a propaganda campaign aimed against it. It is reasonable to conclude that the taking of prisoners is a good indication of effectual psychological operations. It is also reasonable to conclude that since Japanese soldiers were thoroughly indoctrinated with the belief that surrender was utterly dishonorable, they were less likely to surrender than Germans, who were familiar with international law and waged war by a code of conduct that permitted surrender under certain conditions.

Allied propagandists succeeded in finding the means to write convincing propaganda texts. Their use of the Japanese language improved dramatically over time, and by early 1945 Japanese troops no longer criticized Allied leaflets as "childish" but instead focused on the content of the message. An FMAD study in October 1944 reported that Japanese often found Allied propaganda "naive and childlike, stressing the American point of view rather than appealing to Japanese psychology."[50] However, FMAD's 1945 reports reveal a consensus among Japanese prisoners, diarists, and military leaders that Allied leaflets were well written, though they occasionally criticized leaflet writers for using characters that might be too difficult for uneducated troops to read. The following entries from a diary captured on Luzon reveal that Allied leaflets improved over time and that Japanese troops had much more frequent contact with them.

> 8 April 45: Saw more than 10 different kinds of American propaganda leaflets. Their propaganda is excellent. It seems there are many people who [are] taken in by these propaganda leaflets.
>
> 12 April 45, According to enemy propaganda leaflets, there were naval engagements off Taiwan and off the Philippine islands which I did not know of before. It said that the enemy landed at Lingayen five days after the naval battle.[51]

ATIS interrogations likewise produced frequent POW references to the effectiveness of Allied propaganda and assertions that the *Rakkasan News* was particularly influential because it could be verified by independent sources.

A lance corporal who surrendered 25 April 1945 on Luzon identified a number of leaflets with which he had had contact prior to his decision to surrender and remarked that the leaflets "depressed" him. He then reported that additional leaflets, which he identified by name and contents,

> convinced him of the hopeless situation with which they were faced. . . . He was thoroughly impressed and swayed by these which made more specific mention of the circumstances in which he found himself at the time. It was about this time that the PW [prisoner of war] read of the Okinawa landing in the "Parachute News" [i.e., the *Rakkasan News*] and was able to confirm it from other sources. With the realization that whether he fought to the last or not could no longer affect the course of the war in any way came his decision to surrender himself. PW carried with him an "I Cease Resistance" leaflet.[52]

Another prisoner who surrendered voluntarily in the Philippines, on 9 July 1945, reported that he had seen many enemy propaganda leaflets. The ATIS interrogator summarized the prisoner's reaction to them as follows:

> Although at first there was no positive reaction, the consistency with which they were dropped and the authenticity of the written articles gradually convinced the Jap that the situation on Luzon is hopeless. The events mentioned in the "Parachute News" were often verified by persons who had a personal knowledge of the incidents. A leaflet which described the utter defeat of the Japanese naval forces in the Philippine battle was questioned and doubted at first, but when the statements were verified by navy men who survived the

ordeal, the minds of the men revolted against the High Command's erroneous propaganda.[53]

A Sixth Army report for the week of 13–19 May 1945 summarized POW impressions of Allied propaganda. Several Japanese prisoners from the Thirty-eighth Infantry Division reportedly had read "numerous leaflets" and been "strongly impressed by them." Others said they had "believed and admired their contents" or stated that the enlisted men had been "spiritually" influenced by enemy leaflets, which were particularly persuasive "after a heavy artillery barrage and bombing." Others commented that leaflets "containing relationships and differences in environments between officers and EM [enlisted men] were most effective." Many prisoners remembered the specifics of leaflets they had read and could paraphrase the texts of several.

Japanese prisoners often disagreed on the most effective propaganda themes. Individuals reacted differently based on their own personality, experiences, and predispositions. But where there was consensus propagandists responded quickly. They replaced the standard surrender leaflet with one entitled "I Cease Resistance," initiated widespread distribution of leaflets containing the terms of the Geneva Convention's provisions relevant to the treatment of prisoners, wrote leaflets clearly defining the steps one must take to surrender safely, and described what life was like for Japanese soldiers already in captivity. Propagandists also incorporated suggestions that leaflets should focus on developments in Japan and the Pacific rather than on events in Europe, that propaganda written or broadcast by Japanese POWs would be more credible, and that propaganda should make more use of situation maps, which were of great interest to soldiers in the field.

PWB and FELO also anticipated upcoming events to ensure rapid distribution of leaflets announcing significant turning points in the war. Seven million copies of "The Red Army Strikes" were dropped the day the Soviet Union declared war on Japan. They had been prepared four months in advance of the actual event. Anticipating the unconditional surrender of Germany several weeks prior to the end of the war in Europe, PWB produced millions of leaflets announcing Nazi capitulation. By 1945 SWPA's propaganda machine was efficient enough to write, reproduce, and distribute 7 million copies of the Potsdam Declaration within seventy-two hours of receiving word of the conference's results. A FELO operative recalled that within twenty minutes of the announcement of Japan's capitulation FELO planes were airborne, loaded with leaflets reporting the end of hostilities: "The drop was completed by noon and not another shot was fired on Bougainville, although the Japanese General Kanda was unable to contact his units and call them off until 7 a.m. the following day. The finale more than proved, wherever it had been in doubt, that FELO propaganda was effective, and that the Japanese believed us."[54] To ensure that the news spread rapidly throughout the theater, PWB and FELO printed and disseminated millions of copies of the imperial rescript ending the war.

Allied propagandists eventually succeeded in persuading the Allied air forces, the commanders of the Sixth and Eighth Armies, and Allied combat forces of the value of psychological warfare. PWB and FELO managed to convince many skeptics that propaganda played a useful supporting role in the war against Japan by demonstrating the intelligence value of POWs and, most importantly, by presenting plausible arguments that psywar saved Allied lives. Fellers reported that by the end of the war Allied field commanders were asking for more psywar support than PWB could provide.[55] In March 1945 General Krueger, of the Sixth Army, displayed his belief in the increasing effectiveness of leaflets in a memo issued to all subordinate commands in the Philippines: "There are indications that the intensive use of Japanese surrender leaflets is becoming increasingly effective. A substantial increase in the number of prisoners captured will constitute a direct indication of a breaking point in enemy morale, and a successful undermining of his whole military system which, if properly exploited, may lead to the surrender of large groups or units."[56] Education efforts bore fruit almost immediately, beginning in August 1944, when systematic efforts began to convince troops of the immense value of taking prisoners and the irredeemable damage done by killing those attempting to surrender. At that time all combat troops in the Aitape sector of New Guinea received copies of surrender leaflets so that they would recognize them in the heat of battle. An intelligence report dated 18 August 1944 confirmed the benefits that accrued from the effort.

> Within the past week approximately 20 prisoners of war have been taken by our troops. Most of these prisoners of war had surrender leaflets in their possession and walked into our lines for the purpose of surrendering. The fact that our front-line troops did take these Japanese prisoners instead of killing them seems to indicate that our troops have become very prisoner-conscious

since the informal talks given to them. . . . The surrender of Japs during the week in relatively large numbers also indicates the effectiveness of dropping surrender leaflets over enemy lines.[57]

The Seventy-seventh Division experienced similar results after its troops were "indoctrinated regarding the value of prisoners." In January 1945 the division reported that its soldiers exhibited a greater willingness to take POWs and that more prisoners were being taken as a result of troop training.[58]

Allied psychological warfare operations also helped prepare Japanese for the Allied occupation. The imperial rescript announcing Japan's surrender was unexpected by a great many Japanese who knew the nation had never experienced defeat in war and who had been led to believe that Japan would fight to the bitter end. Yet it was not nearly the great shock it might have been. For months Japanese troops (and civilians) had been reading leaflets that displayed evidence, often in graphic forms, that they were losing the war, that it was just a matter of time until the empire would collapse under the strain of a total war the likes of which the world had never seen. Fellers argued that the surrender of 7 million Japanese soldiers following the imperial rescript of 14 August 1945 shortened the war by twelve to eighteen months and saved 450,000 American battle casualties.[59] That they did not continue the struggle was the result of imperial sanction and an awareness of their own desperate circumstances. But the propaganda war made Japan's surrender easier for the Japanese to accept. For months, and with considerable precision, Allied propagandists had reported the devastation inflicted on the home islands and on Japanese combat forces throughout Asia and the Pacific.

Even before the surrender Allied propaganda informed Japanese soldiers and civilians of Allied intentions for the occupation. Leaflets described, to every extent possible, what was meant (or not meant) by the term *unconditional surrender*. And while most Japanese combatants feared that surrender would lead to a brutal occupation, Allied claims to the contrary, they could still hope that Allied propaganda was as reliable in its promise of a period of rebuilding rather than retribution after the war as it had been in foretelling Japan's defeat. Allied propagandists' adherence to the strategy of truth during the war likely made the Japanese more willing to trust the promises of the Allied occupation authorities as well. Finally, because psychological warfare required a thorough understanding of the enemy and the means for communicating with him, the propaganda war produced a substantial number of Allied personnel who were familiar with Japanese culture and who could provide information and language services during the occupation, thus easing the transition from war to peace.

. . .

A number of general conclusions regarding the nature of combat propaganda as it was employed against the Japanese army in the Southwest Pacific are clear. First, propaganda was highly effective under certain circumstances. When enemy troops had experienced frequent military defeats, were short on supplies, were alienated from their officers, or had experienced a loss of unit cohesion, they were susceptible to propaganda appeals.

Second, propaganda had a cumulative effect. Psychological warfare was most effective if the target audience had been in frequent contact with enemy propaganda over a prolonged period. The volume of Allied propaganda did increase steadily over the course of the war. Between November 1942 and the war's end PWB distributed 333 million leaflets in SWPA and FELO disseminated 58,652,135. Of the total, roughly 80 million leaflets were disseminated in the Philippine Islands (60 million to combat troops) between 20 October 1944 and 14 July 1945 alone. More prisoners were taken in the Philippines (12,181) than in any other campaign in the Pacific. By contrast, the Allies distributed 3.24 billion leaflets (targeting both civilians and combatants) in the ETO between D-Day and V-E Day. In sheer volume, then, there is no question but that propagandists in SWPA lagged behind their counterparts in Europe. Nonetheless, the propaganda war against Japan was simultaneously being conducted in the Pacific Ocean Areas as well as in the China-Burma-India theater. Moreover, the language barrier confronting propagandists in the Pacific was much more difficult to overcome. In addition to Japanese, propagandists in SWPA distributed leaflets in a variety of other languages, including British Malay, Dutch Malay, Pidgin, Chinese, Portuguese, Dutch, and several native dialects.

Third, propaganda had to be accurate, verifiable, and believable. It had to be tailored to the target audience's experiences and mind-set. Effective combat propaganda accurately described the battlefield situation and provided viable options or convincing arguments to persuade the target audience to act in a particular way. Propaganda leaflets designed to incite despair by commiserating with starving enemy troops were ridiculed by soldiers who had enough to eat. Less obvious were those instances when the message was accurate but the truth was so incredible that the audience simply could not believe it. German soldiers, for example, could not bring themselves to believe Allied statements that POWs received eggs for breakfast. For Japanese troops, assertions that Allied troops would not brutalize or murder prisoners of war were beyond belief.

Fourth, there were limits to what the propaganda war could accomplish. Material and practical concerns that directly affected the personal well-being of combat troops (food and supplies, combat losses, officer malfeasance, air and naval support) could be manipulated via propaganda mechanisms. The ideological foundations of morale, which were based on emotional and spiritual beliefs (righteousness of the cause, spiritual superiority, ultimate victory, confidence in national leaders), were much more difficult to weaken unless those beliefs were refuted by observable "facts" or personal experience. Japanese confidence in their spiritual superiority, for example, became less certain the longer the war continued. Soldiers' observations and experience "proved" that material shortages led to military defeat despite the strength of "Japanese spirit." Similarly, Japanese troops' faith in their racial superiority was called into question when they observed that Americans and Australians fought with a great deal more determination and strength of spirit than Japanese had been led to believe. Personal experience also led Japanese troops to question the credibility and capabilities of their military leaders, who often lied about the war's progress, abandoned soldiers in field, failed to provide adequately for their men, or proved incompetent or cowardly. As the front drew nearer to the home islands and Japanese forces realized firsthand that the imperial forces were being forced to retreat everywhere, they saw proof that Japan's great warrior tradition was perhaps not infallible.

Propagandists did shake the Japanese soldier's faith in material and practical factors because they made claims that could be verified by observation and fact. This was not the case with matters of a spiritual or emotional nature, which were more often articles of faith that no litany of "facts" could diminish. For example, experience proved that Allied technological superiority and material abundance could overwhelm Japanese spirit, but that did not lead the Japanese to believe that the Americans had more spiritual substance than they did. It proved only that spiritual prowess can be overwhelmed by material factors in wartime. That being the case, however, propagandists managed to persuade many Japanese that they were fighting a losing battle.

Ideological appeals proved generally ineffective and of little interest to Japanese soldiers. FMAD reported that "themes relating to larger issues such as the meaning of the war, the deception of the Emperor by the military clique, and the appeal to building a new and greater Japan after this war seem to have produced few results." The best propaganda lines dealt with the immediate situation and addressed issues that enemy soldiers could check for themselves. Ideological appeals roused little interest because they were remote from the individual soldier, who was powerless to influence grand strategy or national policy even in the rare instance when he might be so inclined. Soldiers in combat theaters were most interested in information that clarified their own position in the grand scheme of things, not grand expostulations on the purpose of the war.[60]

This conclusion holds true for the Wehrmacht as well. German soldiers were disinterested in ideological appeals and exhibited "extensive strategic indifference." Only 10 percent of German prisoners who had contacts with Allied propaganda during the final months of the war remembered leaflets of a political nature, whereas 76 percent remembered good-treatment leaflets. Attacks on Nazi ideology "seem to have been of little avail," and themes regarding the justness of the war "fell on deaf ears."[61] The Wehrmacht, like the IJA, was made up of individuals who focused on their own well-being and that of their immediate group. Beyond that their concerns were few indeed.

Fifth, Allied psywar operations revealed much about the cultural predispositions of the belligerents. Americans demonstrated their obsession with material factors in the way they fought as well as in the way they attempted to persuade the enemy to cease fighting. Whereas Japanese military indoctrination emphasized matters of the spirit as the paramount factor in war, American armed forces consciously or unconsciously exhibited a profound faith that superior technology, greater productive capacity, and overwhelming industrial might would ultimately decide the issue. Allied propaganda was in large part designed to convert the Japanese to that belief.

The most pervasive theme employed by propagandists in SWPA was that of Allied material and industrial superiority. In every propaganda category—despair, divisive, subversive, and enlightenment—leaflet writers informed enemy combatants that their much-touted "Japanese spirit" was no match for the material resources of the Allied powers. Propaganda of despair constantly illustrated Allied superiority in industrial, material, and human resources. It hammered away at Japan's inferior air and naval power, its lack of shipping and the consequent severe supply shortages on the front lines, and its loss of access to resource rich areas of the empire. The objective was to provide positive proof that Japan could not equal the productive capacity of the Allies and thus evoke such an overwhelming sense of hopelessness and fatalism that the troops would see little reason to continue the struggle.

Divisive propaganda texts likewise dwelled on the theme of material deficiencies by attacking Japan's military leaders for failing to protect the army and the supply lines it depended upon. They also exploited army-navy schisms by capitalizing on the theme of abandonment: Japanese soldiers could expect no air support, supplies, or reinforcements because the Allies had control of the sea and air due to their superior material resources. Propagandists also employed this theme to heighten tensions between officers and enlisted men. They argued that deficient planning and supply efforts by field officers or even out-and-out corruption had led to the shortages of food, weapons, equipment, and medical supplies that plagued front-line troops.

One of the chief objectives of subversive propaganda was to undermine Japanese confidence in the basic principles of their military indoctrination. Again, propagandists repeatedly argued that indoctrination regarding Japanese spiritual superiority was dangerously misleading. The propaganda war was replete with assertions that Japanese spiritual strength could not make up for the loss of fighting strength resulting from supply shortages and inferior weaponry. "War cannot be won by courage alone," pronounced Allied propagandists. One could not expect to defeat a massively armed, modern, mechanized enemy with outmoded equipment and starving troops, regardless of one's level of determination. "You can't fight our unlimited forces and equipment with your bare bodies." "Modern wars are won not by spirit," avowed leaflet writers, "but by overwhelming industrial production." The Allied view of modern war was aptly and succinctly summarized in the leaflet text that stated simply, "You can't fight tanks with bayonets."

Finally, enlightenment propaganda was similarly designed to increase Japanese awareness of Allied intentions and capabilities. This genre of propaganda also aimed to convince Japanese that their inferior productive capabilities and collapsing logistical apparatus made defeat inevitable. Propagandists thus sought to "enlighten" the Japanese with irrefutable evidence of Allied material prowess.

In every aspect of the psychological warfare campaign propagandists targeted Japan's material deficiencies as a promising means of destroying enemy morale. The primary reason, of course, was that intelligence sources had revealed relatively early in the war that inadequate production and a deficient logistical system had led to supply shortages that adversely affected soldiers' attitudes toward nearly every aspect of their military service. The hunger and disease that pervaded Japanese units were just as surely the allies of propagandists as were the bombs and bullets of the massive Allied military machine.

In the end, Allied combat propaganda achieved considerable successes but failed to convince most Japanese soldiers to reject the fundamental tenets of their military indoctrination and spiritual training. Propagandists succeeded in eroding enemy morale and confidence in matters of practical and material concern to Japanese soldiers. They failed, for the most part, to destroy the Japanese army's faith in matters of the spirit. Thus, although Allied propaganda helped convince many enemy troops that Japan could not win the war, Japanese soldiers continued to believe in the righteousness of their cause. Propagandists likewise caused the enemy to doubt that spiritual strength could compensate for Allied material superiority, but this did not dissuade the great masses of imperial troops from fulfilling what they perceived as their duty to their emperor and nation.

The work of propagandists was arduous, primarily because of the cultural and linguistic barriers that separated them from their target audience. They nonetheless made effective use of intelligence to keep abreast of Japanese reactions to Allied propaganda and the changing complexion of enemy morale. They also capitalized on opportunities to improve their methods and output. In the process, they discovered that imperial soldiers were neither uniformly devoted to the cause of victory nor psychologically invulnerable to propaganda. They discovered that the Imperial Japanese Army, like all armies, was composed of a multitude of individuals who had the same physical needs as soldiers everywhere but varying degrees of commitment and endurance. And like soldiers everywhere, they struggled to resolve the inherent conflict between two overwhelming and competing human emotions—the desire to preserve one's life and the obligation to fulfill one's duty.

Notes

Introduction

1. PWB, SWPA, Daily Collation Summary, "Challenge Adequacy of Spiritual Force Alone," 19 November 1944, box 12, entry 283L, RG 331, NARA.

2. John W. Dower, *War without Mercy: Race and Power in the Pacific War* (New York: Pantheon, 1986), 53.

3. Dower, *War without Mercy*, 77.

4. Memo, Lt. Col. Benjamin Stern to Director, OWI, "Re: OWI Pacific Command Team," 27 March 1943, box 11, entry 6G, RG 208, NARA. This quotation was said to summarize Adm. William Halsey's attitude toward psywar in March 1943.

5. Dower, *War without Mercy*, 53; James J. Weingartner, "Trophies of War: U.S. Troops and the Mutilation of Japanese War Dead, 1941–1945," *Pacific Historical Review* 61 (1992): 55.

6. Bonner F. Fellers, "Report on Psychological Warfare in the Southwest Pacific Area, 1944–1945" (Washington DC: U.S. Army Center of Military History, Historical Records Division, 1946), 2. This report is located in the U.S. Army Center of Military History, Historical Records Branch, Washington DC; the MacArthur Memorial Bureau of Archives, Norfolk VA; and the Bonner F. Fellers Papers, Hoover Institution on War, Revolution, and Peace, Palo Alto CA.

1 · Tracing the Historical Roots of Propaganda

1. Sun Tzu, *The Art of War,* trans. Thomas Cleary (Boston: Shambhala, 1988), 67, 72; Carl von Clausewitz, *War, Politics, and Power: Selections from On War, and I Believe and Profess,* ed. Edward M. Collins (South Bend IN: Gateway, 1962), 177–78; Peter Paret, "Clausewitz," in *Makers of Modern Strategy: From Machiavelli to the Nuclear Age,* ed. Peter Paret (Princeton: Princeton Univ. Press, 1986), 204.

2. H. C. Peterson, *Propaganda for War: The Campaign against American Neutrality, 1914–1917* (Norman: Oklahoma Univ. Press, 1939); Frederick E. Lumley, *The Propaganda Menace* (New York: Century, 1933); and George Sylvester Viereck, *Spreading Germs of Hate* (New York: Horace Liveright, 1930), describe the dangers of state-sponsored propaganda efforts in the aftermath of World War I. Harold D. Lasswell, *Propaganda Technique in the World War* (New York: Knopf, 1927); and George C. Bruntz, *Allied Propaganda and the Collapse of the German Empire in 1918* (Stanford: Stanford Univ. Press, 1938), provide more dispassionate accounts of the nature and impact of World War I propaganda.

3. Executive Order 9182, 13 June 1942, in U.S. Office of the Federal Registrar, *Code of Federal Regulations, 1938–1943 Compilation* (Washington DC: USGPO, 1968), 1169–70.

4. Executive Order 9182, 13 June 1942, 1169–70.

5. Ronald H. Spector, *Eagle against the Sun: The American War with Japan* (New York: Free Press, 1984), 460. See also Corey Ford, *Donovan of OSS* (Boston: Little, Brown, 1970), 125.

6. Executive Order 9312, 13 March 1943, *Federal Regulations,* 1259–60.

7. NARA, *Federal Records of World War II,* vol. 2, *Military Agencies* (Washington DC: USGPO, 1950), entry 181. Clayton D. Laurie argues that these War Department agencies were relatively powerless since theater commanders controlled psywar operations in the field. See Laurie, *The Propaganda Warriors: America's Crusade against Nazi Germany* (Lawrence: Univ. Press of Kansas, 1996), 148–49.

8. For more detailed descriptions of the nature of various theater psywar organizations see Paul M. A. Linebarger, *Psychological Warfare* (Washington DC: Infantry Journal, 1948), 40–60; Daniel Lerner, *Sykewar: Psychological Warfare against Germany, D-Day to VE-Day* (New York: George W. Stewart, 1949), 168–91; and William E. Daugherty, "U.S. Psychological Warfare Organizations in World War II," in *A Psychological Warfare Casebook: A Review of U.S. Historical Experience with Civil Affairs, 1776–1954,* ed. William E. Daugherty and Morris Janowitz (Baltimore: Johns Hopkins Univ. Press, 1958), 126–35. For more details on the organizational dynamics of the psywar apparatus in the ETO see Laurie, *Propaganda Warriors.*

9. See James P. Warburg, *Unwritten Treaty* (New York: Harcourt, Brace, 1946); Alfred H. Paddock Jr., *U.S. Army Special Warfare, Its Origins: Psychological and Un-*

conventional Warfare, 1941–1952 (Washington DC: National Defense Univ. Press, 1982); and Alan M. Winkler, *The Politics of Propaganda: The Office of War Information, 1942–1945* (New Haven: Yale Univ. Press, 1946).

10. Warburg, *Unwritten Treaty,* 101; Lerner, *Sykewar,* 47–48, quotation on 43.

11. Ford, *Donovan of OSS,* 265–75; Spector, *Eagle against the Sun,* 461–63; Robert Lee Bishop, "The Overseas Branch of the Office of War Information" (Ph.D. diss., University of Wisconsin, 1966).

12. Memo, Stern to Director, OWI, "Re: OWI Pacific Command Team," 27 March 1943.

13. Bishop, "Overseas Branch of the Office of War Information," 352; William Henry Vatcher Jr., "Combat Propaganda against the Japanese in the Central Pacific" (Ph.D. diss., Stanford University, 1950) 17–26; Spector, *Eagle against the Sun,* 460.

14. Charles A. Willoughby and John Chamberlain, *MacArthur, 1941–1951* (New York: McGraw-Hill, 1954), 144–45, 176; Allison Ind, *Allied Intelligence Bureau: Our Secret Weapon in the War against Japan* (New York: David McKay, 1958); Eric A. Feldt, *The Coastwatchers* (New York: David McKay, 1946). MacArthur saw OWI as "administrative conspiracy" (see Winkler, *Politics of Propaganda,* 137). On AIB's integration into MacArthur's command see Charles A. Willoughby, "Intelligence in War: A Brief History of MacArthur's Intelligence Service, 1941–1951," reprinted in his *Guerrilla Resistance Movement in the Philippines: 1941–1945* (New York: Vantage, 1972), 71.

15. Quotation from Ind, *Allied Intelligence Bureau,* 12. See also Willoughby, "Intelligence in War," 71; and Willoughby and Chamberlain, *MacArthur,* 144.

16. Fellers, "Report on Psychological Warfare," 3.

17. Fellers, "Report on Psychological Warfare," 2.

2 · Building a Psychological Warfare Capability

1. For a more detailed discussion of the organizational relationship between FELO and AIB see Alan Powell, *War by Stealth: Australians and the Allied Intelligence Bureau, 1942–1945* (Melbourne: Melbourne Univ. Press, 1996).

2. "Report of Activities of Far Eastern Liaison Office for Period June 1942 to September 1945," p. 39, box 2, Fellers Papers.

3. Memo, "History of Relations of OWI with GHQ," 5 May 1943, p. 1, box 10, entry 283K, RG 331, NARA.

4. Michael L. Stiver (OWI) to MacArthur, 30 December 1942; MacArthur to George C. Marshall, 6 March 1943; and MacArthur to Stiver, 6 January 1943, all in box 16, RG 4, MMBA.

5. Memo, "History of Relations of OWI with GHQ," 5 May 1943; "OWI in Australia," 30 September 1944, box 5, entry 6J, RG 208, NARA.

6. Discussion of FELO training is based on "Notes Recorded on Indoctrination Course in Psychological Warfare Given by officers of FELO," "Introduction to Psychological Warfare," "Planning a Particular Propaganda Operation," and "Principles of Propaganda," box 31, entry 283L, RG 331, NARA.

7. Fellers, "Report on Psychological Warfare"; memo, Fellers to G-5, GHQ, 6 November 1944, and Fellers to Chief of Staff, SWPA, 29 June 1944, both in box 3, Fellers Papers. See also Powell, *War by Stealth*, esp. chapter 9, on FELO's field operations.

8. Press Release, GHQ, SWPA, 30 March 1944, box 49, RG 4; Fellers to MacArthur, 12 August 1941, box 4, RG 10; and telegrams, Marshall to MacArthur, 31 August 1943, and MacArthur to Marshall, 1 September 1943, box 16, RG 4, all in MMBA.

9. Fellers, "Report on Psychological Warfare," 1 and annex 4, "Basic Military Plan for Psychological Warfare in the Southwest Pacific Area," 2 August 1944.

10. OSS Planning Group, "Memorandum on Basic Military Plan for Psychological Warfare in the Southwest Pacific Area," 15 September 1944, box 24, Fellers Papers.

11. Memo, Fellers to Collation Section, 29 August 1944, box 2, entry 283K, RG 331, NARA.

12. Memo, J. Woodall Greene to Planning Department, 9 October 1944, box 10, entry 283K, RG 331, NARA; memo, "Organization of Planning Section," box 3, Fellers Papers.

13. Fellers, "Report on Psychological Warfare," 7; "PWB Activities," 11–17 March 1945, box 14, entry 283K, RG 331, NARA.

14. Fellers, "Report on Psychological Warfare," annex 4, "Basic Military Plan," app. A, "Steps in Planning."

15. Fellers, "Report on Psychological Warfare," 56 and annex 2, "PWB Organizational Chart"; Daugherty, "U.S. Psychological Warfare Organizations in World War II," 134.

16. Fellers, "Report on Psychological Warfare," annex 6, "Basic Military Plan for Psychological Warfare against Japan with Appendices and Minutes of the Conference on Psychological Warfare against Japan, 7–8 May 1945," 54–55.

17. Claude E. Hawley, Detachment Commander, field memo no. 5, 22 January 1945, box 10, entry 283K, RG 331, NARA.

18. Memo, Fellers to Field Units, 13 September 1944, box 3, Fellers Papers.

19. HQ, Sixth Army, Office of the Assistant Chief of Staff, G-2, "Basic Sixth Army Plan for Psychological Warfare," approved 11 September 1944, located in both the John R. Sandberg and Frank Hallgren Collection, Love Library, Special Collections, University of Nebraska–Lincoln, and box 1, entry 283K, RG 331, NARA. In the event, *Rakkasan News* was written chiefly by Japanese prisoners for dissemination to their former comrades.

20. John R. Sandberg, interview by author, 25 June 1984, Lincoln NE. Sandberg recalled that while he was on detached service with the 308th Bomb Wing, unless it received special instructions the bomb wing determined where PWB would make leaflet drops. "We went where the Bomb Wing was going," he said.

21. "General Procedures," describing the procedures of the PWB team on detached service with the 308th Bomb Wing, Sandberg-Hallgren Collection.

22. Sandberg, interview, 25 June 1984. For a more thorough discussion of the methods employed to distribute leaflets in SWPA see H. N. Walker, "Psychological Warfare in the South-West Pacific," *Army Journal* (Australian), no. 298 (March 1974): 58–60.

23. Capt. James A. Matthews, "Employment of the Fifth Air Force in the Conduct of Psychological Warfare in the SWPA," 9 December 1944, box 16, entry 283K, RG 331, NARA.

24. "Psychological Warfare Functions, Sixth Army–Fifth Air Force," 22 September 1944, box 16, entry 283K, RG 331, NARA.

25. "Notes for Air Liaison Officers," box 21, entry 283L; memo, Sgt. James M. Taylor, FELO, 308th Bomb Group, to Lt. A. A. Fisher, FELO, Thirteenth Air Force, 12 January 1945, box 14, entry 283K, both in RG 331, NARA.

3 ▪ Getting to Know the Enemy

1. The most famous national-character study of the Japanese was Ruth Benedict, *The Chrysanthemum and the Sword: Patterns of Japanese Culture* (Boston: Houghton Mifflin, 1946). See also Geoffrey Gorer, "Themes in Japanese Culture," *Transactions of the New York Academy of Sciences,* 2d ser., 5 (November 1943): 106–24; Richard H. Minear, "Cross-Cultural Perception and World War II: American Japanists of the 1940s and Their Images of Japan," *International Studies Quarterly* 24 (December 1980): 555–80; and idem, "The Wartime Studies of Japanese National Character," *Japan Interpreter,* summer 1980, 36–59.

2. Nyozekan Hasegawa, "Our 'Emaciated Endurance,' " *Contemporary Japan* 12 (May 1943): 570–76. See also Dower, *War without Mercy,* 30–31, 221. Dower argues that the government emphasized the idea of "100 million hearts beating as one" not because there was no individuality in Japan but rather because the government wished to eradicate individuality and create the kind of uniformity its propaganda espoused.

3. Carol Gluck, *Japan's Modern Myths: Ideology in the Late Meiji Period* (Princeton: Princeton Univ. Press, 1985), 73.

4. Dower, *War without Mercy,* 282.

5. Dower, *War without Mercy,* 279–83.

6. Dower, *War without Mercy,* 223–24; Otto D. Tolischus, "The Way of the Subjects," in *Tokyo Record* (New York: Reynal & Hitchcock, 1943), 423.

7. Saburo Ienaga, *The Pacific War: World War II and the Japanese, 1931–1945* (New York: Pantheon, 1978), 19–20, 22.

8. Toshio Iritani, *Group Psychology of the Japanese in Wartime* (New York: Kegan Paul International, 1991), 160–84; Ienaga, *Pacific War,* 22–32.

9. Edward J. Drea, "In the Army Barracks of Imperial Japan," *Armed Forces and Society* 15 (spring 1989): 335–36.

10. Ienaga, *Pacific War,* 49; ATIS, SWPA, Research Report no. 76, pt. 3, "The Warrior Tradition as a Present Factor in Japanese Military Psychology," 30 October 1944, p. 11, box 119, RG 3, MMBA; Drea, "In the Army Barracks of Imperial Japan," 330.

11. Drea, "In the Army Barracks of Imperial Japan," 343–44.

12. Imperial Rescript to Soldiers and Sailors (1882), box 104, entry 148, RG 226, NARA.

13. Drea, "In the Army Barracks of Imperial Japan," 335–36; Alvin D. Coox, "The Japanese Army Experience," in *New Dimensions in Military History,* ed. Russell F. Weigley (San Rafael CA: Presidio, 1975), 133–34.

14. Coox, "Japanese Army Experience," 133.

15. Coox, "Japanese Army Experience," 133.

16. Richard J. Smethurst, *A Social Basis for Prewar Japanese Militarism: The Army and the Rural Community* (Berkeley: Univ. of California Press, 1974), xviii, 179–84.

17. Quotation from a 1908 IJA handbook, cited in Drea, "In the Army Barracks of Imperial Japan," 335.

18. Drea, "In the Army Barracks of Imperial Japan," 334–35.

19. Dower, *War without Mercy,* 121.

20. Fellers, "Report on Psychological Warfare." Fellers's official report on PWB includes as an annex his 1935 study "The Psychology of the Japanese Soldier," upon which the following discussion is based.

21. For a thorough analysis of Japanese psychology written early in the war see OSS, R&A, Report no. 679, "Preliminary Survey of Japanese Social and Psychological Conditions: Background for the Formulation of Plans for Psychological Warfare," 1942 (microfilm).

22. An English translation of *Nippon Shindo Ron,* "The Way of the Subjects," is included in Tolischus, *Tokyo Record* as app. 1. *Nippon Shindo Ron* was extracted from the *Kojiki* (Record of ancient matters) and *Nihongi* (Chronicles of Japan), the primary sources of ancient Japanese mythology.

23. ATIS, SWPA, Research Report no. 76, pt. 2, "The Emperor Cult as a Present Factor in Japanese Military Psychology," 21 June 1944, p. 11, box 119, RG 3, MMBA.

24. COI, R&A, Report no. 614, "Morale in the Japanese Military Services," 1942 (microfilm), 1; OSS, R&A, Report no. 679, "Preliminary Survey of Japanese Social

and Psychological Conditions," 32–37; Fellers, "Report on Psychological Warfare," app. 23, 24.

25. COI, R&A, Report no. 614, "Morale in the Japanese Military Services," 17–19; OSS, R&A, Report no. 679, "Preliminary Survey of Japanese Social and Psychological Conditions," 38–45; and Peter DeMendelssohn, *Japan's Political Warfare* (London: Allen & Unwin, 1944), all provided details on how Japanese society inculcated a belief in loyalty and obedience. Hillis Lory, *Japan's Military Masters: The Army in Japanese Life* (New York: Viking, 1943), discussed the "mystic coalition" between the army and the emperor. Otto D. Tolischus provided a detailed analysis of the Japanese army's rise to dominance in *Tokyo Record*, 264–78. Ian Morrison, *Our Japanese Foe* (New York: G. P. Putnam's Sons, 1943), discussed bushido, as did ATIS, SWPA, Research Report no. 76, pt. 3, "The Warrior Tradition as a Present Factor in Japanese Military Psychology."

26. For wartime discussions of the ties between the army and the civilian population see Hillis Lory, "Japan's Army of the People," in Lory, *Japan's Military Masters*, 15–31; and John Andrew Goette, *Japan Fights for Asia* (New York: Harcourt, Brace, 1943), 42–47.

27. Sadao Araki, quoted in ATIS, SWPA, Research Report no. 76, pt. 3, "The Warrior Tradition as a Present Factor in Japanese Military Psychology," 1.

28. Fellers, "Report on Psychological Warfare," annex 3, "Answer to Japan," 11; ATIS, SWPA, Research Report no. 76, pt. 3, "The Warrior Tradition as a Present Factor in Japanese Military Psychology," 6.

29. Benedict, *Chrysanthemum and the Sword*, 24; ATIS, SWPA, Research Report no. 76, pt. 3, "The Warrior Tradition as a Present Factor in Japanese Military Psychology," 9.

30. ATIS, SWPA, Research Report no. 76, pt. 2, "The Emperor Cult as a Present Factor in Japanese Military Psychology," 3–4; OSS, R&A, Report no. 679, "Preliminary Survey of Japanese Social and Psychological Conditions," 75; Tolischus, *Tokyo Record*, 186–88.

31. OSS, R&A, Report no. 679, "Preliminary Survey of Japanese Social and Psychological Conditions," 75.

32. Tolischus, "The Way of the Subjects," 409–10, 420–23.

33. OWI, FMAD, Semi-Monthly Report 14, "The Influence of Allied Propaganda as Revealed in 1025 Interrogation Reports of Japanese Prisoners of War Captured prior to September 1, 1944 and in Approximately 500 Captured Documents, and Other Sources," 15 December 1944, box 335, entry 172, RG 165, NARA.

34. OWI, FMAD, Semi-Monthly Report 15, "Persistent and Changeable Attitudes of the Japanese Forces and Their Implications for Propaganda Purposes," 1 January 1945, pp. 15–24, box 444, entry 378, RG 208, NARA; and Report 26, "Principal Find-

ings Regarding Japanese Morale during the War," 20 September 1945, p. 7, box 335, entry 172, RG 165, NARA.

35. OWI, FMAD, Report 18, "Aspects of Japanese Fighting Morale during the Papuan Phase of the New Guinea Campaign," 23 April 1945, box 9, entry 283K, RG 331, NARA; and Report 26, "Principal Findings Regarding Japanese Morale during the War," 7.

36. Telegrams, JCS to MacArthur, 19 June 1943, and MacArthur to Chief of Staff, War Department, 22 June 1943, box 16, RG 4, MMBA.

37. Greene to Fellers, 10 September 1944, box 3, Fellers Papers; Capt. William R. Beard to Capt. Alfred G. Hall, 2 December 1944, box 16, entry 283K, RG 331, NARA.

38. HQ, Eighth Army, PWB, Asst. Chief of Staff, G-2, Weekly Report no. 6, 6 January 1945, 1; "Fifth Air Force, History, January-February 1945—PWB Unit"; Matthews to Hawley, PWB, Sixth Army, 2 October 1944; Matthews quotation from his "Employment of the Fifth Air Force," all in box 16, entry 283K, RG 331, NARA.

39. Memo, James Taylor to Fisher, 12 January 1945, 3.

40. AMF, Weekly Intelligence Review, no. 9 (2 October 1942): app. E, p. 1, in box 2, RG 23A, MMBA; telegram, MacArthur to Commanding General, Alamo Force, 14 May 1944, box 3, entry 283J, RG 331, NARA.

41. Beard, PWB, G-2, HQ, Tenth Corps, to Fellers, 2 December 1944, box 16, entry 283K, RG 331, NARA.

42. *Intelligence Bulletin* 1, no. 3 (1942): 1.

43. *Intelligence Bulletin* 3, no. 1 (1944): 33; 3, no. 3 (1944): 24; and 3, no. 7 (1945): 55.

44. Beard to Fellers, 3 January 1945, box 16, entry 283K, RG 331, NARA.

45. Memo, Lt. Col. Arthur Murphy for Commanding Officer, United States Army Forces in the Philippines, North Luzon, to Commanding General, Sixth Army, and Maj. Paul T. Anderson, PWB, G-2, 11 February 1945, box 1, entry 283K, RG 331, NARA.

46. Beard to Fellers, 3 January 1945.

47. Beard to Fellers, 3 January 1945.

48. Ken R. Dyke, I&E Officer, USAFFE, to G-1, GHQ, 28 May 1944; and Greene to Fellers, 10 September 1944, both in box 3, Fellers Papers.

49. Charles A. Willoughby to H. V. White, 13 May 1944, box 3, entry 283J, RG 331, NARA.

50. White to Willoughby, 18 May 1944, box 3, entry 283J, RG 331, NARA.

51. Memo, Lt. Col. Charles W. Clegg, by command of Lt. Gen. Walter Krueger for broadest circulation, "Accepting Surrender of Japanese Military Personnel," 18 March 1945, box 1, entry 283K, RG 331, NARA.

52. The U.S. Navy did not include psywar instruction in its orientation for aircrews until March 1945 (*Leaflet Newsletter* 1, no. 4 [4 May 1945]: 17, in box 21, entry 283L, RG 331, NARA).

53. PWB, G-2, Summary Report, "A Short—Cut to Victory," box 2, entry 283J, RG 331, NARA.

54. Greene to Beard, 16 December 1944, box 3, Fellers Papers.

55. G-2 Summary, box 3, Fellers Papers.

56. Leaflet 2-A-8, "Troops of 40th Division," box 10, entry 283K, RG 331, NARA. See also leaflet 1-A-8, "Take Prisoners," 31 January 1945, in the same location.

57. FELO, SWPA, Weekly Narrative 60-30.1.45, cited in HQ, SACSEA, PWD, Information Review, no. 14 (February 1945): 7, in box 18, entry 283L, RG 331, NARA; memo, G-2, USAFFE, to G-1, GHQ, and FELO, "Effect of Allied Surrender Leaflets," 18 August 1944, box 3, entry 283J, RG 331, NARA.

58. Memo, Robert Kleiman to George Taylor, OWI, 17 January 1945, box 4, entry 283K, RG 331, NARA.

59. HQ, SACSEA, PWD, Information Review, no. 18 (June 1945), box 18, entry 283L, RG 331, NARA.

60. Sandberg, interview, 25 June 1984.

61. War Department, MIS, Captured Personnel and Material Branch, "Suggestions for American Propaganda Leaflets," 23 September 1944, and "Criticism of Leaflets 404 to 1003: Psychological Warfare, Part II—Propaganda Material," 25 September 1944, both in box 7, entry 283K, RG 331, NARA; "General Criticisms of American Leaflets by Okano," for Propaganda Committee of the Japanese People's Emancipation League at Yenan, 7 November 1944, box 20, entry 148, RG 226, NARA.

62. Sidney F. Mashbir, *I Was an American Spy* (New York: Vantage, 1953), 339; HQ, SACSEA, PWD, Information Review, quoted in memo, Maj. Harold G. Henderson to Greene, 30 October 1944, box 14, entry 283K, RG 331, NARA.

63. OWI, FMAD, Semi-Monthly Report 13, "Reactions to Allied Propaganda Themes as Revealed in 1025 Interrogation Reports," 1 December 1944, p. 2, box 9, entry 6G, RG 208, NARA.

64. Memo, FMAD to Harold M. Vinacke, OWI, Area 3, Japan Section, 27 November 1944, box 443, entry 378, RG 208, NARA; OWI, FMAD, Semi-Monthly Report 14, "Influence of Allied Propaganda," 15 December 1944, pp. 17–19, box 335, entry 172, RG 165, NARA.

65. FELO, SWPA, Reactions to Propaganda, no. 15 (15 December 1944): 6, in box 4, entry 283K, RG 331, NARA.

4 · Searching for Weaknesses

1. OWI, FMAD, "Outline of a Method for Studying Japanese Army Morale as Reflected in Intelligence Reports," box 335, entry 172, RG 165, NARA.

2. See Samuel A. Stouffer et al., *Studies in Social Psychology in World War II*, vol. 2, *The American Soldier: Combat and Its Aftermath* (Princeton: Princeton Univ.

Press, 1949); and Edward A. Shils and Morris Janowitz, "Cohesion and Disintegration in the Wehrmacht in World War II," in *Public Opinion and Propaganda: A Book of Readings*, ed. Daniel Katz (New York: Holt, Rinehart & Winston, 1954).

3. Edward A. Shils and Morris Janowitz compared the 10–15 percent of "hard core" enlisted men who were zealous with the "soft core" that was a "source of infection" in the German army in their "Cohesion and Disintegration in the Wehrmacht." See also Alexander H. Leighton, *Human Relations in a Changing World: Observations on the Use of the Social Sciences* (New York: E. P. Dutton, 1949).

4. See, e.g., Department of the Navy, ONI, Special Warfare Branch, "Indication of Japanese Deterioration of Morale Shown in Neglect of Combat Weapons," 10 September 1943; and "Further Deterioration of Japanese Army Morale," 20 September 1943, both in box 110, entry 358, RG 208, NARA. See also AMF, Weekly Intelligence Review, no. 64 (22 October 1943), in app. D, "Discipline in the Japanese Army," box 3, RG 23A, MMBA.

5. Lerner, *Sykewar*, 46.

6. OWI, FMAD, Report 18, "Aspects of Japanese Fighting Morale during the Papuan Phase of the New Guinea Campaign," 23 April 1945, box 9, entry 283K, RG 331, NARA.

7. OWI, FMAD, Report 19, "Group and Individual Morale of the Japanese during the Lae–Salamaua Campaign," 12 May 1945, box 9, entry 283K, RG 331, NARA.

8. HQ, Allied Air Forces, SWPA, Intelligence Summary, no. 175 (22 January 1944): 23, in box 39, RG 30, MMBA.

9. HQ, Allied Air Forces, SWPA, Intelligence Summary, no. 189 (11 March 1944), box 40, RG 30, MMBA.

10. ATIS, SWPA, Research Report no. 76, pt. 3, "The Warrior Tradition as a Present Factor in Japanese Military Psychology," 5.

11. ATIS, SWPA, Current Translation no. 14, 18 January 1943, p. 21, box 119, RG 3, MMBA.

12. HQ, Sixth Army, undated report issued by the Asst. Chief of Staff, G-2, Sandberg-Hallgren Collection.

13. FELO, SWPA, Reactions to Propaganda, no. 15 (15 December 1944): 3–5. See also FELO's monthly Reactions to Propaganda, box 4, entry 283K; OWI's monthly *Leaflet Newsletter*, box 21, entry 283L; and PWB's periodic Psychological Warfare Reactions and Developments, box 31, entry 283L, all in RG 331, NARA.

14. AMF, Weekly Intelligence Review, no. 19 (10 November 1944): 20, in box 5, RG 23A, MMBA.

15. ATIS, SWPA, Research Report no. 76, pt. 1, "Self-Immolation as a Factor in Japanese Military Psychology," 30 October 1944, p. 27, box 119, RG 3, MMBA.

16. HQ, Allied Air Forces, SWPA, Intelligence Summary, no. 187 (4 March 1944): 21, in box 40, RG 30, MMBA.

17. AMF, Weekly Intelligence Review, no. 145 (28 July 1945): 16, in box 6, RG 23A, MMBA.

18. OWI, FMAD, Weekly Summary, no. 9 (29 September–5 October 1944), box 9, entry 283K, RG 331, NARA.

19. OWI, FMAD, Report 20, "Factors Affecting Japanese Morale during the Aitape-Hollandia Campaign," 10 June 1945, pp. 6–7, 19, box 9, entry 283K, RG 331, NARA. Excerpts of POW interrogations and captured Japanese documents taken from ATIS, SWPA, Research Report no. 94, "Psychological Effect of Allied Bombing on the Japanese," 21 September 1944, box 119, RG 3, MMBA; and PWB, SWPA, Daily Collation Summary, "Challenge Adequacy of Spiritual Force Alone," 19 November 1944, box 12, entry 283L, RG 331, NARA.

20. ATIS, SWPA, Research Report no. 94, "Psychological Effect of Allied Bombing on the Japanese," 6–8; OWI, FMAD, Report 20, "Aitape-Hollandia Campaign," 7–10.

21. OWI, FMAD, Report 19, "Lae-Salamaua Campaign," 11; HQ, Allied Air Forces, SWPA, Intelligence Summary, no. 175 (22 January 1945): 23, in box 39, RG 30, MMBA; Department of the Navy, ONI, Special Warfare Branch, "Japanese Army Pilots Openly Admit Inferiority of Japanese Planes in Both Quality and Quantity," 13 July 1944, box 110, entry 358, RG 208, NARA; ATIS, SWPA, Research Report no. 76, pt. 1, "Self-Immolation as a Factor in Japanese Military Psychology," 29.

22. HQ, Allied Air Forces, SWPA, Intelligence Summary, no. 175 (22 January 1944): 23, and no. 187 (4 March 1944): 21, in boxes 39 and 40, RG 30, MMBA.

23. PWB, SWPA, Daily Collation Summary, "Spread Antagonism among the Army, Navy, and Air Force," 13 January 1945, box 14, entry 283L, RG 331, NARA. See also Department of the Navy, ONI, Special Warfare Branch, "Friction between the Japanese Army and Navy," 16 December 1944, and "Internal Dissension between Japanese Army and Navy," 21 August 1943, both in box 110, entry 358, RG 208, NARA.

24. HQ, Allied Air Forces, SWPA, Intelligence Summary, no. 187 (4 March 1944): 25, in box 40, RG 30, MMBA; Department of the Navy, ONI, Special Warfare Branch, "Indication of Japanese Deterioration of Morale Shown in Neglect of Combat Weapons," 10 September 1943; ATIS, SWPA, "M Report," 14 July 1944, p. 2, box 1, entry 283K, RG 331, NARA.

25. OWI, FMAD, Report 19, "Lae-Salamaua Campaign," 1, 22; OWI, FMAD, Weekly Summary, no. 6 (8–14 September 1944): 1–2, in box 9, entry 283K, RG 331, NARA; AMF, Weekly Intelligence Review, no. 74 (23–31 December 1943), box 4, RG 23A, MMBA; HQ, SACSEA, PWD, Information Review, no. 11 (9 December 1944): 3, in box 18, entry 283L, RG 331, NARA.

26. Speech by General Koiso, 1944, cited in Department of the Navy, ONI, Special Warfare Branch, "Japanese Defeatist Attitudes and Victory Claims," 16 November

1944, pp. 4–5, box 110, entry 358, RG 208, NARA; speech by Masanori Ito, 15 May 1945, cited in OWI, Overseas Branch—San Francisco, "Tokyo—Then and Now," 26 May 1945, p. 2, box 10, entry 283K, RG 331, NARA.

27. Unless otherwise noted, this example and those in the following paragraphs are extracted from ATIS, SWPA, Research Report no. 122, "Antagonism between Officers and Men in the Japanese Armed Forces," 19 April 1945, box 120, RG 3, MMBA.

28. AMF, Weekly Intelligence Review, no. 110 (8 September 1944): 13, in box 5, RG 23A, MMBA; FELO, SWPA, Survey of Reactions to Leaflet Propaganda, 1 January 1945, p. 5, box 4, entry 283K, RG 331, NARA; PWB, SWPA, Psychological Warfare Reactions and Developments, no. 4 (15 November 1944): 2, in box 31, entry 283K, RG 331, NARA.

29. SEATIC, Publication no. 138, Ground Operations Bulletin, item 1514, 5 May 1945, pp. 39–40, box 5, entry 283L, RG 331, NARA.

30. Department of the Navy, ONI, Special Warfare Branch, "Combat Wariness of Japanese Officers," 15 January 1944, box 110, entry 358; and FELO, SWPA, Information Review, no. 5 (1 September 1943): 1, in box 228, entry 366A, both in RG 208, NARA.

31. ATIS, SWPA, Research Report no. 76, pt. 4, "Prominent Factors in Japanese Military Psychology," pp. 9–10, box 119, RG 3, MMBA.

32. ATIS, SWPA, Research Report no. 122, "Antagonism between Officers and Men in the Japanese Armed Forces," 10–11.

33. ATIS, SWPA, Research Report no. 122, "Antagonism between Officers and Men in the Japanese Armed Forces," 10–11.

34. ATIS, SWPA, Enemy Publication no. 237, "Personal Punishment and Military Discipline," 3 December 1944, pp. 1–11, box 132, RG 3, MMBA.

35. ATIS, SWPA, Enemy Publication no. 336, "Extralegal Punishment," 25 March 1945, pp. 1–7, box 136, RG 3, MMBA.

36. FELO, SWPA, Information Review, no. 3 (11 August 1943): 4, in box 228, entry 366A, RG 208, NARA; ATIS, SWPA, Research Report no. 76, pt. 4, "Prominent Factors in Japanese Military Psychology," 25, and Research Report no. 123, "Control by Rumor in the Japanese Armed Forces," 20 April 1945, p. 3, box 120, both in RG 3, MMBA; OWI, FMAD, Report 26, "Principal Findings Regarding Japanese Morale during the War," 6; ATIS, SWPA, Research Report no. 76, pt. 1, "Self-Immolation as a Factor in Japanese Military Psychology," app. D, 41.

37. ATIS, SWPA, Research Report no. 123, "Control by Rumor in the Japanese Armed Forces," 8–10.

38. On censorship in the Japanese army see ATIS, SWPA, Information Request Report, nos. 79 (28 August 1943) and 120 (15 November 1945), in box 122 and 120, respectively, RG 3, MMBA.

39. FELO, SWPA, Survey of Reactions to Leaflet Propaganda, 1 January 1945, 4; FELO, SWPA, Reactions to Propaganda, no. 10 (15 July 1944): 2, in box 225, entry 366A, RG 208, NARA.

40. PWB, SWPA, Psychological Warfare Reactions and Developments, no. 11 (1 June 1945): 1, 3–4, in box 31, entry 283L, RG 331, NARA; AMF, Weekly Intelligence Review, no. 140 (23 June 1945): 23–24, in box 6, RG 23A, MMBA.

41. See ATIS, SWPA, Enemy Publication nos. 80 and 82, "Morale Lectures," 29 and 31 January 1944, box 125, RG 3, MMBA. Extract from captured "Order of the Day," 23 June 1945, cited in AMF, Weekly Intelligence Review, no. 146 (4 August 1945): 16, in box 6, RG 23A, MMBA.

42. HQ, SACSEA, PWD, Information Review, no. 14 (February 1945): 3, in box 18, entry 283L, RG 331, NARA; OWI, FMAD, Report 19, "Lae-Salamaua Campaign," 22; FELO, SWPA, Information Review, no. 3 (11 August 1943): 3, in box 228, entry 366A, RG 208, NARA.

43. OWI, FMAD, Report 19, "Lae-Salamaua Campaign," 33. ATIS reports of interrogations of Japanese POWs are in boxes 111–16, RG 3, MMBA.

44. OWI, FMAD, Report 19, "Lae-Salamaua Campaign," 16; ATIS, SWPA, Research Report no. 76, pt. 1, "Self-Immolation as a Factor in Japanese Military Psychology," 8.

45. ATIS, SWPA, POW Interrogation Report 31, serial no. 45, p. 9, box 111, and POW Interrogation Report 115-B, serial no. 248, p. 26, box 112, RG 3, MMBA.

46. ATIS, SWPA, Research Report no. 76, pt. 1, "Self-Immolation as a Factor in Japanese Military Psychology," 17; ATIS, SWPA, POW Interrogation Report 133, serial no. 211, p. 4, box 112, RG 3, MMBA. On the Japanese army's practice of disposing of the sick and wounded see ATIS, SWPA, Research Report no. 117, "Infringement of the Laws of War and Ethics by the Japanese Medical Corps," 26 January 1945, box 120, RG 3, MMBA.

47. AMF, Intelligence Summary, no. 188 (31 July 1942): 4, in box 1, RG 23A, MMBA; OWI, FMAD, Report 18, "Papuan Phase of the New Guinea Campaign," 7.

48. Ienaga, *Pacific War*, 49.

49. See, e.g., OWI, Area 3, Japan Section, "Study of the 'No-Surrender' Slogan and 'Self-Sacrifice' Principal of the Japanese," 23 March 1945, box 228, entry 366A, RG 208, NARA.

50. ATIS, SWPA, Research Report no. 76, pt. 1, "Self-Immolation as a Factor in Japanese Military Psychology," 21.

51. ATIS, SWPA, Research Report no. 76, pt. 1, "Self-Immolation as a Factor in Japanese Military Psychology," 21, 32–33.

52. ATIS, SWPA, Report no. 18, "Papuan Phase of the New Guinea Campaign," 7.

53. AMF, Weekly Intelligence Review, no. 137 (2 June 1945): 23–24, in box 6, RG 23A, MMBA.

54. The propaganda work of Japanese POWs is discussed in Allison B. Gilmore, " 'We Have Been Reborn': Japanese Prisoners and the Allied Propaganda War in the Southwest Pacific," *Pacific Historical Review* 64 (1995): 195–215.

55. ATIS, SWPA, Report no. 76, pt. 1, "Self-Immolation as a Factor in Japanese Military Psychology," 33; OWI, FMAD, Report 19, "Lae-Salamaua Campaign," 25, 30.

56. OWI, Area 3, Far East, *Leaflet Newsletter* 1, no. 5 (18 May 1945): 19, in box 21, entry 283L, RG 331, NARA.

57. AMF, Weekly Intelligence Review, no. 145 (28 July 1945): 16, and no. 101 (3 June 1944–7 July 1944): 11, in box 6, RG 23A, MMBA.

58. AMF, Weekly Intelligence Review, no. 108 (18–25 August 1944): 12–13, in box 5, RG 23A, MMBA; PWB, SWPA, Daily Collation Summary, "Futility of Soldiers Seeking Death," 2 January 1945, box 13, entry 283L, RG 331, NARA; OWI, Area 3, Japan Section, "Study of the 'No-Surrender' Slogan and 'Self-Sacrifice' Principal," 20.

5 · Exploiting the Weaknesses

1. Fellers, "Report on Psychological Warfare," 2.

2. Linebarger, *Psychological Warfare*, 46–47.

3. Lerner, *Sykewar*, 202. The three themes that World War II planners rejected, he contends, were propaganda of hope, particularistic propaganda, and revolutionary propaganda.

4. Fellers, "Report on Psychological Warfare," 1 and annex 4, "Basic Military Plan," 5.

5. Memo, Fellers to PWB planners, 16 January 1945, box 10, entry 283K, RG 331, NARA.

6. *Public Papers of the President of the United States: Containing the Public Messages, Speeches, and Statements of the President—Harry S. Truman, April 12 to December 31, 1945* (Washington DC: USGPO, 1961), 45, 50.

7. See Ellis M. Zacharias, *Secret Missions: The Story of an Intelligence Officer* (New York: G. P. Putnam's Sons, 1946); and Morris Janowitz, "Captain Zacharias's Broadcasts to Japan," in Daugherty and Janowitz, *Psychological Warfare Casebook*, 279–91.

8. PWB, SWPA, "Peace with Honor," Sandberg-Hallgren Collection.

9. Memo, Fellers to Greene, "Concerning Weekly Military Plan for Psychological Warfare, 13–19 May 1945," 14 May 1945, box 3, entry 283J, RG 331, NARA.

10. Memo, Fellers to Greene, "Comment on Weekly Military Plan for Psychological Warfare, 20–26 May 1945," 24 May 1945, box 3, entry 283K, RG 331, NARA.

11. Willoughby to Stiver (OWI), 27 February 1943, box 1, entry 6G, RG 208, NARA; Kenney to Deputy Chief of Staff, GHQ, 20 November 1943, box 3, entry 283J, RG 331, NARA.

12. Memo, Leighton to Vinacke, "Annex on Treatment of Japanese Emperor," 21 November 1944; and memo, Leighton to George Taylor, "The Japanese Emperor," 13 July 1945, both in box 443, entry 378, RG 208, NARA.

13. Memo, Leighton to Vinacke, "Annex on Treatment of Japanese Emperor," 21 November 1944. See also memo, John K. Fairbank to George Taylor, "The Japanese Emperor," box 443, entry 378, RG 208, NARA.

14. Memo, Sidney F. Mashbir to Willoughby, 9 November 1943, box 3, entry 283J, RG 331, NARA; OWI, FMAD, Report 27, "The Japanese Emperor," 31 October 1945, pp. 5, 59–60, box 335, entry 172, RG 331, NARA.

15. APWC, "Directive for Political Warfare against the Japanese," 15 April 1942, box 3, entry 283J, RG 331, NARA.

16. Fellers, "Report on Psychological Warfare," annex 4, "Basic Military Plan," app. A, "Steps in Planning," 6; and annex 3, "Answer to Japan," 21–22.

17. FELO, SWPA, Reactions to Propaganda, no. 15 (15 December 1944): 5–6, in box 4, entry 283K, RG 331, NARA; FELO, SWPA, Reactions to Propaganda, no. 12 (15 September 1944): 2–3, in box 334, entry 172, RG 165, NARA; OWI, FMAD, Report 19, "Lae-Salamaua Campaign," 35; HQ, Allied Air Forces, SWPA, Intelligence Summary, no. 175 (22 January 1945): 23, in box 39, RG 30, MMBA; FELO, SWPA, Survey of Reactions to Leaflet Propaganda, 1 January 1945, 2.

18. FELO, SWPA, "Report on FELO Leaflet Activities," 12 May 1944, p. 1, box 225, entry 366A, RG 208, NARA; Bonner F. Fellers, "Special Military Plan for Psychological Warfare, Implementation to Appendix E, Basic Military Plan for Psychological Warfare in the Southwest Pacific Area," pp. 3–4, box 3, entry 283J, RG 331, NARA.

19. Fellers, "Report on Psychological Warfare," annex 4, "Basic Military Plan," app. A, "Steps in Planning," 3.

20. FELO, SWPA, serial no. 403, Sandberg-Hallgren Collection.

21. FELO, SWPA, serial no. 1005, Sandberg-Hallgren Collection.

22. FELO, SWPA, serial no. 512, Sandberg-Hallgren Collection. See also PWB, SWPA, leaflets 6-J-1, "Lonely Japan," and 42-J-6, "Germany Capitulates," 31 March 1945, both in Sandberg-Hallgren Collection.

23. FELO, SWPA, serial no. 101, Sandberg-Hallgren Collection.

24. PWB, SWPA, leaflet 32-J-1, "One Stride after Another," box 56, RG 4, MMBA.

25. FELO, SWPA, serial no. 504, Sandberg-Hallgren Collection.

26. PWB, SWPA, leaflet 28-J-6, "Luzon," 4 January 1945, Sandberg-Hallgren Collection.

27. FELO, SWPA, "Your Leaders Are Liars!" serial nos. 2022, 2023, and 2024, Sandberg-Hallgren Collection.

28. PWB, SWPA, leaflet 11-J-1, "Japanese Claims," Sandberg-Hallgren Collection.

29. FELO, SWPA, serial no. J-249, box 18, entry 283L, RG 331, NARA.

30. PWB, SWPA, leaflet 1-J-10, "X Corps Prisoner of War Leaflet," 1 November 1944, Sandberg-Hallgren Collection.

31. PWB, SWPA, leaflet 21-J-8, "Cebu Prisoner's Surrender No. 1," Sandberg-Hallgren Collection.

32. PWB, SWPA, leaflet 22-J-1, "Watching Fires on the Further Shore," box 56, RG 4, MMBA.

33. PWB, SWPA, leaflet 23-J-1, "Two Strategies," box 56, RG 4, MMBA.

34. PWB, SWPA, leaflet 20-J-1, "General Nogi," box 15, Fellers Papers.

35. PWB, SWPA, leaflet 19-J-1, "One General Gains Fame While Tens of Thousands Die," Sandberg-Hallgren Collection.

36. PWB, SWPA, leaflet 41-J-6, "Who's Chasing Who?" 7 March 1945, Sandberg-Hallgren Collection.

37. FELO, SWPA, serial nos. 1006, 1007, Sandberg-Hallgren Collection.

38. PWB, SWPA, leaflet 7-J-11, "Order to Kill Japanese Sick and Wounded," Sandberg-Hallgren Collection.

39. PWB, SWPA, leaflet 34-J-6, "Empire Day," 7 February 1945, Sandberg-Hallgren Collection.

40. FELO, SWPA, "Open Your Eyes!" serial no. 513, Sandberg-Hallgren Collection.

41. PWB, SWPA, leaflet 101-J-1, "War Has Passed Luzon," Sandberg-Hallgren Collection.

42. PWB, SWPA, leaflet 21-J-1, "Where Is the Japanese Fleet?" box 56, RG 4, MMBA.

43. FELO, SWPA, serial no. 500, Sandberg-Hallgren Collection.

44. FELO, SWPA, "Think It Over Carefully!" serial no. 705, Sandberg-Hallgren Collection.

45. PWB, SWPA, leaflet 4-J-11, "Army Protects Navy," box 56, RG 4, MMBA.

46. PWB, SWPA, leaflet 4-J-3, "The Way to Safety, no. 4," box 15, Fellers Papers.

47. PWB, SWPA, leaflet 106-J-1, box 56, RG 4, MMBA.

48. PWB, SWPA, leaflet 29-J-6, "Luzon Surrender Appeal," 20 January 1945, Sandberg-Hallgren Collection; FELO, SWPA, serial no. 1005, Sandberg-Hallgren Collection; PWB, SWPA, leaflet 33-J-1, "Type 38 Rifle," box 56, RG 4, MMBA; FELO, SWPA, serial no. 504, Sandberg-Hallgren Collection.

49. PWB, SWPA, leaflet 10-J-10, 31 May 1945, Sandberg-Hallgren Collection; FELO, SWPA, serial nos. J.184A and J.224, box 18, entry 283L, RG 331, NARA; HQ, Fourteenth Corps, G-2, "Propaganda Drop no. 10," 3 September 1944, box 28, entry 283L, RG 331, NARA.

50. PWB, SWPA, leaflet 106-J-6, "Personal Surrender Appeal," Sandberg-Hallgren Collection.

51. FELO, SWPA, serial no. 520, Sandberg-Hallgren Collection.

52. PWB, SWPA, leaflet 3-J-11, "General Patrick's Surrender Leaflet," 2 April 1945, and FELO, SWPA, serial no. 518, both in Sandberg-Hallgren Collection; PWB, SWPA, leaflet 111-J-1, "Road to a New Life," box 56, RG 4, MMBA.

53. PWB, SWPA, leaflet 106-J-6, "Personal Surrender Appeal," Sandberg-Hallgren Collection.

54. PWB, SWPA, leaflet 2-J-40, "Negros Surrender," 28 March 1945, box 24, entry 283L, RG 331, NARA.

6 ▪ Fine–tuning the Mechanism and the Message

1. ATIS, SWPA, "Progress Report from Organization, 19 September 1942, to Reorganization, 8 September 1944," 14 September 1944, box 72, RG 3, MMBA.

2. MIS, GHQ, SWPA, FEC, SCAP, *The Intelligence Series*, vol. 5, *Operations of the Allied Translator and Interpreter Section*, GHQ, SWPA, i–ii, 31–35; ATIS, "Progress Report."

3. The most complete set of ATIS reports available to researchers is in RG 3, MMBA.

4. OWI, FMAD, "Report on Wartime Analysis of Japanese Morale," p. 1, box 443, entry 378, RG 208, NARA. For a complete list of FMAD's members and an analysis of its wartime activities see Leighton, *Human Relations in a Changing World*.

5. Many of FMAD's wartime studies are located in box 9, entry 283K, RG 331, NARA. FMAD reports are also dispersed throughout RG 208 and RG 165, NARA.

For reports on Japanese military morale see OWI, FMAD, Report 27, "The Japanese Emperor"; and the following from RG 208, NARA: OWI, FMAD, "Study of the 'No-Surrender' Slogan and 'Self-Sacrifice' Principal of the Japanese," 23 March 1945, box 228, entry 366A; OWI, FMAD, "The Japanese Fighting Man," box 443, entry 378; OWI, FMAD, "Japanese Military Morale," 19 October 1944, box 443, entry 378.

For FMAD studies on the impact of Allied propaganda see OWI, FMAD, Semi-Monthly Reports 13, "Reactions to Allied Propaganda Themes," 14, "Influence of Allied Propaganda," and 15, "Persistent and Changeable Attitudes of Japanese Forces"; memos, Leighton to George Taylor, "Increasing Effectiveness of Allied Propaganda in Inducing Japanese Surrender and Desertion," 7 May 1945, and "Suggestions for Psychological Warfare in Combat Areas," 5 June 1945, box 443, entry 378, RG 208, NARA.

6. Memo, Fellers to Collation Section, 29 August 1944. See also memo, Fellers to Field Units, 13 September 1944.

7. PWB, SWPA, Daily Collation Summary, "Challenge the Adequacy of Spiritual Force Alone," 30 September 1944, box 12, entry 283L, RG 331, NARA.

8. PWB, SWPA, Daily Collation Summary, "Plant Suspicion of Leadership," 31 January 1945, box 14, entry 283L, RG 331, NARA; PWB, leaflet 33-J-1, "Type 38 Rifle."

9. PWB's Daily Collation Summaries are located in boxes 7, 8, 12, and 14, entry 283L, RG 331, NARA.

10. PWB, SWPA, Review of Significant Trends Discerned in Daily Collation Summaries, no. 3 (16 October 1944): 6, in box 7, entry 283L, RG 331, NARA.

11. Patterns, Trends, and Prospective Developments Offering Opportunities for Exploitation and Implementation of Basic Military Plan, and Japanese Trends of Psychological Significance are located in boxes 31 and 21, entry 283L, RG 331, NARA.

12. OWI, China Division, Yenan Report no. 69, "Criticisms of Southwest Pacific Leaflets by Propaganda Department of JPEL," March 1945, box 331, entry 172, RG 165, NARA.

13. Propaganda Committee, "Mechanics of Propaganda," by Koji Ariyoshi, 7 November 1944, box 20, entry 148, RG 226, NARA.

14. AIB, SWPA, "Reports from Allied Intelligence Bureau, 1943," p. 41, box 23, RG 30, MMBA; Fellers, "Report on Psychological Warfare," annex 4, "Basic Military Plan," 3.

15. Department of the Navy, ONI, Special Warfare Branch, memo, Head, Special Warfare Branch, to Overseas Branch, OWI, "Japanese Reliance on Spiritual Superiority," 18 February 1944, p. 2, box 110, entry 358, RG 208, NARA; OWI, FMAD, Semi-Monthly Report 13, "Reactions to Allied Propaganda Themes," 7–9.

16. OWI, FMAD, Report 18, "Papuan Phase of the New Guinea Campaign," 11; memo, Ruth Benedict to Leonard Doob, "Propaganda for Japanese Front-line Surrender," 28 October 1944, box 110, entry 358, RG 208, NARA; OWI, Official Dispatch, John Hiestand (Brisbane) to George Taylor and Vinacke, 9 January 1945, box 110, entry 358, RG 208, NARA.

17. The following discussion on Japanese POWs' reaction to Allied propaganda is based on a variety of sources, especially FELO's Information Bulletins, Information Reviews, and Reactions to Propaganda; OWI's *Leaflet Newsletter*s and FMAD's many reports; PWB's Psychological Warfare Reactions and Developments; SACSEA, PWD's Information Reviews, and SEATIC's Psychological Warfare Bulletins; CINCPAC-CINCPOA bulletins; and ATIS's POW interrogation reports.

18. FELO, SWPA, Reactions to Propaganda, no. 15 (15 December 1944): 6–7.

19. Memo, Information Section, ATIS, GHQ, to Co-ordinator, ATIS, GHQ, "Propaganda Leaflet: Geneva Convention," 31 May 1945, box 3, Fellers Papers.

20. Walker, "Psychological Warfare in the South-West Pacific," 49–64, quotation on 54.

21. PWB, SWPA, Psychological Warfare Reactions and Developments, no. 2 (13 October 1944), box 31, entry 283L, RG 331, NARA.

22. Breckenridge Long to Secretary of War Henry L. Stimson, 12 August 1943, box 333, entry 172, RG 165, NARA.

23. Memo, Acting Chief, Propaganda Branch, to Joint Security Control, "Identifiability of Photographs of Japanese Prisoners," 30 March 1945, box 333, entry 172, RG 165, NARA.

24. Memo, Leaflet Section to Members of the Operations Board, "Field Party's Request for Japanese Surrender Leaflet," 4 September 1944, box 2, entry 283K, RG 331, NARA.

25. Greene to Fellers, 6 September 1944, box 3, Fellers Papers; memo, R. G. Ferguson, HQ, Seventh Infantry Division, to Asst. Chief of Staff, G-2, United States Army Forces, Pacific Ocean Areas, via Asst. Chief of Staff, G-2, Twenty-fourth Corps, "Psychological Warfare," 10 January 1945, box 14, entry 283K, RG 331, NARA.

26. Greene to Fellers, 4 February 1945, box 3, Fellers Papers.

27. OWI, Psychological Warfare Team, India-Burma Theater, Reaction Report 9, "Reasons Why Japanese Soldiers Accept or Reject Allied Propaganda," 20 April 1945, box 18, entry 283K, RG 331, NARA.

28. FELO, SWPA, Reactions to Propaganda, no. 12 (15 September 1944): 1.

29. Greene to Fellers, 10, 19 October 1944, box 3, Fellers Papers.

30. Greene to Fellers, 6 February 1945, box 3, Fellers Papers; "Report of Lt. Col. Edward A. Pagels, China Theater Psychological Warfare Officer to the Psychological Warfare Board on 27 May 1945," box 13, entry 148, RG 226, NARA.

31. OWI, Area 3, Far East, *Leaflet Newsletter* 1, no. 2 (6 April 1945): 14–17, and 1, no. 5 (18 May 1945): 18–21, in box 21, entry 283L, RG 331, NARA. Issues of the *Rakkasan News* are in box 3, entry 283L, RG 331, NARA; and box 56, RG 4, MMBA.

32. PWB, SWPA, Psychological Warfare Reactions and Developments, no. 9 (3 May 1945): 7, in box 31, entry 283L, RG 331, NARA. For other examples of front-line broadcasting see boxes 13, 15, and 18, entry 283K, RG 331; and PWB's Collation Section reports under the title "Effectiveness of Frontline Broadcasts in Inducing Surrender and Lowering Morale," box 4, entry 283K, RG 331, NARA.

33. PWB, SWPA, Psychological Warfare Reactions and Developments, no. 11 (1 June 1945): 2–3, and no. 5 (20 December 1944), in box 31; and FELO, SWPA, Information Bulletin, no. 12 (16 August 1945): 1, in box 16, both in entry 283L, RG 331, NARA.

34. ATIS, SWPA, Information Request Report, no. 96 (25 November 1943): 5, in box 123, RG 3, MMBA.

35. See Masaharu Ano, "Loyal Linguists: Nisei of World War II Learned Japanese in Minnesota," *Minnesota History* 45 (1977): 273–87; Bill Hosokawa, "Our Own Japanese in the Pacific War," *American Legion Magazine*, July 1964; Stanley L. Falk and Warren M. Tsuneishi, eds., *American Patriots: MIS in the War against Japan* (Vienna VA: Japanese American Veterans Association of Washington DC, 1995); Tad Ichinokuchi, ed., *John Aiso and the M.I.S.: Japanese-American Soldiers in the Military Intelligence Service, World War II* (Los Angeles: Military Intelligence Service Club of Southern California, 1988); Joseph D. Harrington, *Yankee Samurai: The Secret Role of Nisei in America's Pacific Victory* (Detroit: Pettigrew, 1979); and Lynn Crost, *Honor by Fire: Japanese Americans at War in Europe and the Pacific* (Novato CA: Presidio, 1994). The Naval Language School in Boulder, Colo-

rado, and the Royal Australian Air Force Language School in Melbourne, Australia, also provided trained linguists for the war effort.

7 • Assessing the Results

1. Fellers, "Report on Psychological Warfare," 16.

2. HQ, SACSEA, PWD, Information Review, no. 18 (19 July 1945): 2, in box 18, entry 283L, RG 331, NARA.

3. FELO, SWPA, Reactions to Propaganda, no. 13 (15 October 1944): 2–7, in box 4, entry 283K, RG 331, NARA.

4. OWI, FMAD, Semi-Monthly Report 14, "Influence of Allied Propaganda," 5; FELO, SWPA, Reactions to Propaganda, no. 16 (1 January 1945): 3–5, in box 225, entry 366A, RG 208, NARA; OWI, FMAD, Report 17, "Recent Trends in Japanese Military Morale as Revealed in Interrogations of 251 Military POWs Captured in the Philippines, 15 January to 15 March 1945," 9 April 1945, p. 4, box 9, entry 283K, RG 331, NARA.

5. OWI, FMAD, Report 2, "The Influence of Allied Propaganda as Revealed in Reports of Interrogations with 556 POWs," p. 5, in box 335, entry 172, RG 165, NARA.

6. FELO, SWPA, Reactions to Propaganda, no. 13 (15 October 1944): 3; PWB, SWPA, Psychological Warfare Reactions and Developments, no. 2 (13 October 1944): 4, and no. 10 (8 May 1945): 2, both in box 31, entry 283L, RG 331, NARA; OWI, Area 3, Far East, *Leaflet Newsletter* 1, no. 8 (29 June 1945): 7, in box 21, entry 283L, RG 331, NARA.

7. HQ, SACSEA, PWD, Information Review, no. 12 (December 1944): 6, in box 18, entry 283L, RG 331; FELO, SWPA, Reactions to Propaganda, no. 13 (15 October 1944): 1.

8. FELO, SWPA, Survey of Reactions to Leaflet Propaganda, 1 January 1945, 3–4.

9. OWI, FMAD, Semi-Monthly Report 14, "Influence of Allied Propaganda," 10; AMF, Weekly Intelligence Review, no. 112 (15–22 September 1944): 13, in box 5, RG 23A, MMBA.

10. AMF, Weekly Intelligence Review, no. 144 (21 July 1945): 19 and no. 145 (28 July 1945): 19, in box 6, RG 23A, MMBA. See also FELO, SWPA, Information Bulletin, no. 12 (16 August 1945): 10, in box 16; and HQ, SACSEA, PWD, Information Review, no. 18 (June 1945): 2, in box 18, both in entry 283L, RG 331, NARA.

11. PWB, SWPA, Psychological Warfare Reactions and Developments, no. 12 (18 June 1945): 1, in box 31, entry 283L, RG 331, NARA.

12. PWB, SWPA, Psychological Warfare Reactions and Developments, no. 7 (10 March 1945): 5–8, in box 31, entry 283L, RG 331, NARA.

13. FMAD, SWPA, Report 17, "Recent Trends in Japanese Military Morale," 4–11.

14. Memo, Greene to Fellers, 9 June 1945, box 3, Fellers Papers.

15. Carl Berger, *An Introduction to Wartime Leaflets* (Washington DC: Special Operations Research Office, The American University, 1959), 115.

16. Fellers, "Report on Psychological Warfare," 11.

17. The numbers of POWs captured annually were compiled from "Japanese Prisoners of War," 19 May 1945, box 333, entry 172, RG 165, NARA; statistical summaries, box 15, Fellers Papers; and Fellers to MacArthur, 5 August 1945, box 14, RG 3, MMBA. The numbers of FELO prisoners are from FELO, SWPA, "Report on Activities of Far Eastern Liaison Office for Period June 1942 to September 1945," box 2, Fellers Papers.

18. HQ, Sixth Army, Office of the Assistant Chief of Staff, G-2, "Basic Sixth Army Plan for Psychological Warfare."

19. Walker, "Psychological Warfare in the South-West Pacific," 49–64, 55.

20. ATIS, SWPA, Research Report no. 76, pt. 4, "Prominent Factors in Japanese Military Psychology," 16.

21. OWI, Area 3, Far East, *Leaflet Newsletter* 1, no. 8 (29 June 1945): 6; and PWB, SWPA, Psychological Warfare Reactions and Developments, no. 6 (25 January 1945): 8, both in box 21, entry 283L, RG 331, NARA.

22. AMF, Weekly Intelligence Review, no. 108 (18–25 August 1944): 12–13, in box 5, RG 23A, MMBA.

23. FELO, SWPA, Reactions to Propaganda, no. 13 (15 October 1944): 2, in box 4, entry 283K; FELO, SWPA, Information Bulletin, no. 12 (16 August 1945): 13, in box 16, entry 283L; and PWB, SWPA, Psychological Warfare Reactions and Developments, no. 8 (10 April 1945): 4, in box 31, entry 283L, all in RG 331, NARA.

24. FELO, SWPA, Survey of Reactions to Leaflet Propaganda, 1 January 1945, pp. 2–3, box 225, entry 366A, RG 208, NARA; OWI, FMAD, Semi-Monthly Report 14, "Influence of Allied Propaganda," 14.

25. PWB, SWPA, Collation Sheets, "Effectiveness of Leaflets in Lowering Enemy Morale," box 5, entry 283K, RG 331, NARA.

26. CINCPAC-CINCPOA, Bulletin no. 107–45, 14 May 1945, Translations & Interrogations, no. 28, "Japanese Propaganda and Counter-Propaganda Techniques," pp. 39–52, box 4, entry 283L, RG 331, NARA.

27. FELO, SWPA, Information Bulletin, no. 2 (16 March 1945): 4, in box 16, entry 283L, RG 331; FELO, SWPA, "Report on FELO Leaflet Activities," 12 May 1944, p. 3, box 225, entry 366A, RG 208; and FELO, SWPA, Information Review, no. 16 (1 August 1944): 8, in box 228, entry 366A, RG 208, all in NARA.

28. FELO, SWPA, Reactions to Propaganda, no. 12 (15 September 1944): 2.

29. FELO, SWPA, Reactions to Propaganda, no. 13 (15 October 1944): 3–4; Walker, "Psychological Warfare in the South-West Pacific," 53.

30. OWI, FMAD, Semi-Monthly Report 14, "Influence of Allied Propaganda," 11;

PWB, SWPA, Psychological Warfare Reactions and Developments, no. 6 (25 January 1945): 6, in box 31, entry 283L, RG 331, NARA.

31. Excerpt from notebook captured on Leyte, 7 December 1944, cited in OWI, Area 3, Japan Section, "Study of the 'No Surrender' Slogan and 'Self–Sacrifice' Principal," 18.

32. CINCPAC-CINCPOA, Bulletin no. 140–45, 7 June 1945, Translations & Interrogations, no. 31, pp. 67–69, box 4, entry 283L, RG 331, NARA.

33. AMF, Weekly Intelligence Review, no. 129 (7 April 1945): 23, in box 6, RG 23A, MMBA; OWI, Area 3, Far East, *Leaflet Newsletter* 1, no. 2 (6 April 1945): 9, in box 21, entry 283L, RG 331, NARA.

34. FELO, SWPA, Information Review, no. 5 (1 September 1943): 2, in box 228, entry 366A, RG 208, NARA; FELO, SWPA, Survey of Reactions to Leaflet Propaganda, 1 January 1945, box 4, entry 283K, RG 331, NARA; AMF, Weekly Intelligence Review, no. 66 (29 October–5 November 1943): 13, in box 3, RG 23A, MMBA.

35. FELO, SWPA, Survey of Reactions to Leaflet Propaganda, 1 January 1945, p. 3, box 4, entry 283K, RG 331, NARA; AMF, Weekly Intelligence Review, no. 98 (9–16 June 1944): 10–11, in box 5, RG 23A, MMBA.

36. PWB, SWPA, Psychological Warfare Reactions and Developments, no. 4 (15 November 1944): 1, in box 31, entry 283L, RG 331, NARA.

37. Report from the Fifty-third Infantry Regiment, IJA, cited in ATIS, SWPA, Research Report no. 76, pt. 4, "Prominent Factors in Japanese Military Psychology," 15.

38. AMF, Weekly Intelligence Review, no. 100 (23–30 June 1944): 20–21, in box 5, RG 23A, MMBA; PWB, SWPA, Psychological Warfare Reactions and Developments, no. 10 (8 May 1945): 6, in box 31, entry 283L, RG 331, NARA.

39. PWB, SWPA, Psychological Warfare Reactions and Developments, no. 4 (15 November 1944): 3, in box 31; HQ, SACSEA, PWD, Information Review, no. 16 (1 August 1944): 3, in box 18; and OWI, Area 3, Far East, *Leaflet Newsletter* 1, no. 8 (29 June 1945): 6–7, in box 21, all in entry 283L, RG 331, NARA.

40. FELO, SWPA, Survey of Reactions to Leaflet Propaganda, 1 January 1945, p. 3, box 4, entry 283K, RG 331, NARA; OWI, FMAD, Semi-Monthly Report 13, "Reactions to Allied Propaganda Themes," 5.

41. ATIS, SWPA, Current Translation no. 126, 23 June 1944, p. 38, box 144, RG 3, MMBA.

42. OWI, FMAD, Report 20, "Aitape-Hollandia Campaign," 13.

43. FELO, SWPA, Reactions to Propaganda, no. 16 (15 January 1945): 1, and no. 15 (15 December 1944): 7.

44. Shils and Janowitz, "Cohesion and Disintegration in the Wehrmacht," 558; OWI, FMAD, Report 30, "Japanese Personality and Reactions as Seen in Soldiers' Diaries," 19 December 1945, p. 22, box 335, entry 172, RG 165, NARA.

45. OWI, FMAD, Report 26, "Principal Findings Regarding Japanese Morale during the War," and Semi-Monthly Report 15, "Persistent and Changeable Attitudes of the Japanese Forces," 4.

46. OWI, FMAD, Report 17, "Recent Trends in Japanese Military Morale," 9–11.

47. PWB, SWPA, Daily Collation Summary, "Did Leaflets Induce Surrender?" June 1945, box 5, entry 283K, RG 331, NARA.

48. Shils and Janowitz, "Cohesion and Disintegration in the Wehrmacht," 563–67.

49. Shils and Janowitz, "Cohesion and Disintegration in the Wehrmacht," 563, 570–72.

50. PWB, SWPA, Psychological Warfare Reactions and Developments, no. 3 (23 October 1944): 5, in box 31, entry 283L, RG 331, NARA.

51. PWB, SWPA, Daily Collation Summary, "Were Leaflets Effective in Lowering Morale of the Men in PW's Unit?" box 5, entry 283K, RG 331, NARA.

52. PWB, SWPA, Daily Collation Summary, "Effectiveness of Leaflets in Inducing Surrender," box 5, entry 283K, RG 331, NARA.

53. PWB, SWPA, Daily Collation Summary, "Were Leaflets Effective in Lowering Morale of the Men in PW's Unit?"

54. Walker, "Psychological Warfare in the South-West Pacific," 63–64.

55. Fellers, "Report on Psychological Warfare," 11.

56. Berger, *Introduction to Wartime Leaflets,* 58.

57. Berger, *Introduction to Wartime Leaflets,* 58.

58. Memo, Robert Kleiman to George Taylor, 17 January 1945, box 4, entry 283K, RG 331, NARA.

59. Fellers, "Report on Psychological Warfare," 15.

60. OWI, FMAD, Semi-Monthly Report 13, "Reactions to Allied Propaganda Themes," 1; and Report 26, "Principal Findings Regarding Japanese Morale during the War," 8.

61. Shils and Janowitz, "Cohesion and Disintegration in the Wehrmacht," 580–82.

Bibliographic Essay

Although a great many secondary sources have been published on the Pacific War generally as well as on specialized topics pertaining to that conflict, no comprehensive history of psychological warfare against Japan exists. Therefore, this study is based chiefly on primary sources. Nonetheless, many secondary works proved useful. This essay does not provide a comprehensive bibliography of the available literature but is intended, first and foremost, to give the reader a clear understanding of the archival research that provided the foundation for this book, as well as a few of the most useful published sources.

Archival and Manuscript Sources

The primary-source research for this book was conducted at several archives. The collections of the MacArthur Memorial Bureau of Archives (MMBA), in Norfolk, Virginia, were indispensable. Most useful was Record Group (RG) 3, Records of Headquarters, South West Pacific Area, 1942–1945 (199 boxes), which includes more than 70 boxes of materials pertaining to the intelligence work of ATIS. ATIS research reports, translations of captured documents, POW interrogations, and bulletins shed much light on the Japanese army as an institution and the morale of its soldiers and were the most influential source of intelligence for psywar personnel in SWPA. RG 3 also includes the records of the Office of the Military Secretary (Brig. Gen. Bonner F. Fellers) and intelligence summaries issued by the Military Intelligence Service.

RG 4, Records of General Headquarters (GHQ), United States Army Forces Pacific (USAFPAC), 1942–1947 (57 boxes), is a significant repository of the propaganda leaflets and newspapers produced and disseminated in the theater. It also includes documents pertaining to intelligence and operations, as well as communiqués and press releases. RG 23, Papers of Major General Charles A. Willoughby, United States Army (23 boxes), and RG 23A, Facsimiles of Papers of Major General Charles A. Willoughby, United States Army, from the National Archives, 1942–1945 (6 boxes), contain issues of the AMF Weekly Intelligence Review as well as data on the operations of AIB. The MMBA also houses RG 2, Records of Headquarters, United States Army Forces in the Far East (USAFFE), 1941–1942 (14 boxes), and RG 30, Papers of Lieutenant General Richard K. Sutherland, United States Army, 1941–1945 (45 boxes). These records include issues of the Allied Air Forces Intelligence Summary as well as AIB reports.

The MMBA contains two other official sets of reports essential to a study of intelligence and propaganda operations in SWPA. First, Brig. Gen. Bonner F. Fellers's "Report on Psychological Warfare in the Southwest Pacific Area: 1944–1945" is his official account of the organization and administration of PWB and the planning and conduct of psywar in the theater. It also includes more than thirty annexes pertaining to psywar, including Fellers's own research on Japanese military psychology in the 1930s, a listing of the source materials used by PWB, sample planning documents, and transcripts of radio and front-line broadcasts. (Fellers's report is also available at the U.S. Army Military History Research Collection, Carlisle Barracks, Pennsylvania; the U.S. Army Center of Military History, Washington DC; and in the Fellers Papers at the Hoover Institution on War, Revolution, and Peace, Palo Alto, California.)

Another useful source is *The Intelligence Series: G-2, USAFFE, SWPA, AFPAC, FEC, SCAP*, prepared by MIS, GHQ, Far East Command (FEC), Tokyo, 1948. The series comprises ten volumes plus documentary appendixes and was edited by MacArthur's General Staff, chiefly Maj. Gen. Charles A. Willoughby, who was intent both on proving the successes of the intelligence apparatus in SWPA and on voicing his contempt for the ad hoc structure of semiautonomous intelligence bureaus that resisted centralized control during the war. Volume 5, *Operations of the Allied Translator and Interpreter Section, GHQ, SWPA*, is most useful for those interested in understanding the vital wartime role of linguists. For the evolution of the theater's intelligence apparatus and its "diverse Allied intelligence agencies and bureaus" see volume 3, *Operations of the Military Intelligence Section, GHQ, SWPA & FEC/SCAP*, and volume 4, *Operations of the Allied Intelligence Bureau, GHQ, SWPA*. (*The Intelligence Series* can also be found in several other locations, including the U.S. Army Military History Research Collection, the U.S. Army Center of Military History, and the National Archives.)

The U.S. National Archives and Records Administration (NARA), in Washington DC, was also an invaluable repository of information on psywar against Japan. Most helpful was RG 331, Allied Operational and Occupational Headquarters, World War II, General Headquarters, South West Pacific Area. The records of PWB are located in RG 331, entry 283L (Publications File, 1943–1945, 33 boxes) and entry 283K (General File, 1944–1945, 18 boxes). Entry 283L includes what must be a nearly complete collection of the propaganda produced by both PWB and FELO for dissemination to civilian and military populations throughout the theater, as well as PWB's Daily Collation Summaries, which systematically collected intelligence of use to propagandists and applied it to specific propaganda objectives. It also includes many other pertinent reports, such as FELO's Information Bulletin and weekly summaries of PWB operations and output.

PWB records in RG 331 also include intelligence and psywar materials produced in other theaters of the war against Japan, including PWD, SACSEA (Psychological Warfare Division, Supreme Allied Command, Southeast Asia) Information Reviews, which summarized propaganda operations and their results in that theater; the Southeast Asia Translation and Interrogation Center (SEATIC) bulletins; and CINCPAC-CINCPOA's bulletins, which include Information Bulletins, Translations & Interrogations, Special Translations, and Psychological Warfare Developments and Responses. In addition to revealing much about the conduct of psywar in Asia and the Pacific, these records demonstrate the considerable interchange that existed among Allied psywar agencies.

RG 165, War Department General Staff, Military Intelligence Division (G-2), contains Correspondence of the Propaganda Branch (1939–1945). It also includes issues of OWI's *Leaflet Newsletter* and FELO's Reactions to Propaganda, both of which were essential to evaluating the scope and diversity of propaganda operations in SWPA and the Japanese response to them. RG 208, Records of the Office of War Information, was also quite useful, particularly those records relating to the activities of the Bureau of Overseas Intelligence but also materials collected in the Records of the Historian and Outpost Records. Most helpful were the materials documenting the work of FMAD, whose analyses were as vital to propagandists during the war as they are to historians now interested in understanding trends in Japanese morale. RG 208 contains the best available collection of FMAD's numerous studies of Japanese wartime morale, as well as copies of OWI's many publications, such as the *Leaflet Newsletter*.

Although OSS did not operate in SWPA, RG 226, Records of the Office of Strategic Services, nonetheless provides information on the OSS Research and Analysis Branch (R&A), which produced a variety of reports on morale in the enemy's armed forces and among civilian populations, as well as conditions in enemy nations that were used by propagandists in SWPA. OSS records also include interesting insights into the training of personnel and planning for morale operations throughout Asia and the Pacific.

The University of Nebraska–Lincoln's Love Library also has an impressive collection of propaganda materials from the Southwest Pacific. Accumulated during the war by John R. Sandberg and Frank Hallgren, who served with PWB, the Sandberg–Hallgren Collection includes Sandberg's diary, a large collection of PWB and FELO leaflets, and assorted documents pertaining to the organization and administration of PWB units operating with the U.S. Sixth Army.

Finally, the Hoover Institution on War, Revolution, and Peace, Stanford University, Palo Alto, California, maintains several collections of interest to students of psywar, including the G. William Gahagan Papers (assistant to the director of OWI, San Francisco), the William Henry Vatcher Jr. Papers (collections of propaganda materials pertaining to operations in the Central Pacific during World War II, as well as propaganda from the Korean War era), and the Paul Myron Anthony Linebarger Papers (Far Eastern specialist for OWI during World War II and author of several books and articles on psywar). For the purposes of this study, however, the Bonner Frank Fellers Papers (15 boxes) were most useful. The collection includes Fellers's correspondence and administrative reports during his tenure as head of PWB; weekly planning documents for PWB operations throughout the theater, including radio broadcasts to the Philippines and propaganda aimed at the home islands; and a sizable collection of the propaganda distributed in the Southwest Pacific.

Published Sources

For contemporary accounts of the rise of Japanese militarism by Western observers see Otto Tolischus, *Through Japanese Eyes* (New York: Reynal & Hitchcock, 1945) and *Tokyo Record* (New York: Reynal & Hitchcock, 1943); John Maki, *Japanese Militarism: Its Cause and Its Cure* (New York: Knopf, 1945); Thomas Arthur Bisson, *Shadow over Asia: The Rise of Militant Japan* (New York: Foreign Policy Association, 1942); Hugh Byas, *The Japanese Enemy: His Power and His Vulnerability* (New York: Knopf, 1942); Douglas Haring, *Blood on the Rising Sun* (Philadelphia: Macrae Smith, 1943); and Ian Morrison, *Our Japanese Foe* (New York: G. P. Putnam's Sons, 1943). The American ambassador to Japan from 1932 to 1942, Joseph C. Grew, provides an insider's view of diplomatic developments and conditions in Tokyo prior to Pearl Harbor in his *Report from Tokyo* (New York: Simon & Schuster, 1942) and *Ten Years in Japan: A Contemporary Record Drawn from the Diaries and Private and Official Papers of Joseph C. Grew, United States Ambassador to Japan, 1932–1942* (New York: Simon & Schuster, 1944).

Among the numerous significant historical analyses of the rise of Japanese militarism and the road to war in the 1930s the best are Robert J. C. Butow, *Tojo and the Coming of the War* (Princeton: Princeton Univ. Press, 1961); Richard J. Smethurst, *A Social Basis for Prewar Japanese Militarism: The Army and the Rural Community* (Berkeley: Univ. of California Press, 1974); James Crowley, *Japan's Quest for Autonomy: National Security and Foreign Policy, 1930–1938* (Princeton:

Princeton Univ. Press, 1966); Mark R. Peattie, *Ishiwara Kanji and Japan's Confrontation with the West* (Princeton: Princeton Univ. Press, 1975); and Akira Iriye, *The Origins of the Second World War: Asia and the Pacific* (London: Longman, 1987). Richard Smethurst, "The Creation of the Imperial Military Reserve Association," *Journal of Asian Studies* 30 (August 1971): 815–28, and Herbert E. Norman, *Soldier and Peasant in Japan: The Origins of Conscription* (New York: Institute of Pacific Relations, 1943), discuss the ties between the Japanese army and civilian society, and Roger F. Hackett, "The Meiji Leaders and Modernization: The Case of Yamagata Aritomo," in *Changing Japanese Attitudes toward Modernization*, edited by Marius B. Jansen (Princeton: Princeton Univ. Press, 1965), provides a useful analysis of the "father" of the modern Japanese army. A much more recent study of the internal dynamics of the Japanese army during the 1920s is Leonard A. Humphreys, *The Way of the Heavenly Sword: The Japanese Army in the 1920s* (Stanford: Stanford Univ. Press, 1995). See also Ivan Morris, *Japan, 1931–1945: Militarism, Fascism, Japanism?* (Boston: D. C. Heath, 1963); Richard Storry, *The Double Patriots: A Study in Japanese Nationalism* (Boston: Houghton Mifflin, 1957); Sharon Minichiello, *Retreat from Reform: Patterns of Political Behavior in Interwar Japan* (Honolulu: Univ. Press of Hawaii, 1984); Richard Mitchell, *Thought Control in Prewar Japan* (Ithaca: Cornell Univ. Press, 1976); Michio Kitahara, "Psychoanalytic Aspects of Japanese Militarism," *International Interaction* 12 (1985): 1–30.

For case studies of the incidents that catapulted the army into power see Ben-Ami Shillony, *Revolt in Japan: The Young Officers and the February 26, 1936 Incident* (Princeton: Princeton Univ. Press, 1973); James William Morley, ed., *Japan Erupts: The London Naval Conference and the Manchurian Incident, 1928–1932* (New York: Columbia Univ. Press, 1984); and Takehiko Yoshihashi, *Conspiracy at Mukden: The Rise of the Japanese Military* (New Haven: Yale Univ. Press, 1963). Alvin D. Coox's *Nomonhan: Japan against Russia, 1939* (Stanford: Stanford Univ. Press, 1985), assesses Japan's military capabilities in this brief but telling encounter with Russia. For Japanese perspectives on developments in the 1930s see Shigenori Togo, *The Cause of Japan* (Westport CT: Greenwood, 1956); and Mamoru Shigemitsu, *Japan and Her Destiny: My Struggle for Peace,* translated by Oswald White (New York: Dutton, 1958).

JAPANESE HISTORY AND CULTURE

Carol Gluck, *Japan's Modern Myths: Ideology in the Late Meiji Period* (Princeton: Princeton Univ. Press, 1985), provides a marvelous analysis of the ideas that transformed Meiji Japan. Ruth Benedict, *The Chrysanthemum and the Sword: Patterns in Japanese Culture* (Boston: Houghton Mifflin, 1946), is the classic study of Japan's culture and national character, conducted during wartime by a scholar who served in OWI's FMAD. For a discussion of Benedict's methodology and similar national-character studies see Richard H. Minear, "Cross-Cultural

Perception and World War II: American Japanists of the 1940s and Their Images of Japan," *International Studies Quarterly* 24 (December 1980): 555–80.

Inazo Nitobe's *Bushido: The Soul of Japan, an Exposition of Japanese Thought* (New York: G. P. Putnam's Sons, 1905; reprint, Tokyo: Tuttle, 1969) provides an interesting Japanese perspective on the meaning of bushido; and Nyozekan Hasegawa, "Our 'Emaciated Endurance,' " *Contemporary Japan* 12 (May 1943): 570–76, provides an example of Japanese writings that perpetuated the image of Japan as a land of spiritually superior people. Ivan Morris's *Nobility of Failure: Tragic Heroes in the History of Japan* (New York: Farrar, Straus & Giroux, 1988) provides case studies of Japanese heroes (including kamikaze pilots) who chose to die honorably.

For analyses of the wartime role of Emperor Hirohito see Leonard Mosley, *Hirohito, Emperor of Japan* (Englewood Cliffs NJ: Prentice-Hall, 1966); David Bergamimi, *Japan's Imperial Conspiracy* (London: Heinemann, 1971); Toshiaki Kawahara, *Hirohito and His Times: A Japanese Perspective* (New York: Kodansha International, 1990); and Stephen Large, *Emperor Hirohito and Showa Japan* (London: Routledge, 1992).

THE PACIFIC WAR

Contemporary accounts of the war in Asia and the Pacific include Kinoaki Matsuo, *How Japan Plans to Win* (Boston: Little, Brown, 1942); Mark J. Gayn, *The Fight for the Pacific* (New York: William Morrow, 1942) and *Japan Diary* (New York: William Sloane Associates, 1948); John Andrew Goette, *Japan Fights for Asia* (New York: Harcourt, Brace, 1943); George H. Johnston, *The Toughest Fighting in the World* (New York: Duell, Sloan & Pearce, 1943); and Masuo Kato, *The Lost War: A Japanese Reporter's Inside Story* (New York: Knopf, 1946).

The best single-volume military history of the Pacific war is Ronald H. Spector, *Eagle against the Sun: The American War with Japan* (New York: Free Press, 1984); and John Toland's *Rising Sun: The Decline and Fall of the Japanese Empire, 1936–1945* (New York: Random House, 1970) provides an outstanding analysis of the fighting throughout the Far East from a Japanese perspective. John W. Dower's *War without Mercy: Race and Power in the Pacific War* (New York: Pantheon, 1986) is a superb analysis of the impact of cultural stereotypes and racism on the conduct of the war in the Pacific. Saburo Ienaga, *The Pacific War: World War II and the Japanese, 1931–1945* (New York: Pantheon, 1978), offers a critical perspective on the emergence of military dictatorship, the road to war, and the Japanese people at war throughout the Far East; whereas Akira Iriye, *Power and Culture: The Japanese-American War, 1941–1945* (Cambridge: Harvard Univ. Press, 1981), focuses exclusively on the Pacific War.

Saburo Hayashi and Alvin D. Coox, *Kogun: The Japanese Army in the Pacific War* (Quantico VA: Marine Corps Association, 1959), is an operational history of the war in the Pacific, and Coox's chapter "The Japanese Army Experience," in

New Dimensions in Military History, edited by Russell F. Weigley (San Rafael CA: Presidio, 1975), examines the evolution of Japanese armed forces from a group of regional bands to a centralized national army following the Meiji Restoration and defines the special status of the Japanese army in national life. Edward J. Drea, "In the Army Barracks of Imperial Japan," *Armed Forces and Society* 15 (spring 1989): 329–48, offers a fascinating look at the character of the modern Japanese army in his examination of the induction, training, and indoctrination of Japanese soldiers in the 1930s, and Col. Harold Doud's "Six Months with the Japanese Infantry," *Infantry Journal* 44 (January–February 1937): 17–21, summarizes his sentiments about the character of the Japanese army based on his firsthand experiences in Japan.

Several good books have been written about Japanese life during World War II, prominent among them Ben-Ami Shillony, *Politics and Culture in Wartime Japan* (Oxford: Oxford Univ. Press, 1981); Thomas R. H. Havens, *Valley of Darkness: The Japanese People and World War Two* (New York: Norton, 1978); Toshio Iritani, *Group Psychology of the Japanese in Wartime* (New York: Kegan Paul International, 1991); Shunsuke Tsurumi, *An Intellectual History of Wartime Japan, 1931–1945* (London: KPI, 1986); and Christopher Thorne, *The Far Eastern War: States and Societies, 1941–1945* (London: Unwin Paperbacks, 1986).

For a comprehensive history of both the war in SWPA and MacArthur as supreme commander see D. Clayton James, *The Years of MacArthur: Vol. II, 1941–1945* (Boston: Houghton Mifflin, 1975). William Leary, ed., *We Shall Return: MacArthur's Commanders and the Defeat of Japan* (Lexington: Univ. Press of Kentucky, 1988), provides an excellent collection of scholarly essays on MacArthur's subordinate commanders. Christopher Thorne's *Allies of a Kind: The United States, Britain, and the War against Japan, 1941–1945* (New York: Oxford Univ. Press, 1978) assesses the interallied aspects of the conflict; and Edward J. Drea, *MacArthur's ULTRA: Codebreaking and the War against Japan, 1942–1945* (Lawrence: Univ. Press of Kansas, 1992), illuminates the technical aspects of code breaking and the extent to which ULTRA intercepts affected military operations in the theater.

Australian contributions to the war against Japan, which are all too often overlooked by American historians, are highlighted in D. M. Horner, *Crisis of Command: Australian Generalship and the Japanese Threat, 1941–1943* (Canberra: Australian National Univ. Press, 1978) and *High Command: Australia and Allied Strategy, 1939–1945* (Sydney: Allen & Unwin, 1982). For additional Australian perspectives see Gavin Long, *MacArthur as Military Commander* (Princeton: Van Nostrand, 1969), and John Heatherington, *Blamey, Controversial Soldier* (Canberra, 1973), which chronicle the lives of two of SWPA's great military figures.

The dramatic and controversial negotiations that brought the war to an end in 1945 are superbly documented by Robert J. C. Butow in *Japan's Decision to Surrender* (Stanford: Stanford Univ. Press, 1954). Toland's *Rising Sun* also offers an extended discussion of the debates that led to Japan's surrender, as does Lester Brooks, *Behind Japan's Surrender: The Secret Struggle That Ended an Empire* (New York: McGraw-Hill, 1968).

For oral histories of the war in Asia and the Pacific see Theodore F. Cook and Haruko Taya Cook, *Japan at War: An Oral History* (New York: New Press, 1992); and Frank Gibney, ed., *Senso: The Japanese Remember the Pacific War* (New York: M. E. Sharpe, 1995).

AMERICANS OF JAPANESE ANCESTRY

Although the valor of Japanese Americans who fought with the 442d Regimental Combat Team in Europe has received considerable attention, as have the Japanese American internment camps, the contributions of Nisei linguists in the Pacific remain obscure. Joseph D. Harrington's *Yankee Samurai: The Secret Role of Nisei in America's Pacific Victory* (Detroit: Pettigrew, 1979) is devoted solely to the story of Nisei in the war against Japan, but it is largely anecdotal and provides no documentation. Much more recent is Lynn Crost's *Honor by Fire: Japanese Americans at War in Europe and the Pacific* (Novato CA: Presidio, 1994), which is broader in scope but like Harrington somewhat lacking in historical context. More useful are the publications of some of the MIS associations, such as Tad Ichinokuchi, ed., *John Aiso and the M.I.S.: Japanese-American Soldiers in the Military Intelligence Service, World War II* (Los Angeles: Military Intelligence Service Club of Southern California, 1988); Clifford Uyeda and Barry Saiki, eds., *The Pacific War and Peace: Americans of Japanese Ancestry in Military Intelligence Service, 1941–1952* (San Francisco: MIS Association of Northern California and National Japanese-American Historical Society, 1991); Ted T. Tsukiyama and Fumiyo Migimoto, eds., *Secret Valor: M.I.S. Personnel, World War II, Pacific Theater, Pre-Pearl Harbor to Sept. 8, 1951* (Honolulu: MIS Veterans Club of Hawaii, 1993); and Stanley L. Falk and Warren M. Tsuneishi, eds., *American Patriots: MIS in the War against Japan* (Vienna VA: Japanese American Veterans Association of Washington DC, 1995).

Bill Hosokawa, whom the U.S. Army rejected for admission to the U.S. Military Intelligence Service Language School, has written a most useful article entitled "Our Own Japanese in the Pacific War," *American Legion Magazine,* July 1964, 15–17, 44–47, as well as a more general history of Americans of Japanese ancestry during World War II entitled *Nisei: The Quiet Americans* (New York: William Morrow, 1969). For a fascinating discussion of the regimen imposed on language students at the army's language school see Masaharu Ano, "Loyal Linguists: Nisei of World War II Learned Japanese in Minnesota," *Minnesota History* 45 (1977): 273–87.

PROPAGANDA AND PUBLIC OPINION

For general discussions on propaganda theory and methods see Leonard W. Doob, *Propaganda, Its Psychology and Technique* (New York: Henry Holt, 1948) and *Public Opinion and Propaganda* (New York: Henry Holt, 1948); Karin Dovring, *Road of Propaganda: The Semantics of Biased Communication* (New York: Philosophical Library, 1959); Harold D. Lasswell, Daniel Lerner, and Hans Speier, *Propaganda and Communication in World History* (Honolulu: Univ. Press of Hawaii, 1979); Oliver Thomson, *Mass Persuasion in History: An Historical Analysis of the Development of Propaganda Techniques* (Edinburgh: Paul Harris, 1977); and Ernst Kris and Nathan Leites, "Trends in Twentieth Century Propaganda," in *Psychoanalysis and the Social Sciences*, 5 vols. (New York: International Univ. Press, 1947–58), 1:393–409. For assessments of the role of propaganda in wartime see Harold Lavine and James Wechsler, *War Propaganda and the United States* (New Haven: Yale Univ. Press, 1940); and Daniel Lerner, ed., *Propaganda in War and Crisis* (New York: George W. Stewart, 1951; reprint, New York: Arno, 1972).

WORLD WAR I

The uses and abuses of propaganda during World War I have received considerable attention over the years; nonetheless, Harold D. Lasswell's *Propaganda Technique in the World War* (New York: Knopf, 1927) is the most thorough and dispassionate account of wartime propaganda and thus remains the definitive study. For more narrow assessments of British or Allied propaganda efforts see Montagu William Consett, *The Triumph of Unarmed Forces, 1914–1918* (London: Williams & Norgate, 1918); George C. Bruntz, *Allied Propaganda and the Collapse of the German Empire in 1918* (Stanford: Stanford Univ. Press, 1938); and Gary S. Messinger, *British Propaganda and the State in the First World War* (Manchester: Manchester Univ. Press, 1992). The best historical analysis of America's brief foray into the field of war propaganda is James Mock and Cedric Larson, *Words That Won the War: The Story of the Committee on Public Information* (Princeton: Princeton Univ. Press, 1939). See also George Creel, *The Creel Report: Complete Report of the Chairman of the Committee on Public Information* (Washington DC: USGPO, 1920). For an understanding of the Allied personalities involved in waging the propaganda war see Sir Campbell Stuart, *Secrets of Crewe House: The Story of a Famous Campaign* (London: Hodder & Stoughton, 1920); Hamilton Fyfe, *Northcliffe: An Intimate Biography* (London: Allen & Unwin, 1930); and George Creel, *How We Advertised America* (New York: Harper & Bros., 1920).

Propaganda aimed at ending American neutrality is highlighted in James Duane Squires, *British Propaganda at Home and in the United States from 1914 to 1917* (Cambridge: Harvard Univ. Press, 1935); and H. C. Peterson, *Propaganda for War: The Campaign against American Neutrality, 1914–1917* (Norman: Oklahoma Univ. Press, 1939). For interwar accounts that emphasize the evil and overpowering nature of state-sponsored propaganda see George Sylvester Viereck, *Spreading Germs of Hate* (New York: Horace Liveright, 1930); and Frederick E. Lumley, *The Propaganda Menace* (New York: Century, 1933).

WORLD WAR II

Published sources on the use of propaganda and psywar operations during World War II are dominated by studies of the ETO. Nazi propaganda in particular has received considerable attention in Jay W. Baird, *The Mythical World of Nazi War Propaganda, 1939–1945* (Minneapolis: Univ. of Minnesota Press, 1974); Ernest K. Bramsted, *Goebbels and National Socialist Propaganda, 1925–1945* (East Lansing: Michigan State Univ. Press, 1965); Leonard W. Doob, "Goebbels' Principles of Propaganda," *Public Opinion Quarterly* 14 (fall 1950): 419–42; Ladislas Farago, *German Psychological Warfare* (New York: G. P. Putnam's Sons, 1942; reprint, New York: Arno, 1972); Z. A. B. Zeman, *Nazi Propaganda* (London: Oxford Univ. Press, 1973); and Robert E. Herzstein, *The War That Hitler Won: The Most Infamous Propaganda Campaign in History* (New York: G. P. Putnam, 1978).

The best general analysis of Allied psywar in the ETO is still Daniel Lerner, *Psychological Warfare against Nazi Germany; The Sykewar Campaign, D-Day to VE-Day* (Cambridge: MIT Press, 1971), originally published in 1949 as *Sykewar: Psychological Warfare against Germany, D-Day to VE-Day.* Michael Balfour's *Propaganda in War, 1939–1945: Organizations, Policies, and Publics in Britain and Germany* (London: Routledge & Kegan Paul, 1979) compares Nazi and British propaganda techniques. Charles Cruickshank focuses on British psywar operations in *The Fourth Arm: Psychological Warfare, 1938–1945* (London: Davis-Poynter, 1977), whereas Clayton D. Laurie, *The Propaganda Warriors: America's Crusade against Nazi Germany* (Lawrence: Univ. Press of Kansas, 1996), assesses the American propaganda war, though it focuses more on organizational dynamics and the bureaucratic turf war than on propaganda operations per se. James Erdmann's *Leaflet Operations in the Second World War: The Story of the How and the Why of the 6,500,000 Propaganda Leaflets Dropped on the Axis Forces and Homelands in the Mediterranean and European Theaters of Operations* (Denver: Denver Instant Printing, 1969) examines leafleting operations specifically, as does Carl Berger's *Introduction to Wartime Leaflets* (Washington DC: Special Operations Research Office, The American University, 1959).

The classic assessment of German troop morale is Edward A. Shils and Morris Janowitz, "Cohesion and Disintegration in the Wehrmacht in World War II," in *Public Opinion and Propaganda: A Book of Readings,* edited by Daniel Katz (New York: Holt, Rinehart & Winston, 1954). For a very recent analysis and a discussion of the literature see Stephen G. Fritz, "'We are trying . . . to change the face of the world'—Ideology and Motivation in the Wehrmacht on the Eastern Front: The View from Below," *Journal of Military History* 60 (October 1996): 683–710. The most comprehensive study of the attitudes and morale of American soldiers during World War II is Samuel A. Stouffer et al., *Studies in Social Psychology in World War II*, volume 2, *The American Soldier: Combat and Its Aftermath* (Princeton: Princeton Univ. Press, 1949).

Anthony Rhodes, *Propaganda: The Art of Persuasion: World War II* (New York: Chelsea House, 1976), encompasses the propaganda produced by all the major participants and provides the best visual source of the great scope and artistry of wartime propaganda, though its focus is clearly on the home front. Paul M. A. Linebarger, *Psychological Warfare* (Washington DC: Infantry Journal, 1948), is a general study of the theory and methods of American psywar operations in all theaters of war. For an analysis of the U.S. Army's institutional response to the profusion of unconventional operations during World War II and beyond see Alfred H. Paddock Jr., *U.S. Army Special Warfare, Its Origins: Psychological and Unconventional Warfare, 1941–1952* (Washington DC: National Defense Univ. Press, 1982). Charles Roetter, *The Art of Psychological Warfare, 1914–1945* (New York: Stein & Day, 1974), assesses the evolution of psywar techniques through both world wars but emphasizes the ETO. Other studies of World War II psywar include Terence H. Qualter, *Propaganda and Psychological Warfare* (New York: Random House, 1962); Leo Jay Margolin, *Paper Bullets: A Brief History of Psychological Warfare in World War II* (New York: Froben, 1946); Elliott Harris, *The "Un-American" Weapon: Psychological Warfare* (New York: M. M. Lads, 1967); Robert E. Summers, *America's Weapon of Psychological Warfare* (New York: Wilson, 1951); and Gladys Thum and Marcella Thum, *The Persuaders: Propaganda in War and Peace* (New York: Athenaeum, 1972).

In the aftermath of the war a number of analyses of propaganda and psywar emerged, many written by those who had engaged in it. See, for example, Paul M. A. Linebarger (U.S. Army), *A Syllabus of Psychological Warfare* (Washington DC: War Department General Staff, Intelligence Division, Propaganda Branch, 1946) and "Psychological Warfare in World War II," *Infantry Journal* 60 (May–June 1947): 36–39, 41–46; and Daniel Lerner, ed. (intelligence officer, PWD, SHAEF), *Propaganda in War and Crisis* (New York: George W. Stewart, 1951). Indeed much of the published literature on propaganda in wartime has been written by those who experienced it firsthand. This is particularly true of published works on OWI (see below) but also of the studies written by Daniel Lerner, Ladislas Farago, and Harold Lasswell (cited above), all of whom functioned as propagandists of one sort or another. This also applies to Richard H. S. Crossman (British political warfare officer, PWD, SHAEF), whose article "Psychological Warfare" appeared in the *Journal of the Royal United Service Institution* 97 (1952): 319–32. See also a series of articles by Martin F. Herz (chief leaflet writer, PWD, SHAEF): "Some Psychological Lessons from Leaflet Propaganda in World War II," *Public Opinion Quarterly* 13 (fall 1949): 471–86; "The Combat Leaflet—Weapon of Persuasion," *Army Information Digest* 5 (June 1950): 37–43; and "Psychological Warfare against Surrounded Troop Units," *Military Review* 30 (August 1950):

3–9. Saul K. Padover, an OSS officer in Europe, also published articles based in part upon his experiences: "Japanese Race Propaganda," *Public Opinion Quarterly* 7 (summer 1943): 191–204, and "Psychological Warfare and Foreign Policy," *American Scholar* 20 (spring 1951): 151–61.

Three volumes of case studies, many of which were written by participants in propaganda operations, are particularly useful for comparative purposes: Ronald D. McLaurin, ed., *The Art and Science of Psychological Operations: Case Studies of Military Application* (Washington DC: U.S. Department of the Army, 1976) and *Military Propaganda: Psychological Warfare and Operations* (New York: Praeger, 1982); and William E. Daugherty and Morris Janowitz, eds., *A Psychological Warfare Casebook: A Review of U.S. Historical Experience with Civil Affairs, 1776–1954* (Baltimore: Johns Hopkins Univ. Press, 1958).

PSYCHOLOGICAL WARFARE IN THE PACIFIC

By way of contrast, very little scholarly attention has been paid to psywar operations in Asia and the Pacific. With the exception of Charles Cruickshank's *SOE in the Far East* (New York: Oxford Univ. Press, 1983), which assesses the activities of the British Special Operations Executive particularly in Southeast Asia, there are virtually no extensive scholarly treatments of the subject. Students of psywar (as distinct from sabotage, espionage, and other such clandestine operations) in the Pacific have exceedingly few published sources with which to work.

Spector's *Eagle against the Sun* provides the best overview of the American and Allied intelligence apparatus in the war against Japan. Alan Powell's *War by Stealth: Australians and the Allied Intelligence Bureau, 1942–1945* (Melbourne: Melbourne Univ. Press, 1996) is the only scholarly study available on AIB and its subagencies, including FELO. For an American perspective on AIB see Allison Ind, *Allied Intelligence Bureau: Our Secret Weapon in the War against Japan* (New York: David McKay, 1958). Ind was deputy controller of AIB and the highest-ranking U.S. officer in the organization. Eric A. Feldt, *The Coastwatchers* (New York: David McKay, 1946), provides another insider's story of intelligence gathering in SWPA (Feldt, a lieutenant commander in the Royal Australian Navy, was responsible for the development of the coastwatcher network in Papua New Guinea and the Solomons). See also *The Intelligence Series*, volume 4, *Operations of the Allied Intelligence Bureau, GHQ, SWPA*. Sidney F. Mashbir, *I Was an American Spy* (New York: Vantage, 1953), is the only published work that deals at length with ATIS, which Mashbir headed. *The Intelligence Series* also includes a volume on ATIS.

The operations of FELO are absent from the published sources with the exception of Powell's *War by Stealth* (esp. chap. 9) and H. N. Walker's "Psychological Warfare in the South-West Pacific," *Army Journal* (Canberra), no. 298 (March 1974): 49–64. Even more complete is the scholarly neglect of PWB, SWPA, about which nothing has been published. Likewise, the psywar organizations estab-

lished in the Pacific Ocean Areas and on the Asian mainland are thoroughly neglected, with the exception of three doctoral dissertations, which address the
topic of psywar in the Pacific more directly than any other sources. They are W.
H. Vatcher Jr., "Combat Propaganda against the Japanese in the Central Pacific"
(Stanford University, 1950); Allison B. Gilmore, "In the Wake of Winning Armies: Allied Psychological Warfare in the Southwest Pacific Area during WWII"
(Ohio State University, 1989); and Eleanor Sparagana, "The Conduct and Consequences of Psychological Warfare: American Psychological Warfare Operations in the War against Japan, 1941–1945" (Brandeis University, 1990).

For a look at OWI's work in the war against Japan see Alexander H. Leighton
(Chief, FMAD, OWI), *Human Relations in a Changing World: Observations on the
Use of the Social Sciences* (New York: E. P. Dutton, 1949), a valuable exposition of
the methods employed by FMAD to measure the wartime morale of the Japanese
and the division's basic findings, written by the head of the organization. See also
Leighton's "Psychological Warfare and the Japanese Emperor," in *Personalities
and Cultures: Readings in Psychological Anthropology*, edited by Robert Hunt
(Garden City NY: Natural History Press, 1946). Frederic S. Marquardt, who became chief of OWI's activities in SWPA, wrote *Before Bataan and After: A Person-
alized History of Our Philippine Experiment* (New York: Bobbs-Merrill, 1943); unfortunately, its focus on the prewar period makes it virtually useless for scholars
interested in the propaganda war. Ellis M. Zacharias, *Secret Missions: The Story of
an Intelligence Officer* (New York: G. P. Putnam's Sons, 1946), is useful for its recounting of Zacharias's famous broadcasts to the Japanese home islands. See
also his "Eighteen Words That Bagged Japan," *Saturday Evening Post*, 17 November 1945.

English-language sources on Japanese propaganda are Dower's *War without
Mercy*; Peter DeMendelssohn, *Japan's Political Warfare* (London: Allen & Unwin,
1944), a useful wartime study of Japan's attempt to achieve conformity through its
"war on thought and argument" both at home and in occupied territories; and
Joyce C. Lebra, ed., *Japan's Greater East Asia Co-Prosperity Sphere in World War II:
Selected Readings and Documents* (Oxford: Oxford Univ. Press, 1975). See also Lucy
D. Meo, *Japan's Radio War on Australia, 1941–1945* (London: Cambridge Univ.
Press, 1968); Joel V. Berreman (a propaganda analyst with OWI in San Francisco
and Chungking), "Assumptions about America in Japanese War Propaganda to
the United States," *American Journal of Sociology* 54 (1948–49): 108–17; and Selden
Menefee, "Japan's Psychological War," *Social Forces*, May 1943, 425–36.

For a sense of the nature of the wartime reporting of psywar in the Pacific see
Roland Gask, "Japs Do Surrender: Psychological Warfare Somewhere in the
China-Burma-India Theater," *Newsweek*, 30 October 1944, 31–33; Edgar L. Jones,
"Fighting with Words: Psychological Warfare in the Pacific," *Atlantic Monthly*,
August 1945, 47–51; and Alvin M. Josephy, "Some Japs Surrender," *Infantry Jour-
nal* 57 (August 1945): 40–45.

OFFICE OF WAR INFORMATION

For general discussions of the activities of owi see Edward W. Barrett (Overseas Branch, owi, Europe), *Truth Is Our Weapon* (New York: Funk & Wagnalls, 1953); Wallace Carroll (Deputy Director, Overseas Branch, owi, Europe), *Persuade or Perish* (Boston: Houghton Mifflin, 1948); James P. Warburg (Overseas Branch, owi, Europe 1942–44), *Unwritten Treaty* (New York: Harcourt, Brace, 1946); and Alan M. Winkler, *The Politics of Propaganda: The Office of War Information, 1942–1945* (New Haven: Yale Univ. Press, 1946). The most extensive study of owi's overseas operations is Robert Lee Bishop, "The Overseas Branch of the Office of War Information" (Ph.D. diss., University of Wisconsin, 1966), which does not overlook activities in the Pacific. See also Leonard W. Doob, "The Utilization of Social Scientists in the Overseas Branch of the Office of War Information," *American Political Science Review* 41 (August 1947): 649–67; Charles M. Holton, "How the owi Operates Its Overseas Propaganda Machine," *Journalism Quarterly* 19 (December 1942): 349–55; Charles A. H. Thomson, *Overseas Information Service of the U.S. Government* (Washington, D.C.: Brookings Institution, 1948); and J. A. Pollard, "Words Are Cheaper Than Blood: Overseas owi and the Need for a Permanent Propaganda Agency," *Public Opinion Quarterly* 9 (fall 1945): 283–304.

Index

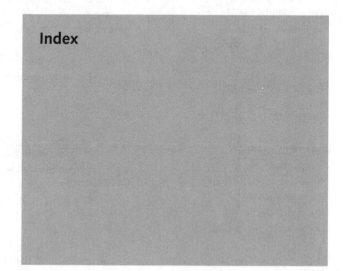